S0-AGF-857

WITHDRAWN

ZORA NEALE HURSTON, EULALIE SPENCE, MARITA BONNER, AND OTHERS

THE PRIZE PLAYS AND OTHER ONE-ACTS PUBLISHED IN PERIODICALS

AFRICAN-AMERICAN WOMEN WRITERS, 1910–1940

HENRY LOUIS GATES, JR. *GENERAL EDITOR*
Jennifer Burton *Associate Editor*

OTHER TITLES IN THIS SERIES

ZORA NEALE HURSTON, EULALIE SPENCE, MARITA BONNER, AND OTHERS

THE PRIZE PLAYS AND OTHER ONE-ACTS PUBLISHED IN PERIODICALS

Introduction by
JENNIFER BURTON

G. K. HALL & CO.
An Imprint of Simon & Schuster Macmillan
New York

Prentice Hall International
London Mexico City New Delhi Singapore Sydney Toronto

The Bog Guide by May Miller is published with the permission of Mrs. Suzanne M. Jefferson

Introduction copyright © 1996 by Jennifer Burton

All rights reserved. No part of this book may be reproduced or transmitted in any form or by any means, electronic or mechanical, including photocopying, recording, or by any information storage and retrieval system, without permission in writing from the Publisher.

G. K. Hall & Co.
An Imprint of Simon & Schuster Macmillan
1633 Broadway
New York, New York 10019

Library of Congress Catalog Card Number: 96-5451

Printed in the United States of America

Printing Number
1 2 3 4 5 6 7 8 9 10

Library of Congress Cataloging-in-Publication Data

Zora Neal Hurston, Eulalie Spence, Marita Bonner, and others : the prize plays and other one-acts published in periodicals / Introduction by Jennifer Burton.
    p.   cm.—(African American women writers, 1910–1940)
    ISBN 0-7838-1436-4 (alk. paper)
    1. American Drama—Afro-American authors. 2. American drama—Women authors. 3. American drama—20th century. 4. Afro-American women—Drama. 5. One-act plays, American. 6. Afro-Americans—Drama. I. Series.
PS628.N4Z67   1996
812'.520809287'08996073—dc20   96-5451
                                                       CIP

This paper meets the requirements of ANSI/NISO Z39.48-1992 (Permanence of Paper).

CONTENTS

CONTENTS

CONTENTS

CONTENTS

GENERAL EDITORS' PREFACE

The past decade of our literary history might be thought of as the era of African-American Women writers. Culminating in the awarding of the Pulitzer Prize to Toni Morrison and Rita Dove and the Nobel Prize for Literature to Toni Morrison in 1993, and characterized by the presence of several writers—Toni Morrison, Alice Walker, Maya Angelou, and the Delaney Sisters, among others—on the *New York Times* Best Seller List, the shape of the most recent period in our literary history has been determined in large part by the writings of black women.

This, of course, has not always been the case. African-American women authors have been publishing their thoughts and feelings at least since 1773, when Phillis Wheatley published her book of poems in London, thereby bringing poetry directly to bear upon the philosophical discourse over the African's "place in nature" and his or her place in the great chain of being. The scores of words published by black women in America in the nineteenth century—most of which were published in extremely limited editions and never reprinted—have been republished in new critical editions in the forty-volume *Schomburg Library of Nineteenth-Century Black Women Writers*. The critical response to that series has led to requests from scholars and students alike for a similar series, one geared to the work by black women published between 1910 and the beginning of World War Two.

African-American Women Writers, 1910–1940 is designed to bring back into print many writers who otherwise would be unknown to contemporary readers, and to increase the availability of lesser-known texts by established writers who originally published during this critical period in African-American letters. This series implicitly acts as a chronological sequel to the Schomburg series, which focused on the origins of the black female literary tradition in America.

In less than a decade, the study of African-American women's writings has grown from its promising beginnings into a firmly established field in departments of English, American Studies, and African-American studies. A comparison of the form and function of the original series and this sequel illustrates this dramatic shift. The *Schomburg Library* was published at the cusp of focused academic investigation into the interplay between race and gender. It covered the extensive period from the publication of Phillis Wheatley's *Poems on Various Subjects, Religious and Moral* in 1773 through the "Black Women's Era" of 1890–1910, and was designed to be an inclusive series of the major early texts by black women writers. The Schomburg Library provided a historical backdrop for black women's writings of the 1970s and 1980s, including the works of writers such as Toni Morrison, Alice Walker, Maya Angelou, and Rita Dove.

African-American Women Writers, 1910–1940 continues our effort to provide a new generation of readers access to texts—historical, sociological, and literary—that have been largely "unread" for most of this century. The series bypasses works that are important both to the period and the tradition, but that are readily available, such as Zora Neale Hurston's *Their Eyes Were Watching God*, Jessie Fauset's *Plum Bun* and *There Is Confusion*, and Nella Larsen's *Quicksand* and *Passing*. Our goal is to provide access to a wide variety of rare texts. The series includes Fauset's two other novels, *The Chinaberry Tree: A Novel of American Life* and *Comedy: American Style* and Hurston's short play *Color Struck*, since these are not yet widely available. It also features works by virtually unknown writers, such as *A Tiny Spark*, Christina Moody's slim volume of poetry self-published in 1910, and *Reminiscences of School Life, and Hints on Teaching*, written by Fanny Jackson Coppin in the last year of her life (1913), a multigenre work combining an autobiographical sketch and reflections on trips to England and South Africa, complete with pedagogical advice.

Cultural studies' investment in diverse resources allows the historic scope of the *African-American Women Writers* series to be more focused that the *Schomburg Library* series, which covered works written over a 137-year period. With few exceptions, the authors included in the *African-American Women Writers* series wrote their major works between 1910 and 1940. The texts reprinted include all of the works by each particular author that are not otherwise readily obtainable. As a result, two volumes contain works originally published after 1940. The Charlotte Hawkins Brown volume includes her book of etiquette published in 1941, *The Correct Thing To Do—To Say—To Wear*. One of the poetry volumes contains Maggie Pogue Johnson's *Fallen Blossoms*, published in 1951, a compilation of all her previously published and unpublished poems.

Excavational work by scholars during the past decade has been crucial to the development of *African-American Women Writers, 1910–1940*. Germinal bibliographical sources such as Ann Allen Shockley's *Afro-American Women Writers 1746–1933* and Maryemma Graham's *Database of African-American Women Writers* made the initial identification of texts possible. Other works were brought to our attention by scholars who wrote letters sharing their research. Additional texts by selected authors were then added, so that many volumes contain the complete oeuvres of particular writers. Pieces by authors without enough published work to fill an entire volume were grouped with other pieces by genre.

The two types of collections, those organized by author and those organized by genre, bring out different characteristics of black women's writings of the period. The collected works of the literary writers illustrate that many of them were experimenting with a variety of forms. Mercedes Gilbert's volume, for example, contains her 1931 collection, *Selected Gems of Poetry, Comedy, and Drama, Etc.*, as well as her 1938 novel, *Aunt Sara's Wooden God*. Georgia Douglas Johnson's volume contains her plays and short stories in addition to her poetry. Sarah Lee Brown Fleming's volume combines her 1918 short novel *Hope's Highway* with her 1920 collection of poetry, *Clouds and Sunshine*.

The generic volumes both bring out the formal and thematic similarities among many of the writings and highlight the striking individuality of particular writers. Most of the plays in the volume of one-acts are social dramas whose tragic endings can be clearly attributed to miscegenation and racism. Within the context of these other plays, Marita Bonner's surrealistic theatrical vision becomes all the more striking.

The volumes of *African-American Women Writers, 1910–1940* contain reproductions of more than one hundred previously published texts, including twenty-nine plays, seventeen poetry collections, twelve novels, six autobiographies, three histories of organizations, three black histories, two anthologies, two sociological studies, a diary, and a book of etiquette. Each volume features an introduction written by a contemporary scholar that provides crucial biographical data on each author and the historical and critical context of her work. In some cases, little information on the authors was available outside of the fragments of biographical data contained in the original introduction or in the text itself. In these instances, editors have documented the libraries and research centers where they tried to find information, in the hope that subsequent scholars will continue the necessary search to find the "lost" clues to the women's stories in the rich stores of papers, letters, photographs, and other primary materials scattered throughout the country that have yet to be fully catalogued.

Many of the thrilling moments that occurred during the development of this series were the result of previously fragmented pieces of these women's histories suddenly coming together, such as Adele Alexander's uncovering of an old family photograph picturing her own aunt with Addie Hunton, the author Alexander was researching. Claudia Tate's examination of Georgia Douglas Johnson's papers in the Moorland-Spingarn Research Center of Howard University resulted in the discovery of a wealth of previously unpublished work.

The slippery quality of race itself emerged during the construction of the series. One of the short novels originally intended for inclusion in the series had to be cut when the family of the author protested that the writer was not of African descent. Another case involved Louise Kennedy's sociological study *The Negro Peasant Turns Inward*. The fact that none of the available biographical material on Kennedy specifically mentioned race, combined with some coded criticism in a review in *Crisis*, convinced editor Sheila Smith McKoy that Kennedy was probably white.

These women, taken together, begin to chart the true vitality, and complexity, of the literary tradition that African-American women have generated, using a wide variety of forms. They tesitfy to the fact that the monumental works of Hurston, Larsen, and Fauset, for example, emerged out of a larger cultural context; they were not exceptions or aberrations. Indeed, their contributions to American literature and culture, as this series makes clear, were fundamental not only to the shaping of the African-American tradition but to the American tradition as well.

Henry Louis Gates, Jr.
Jennifer Burton

ACKNOWLEDGMENTS

Many people have helped to make this volume and this entire series possible. For their comments and ideas on the introduction and works in this volume, I want to thank professors Henry Louis Gates, Jr., and Elaine Scarry of Harvard University, Claudia Tate of George Washington University, Christine R. Gray of the University of Maryland at College Park, Bob West of NCAAT, the National Conference on African American Theatre, and James V. Hatch of the Hatch-Billops Collection. For reading drafts and providing loving support, thanks to Aniruddh Patel, Maribeth Back, Mary Anne Stewart Boelcskevy, Rebecca Carman, Karen Isabelle Halil, Sherry Lovelace, Terri Hume Oliver, and my family, Roger, Gabrielle, Maria, Ursula, Gabrielle, and Charity Burton.

A number of these volumes were greatly aided by Professor Maryemma Graham and Valerie E. M. Elmore in conjunction with Graham's Project on the History of Black Writing at Northeastern University.

The production of the thirty volumes in this series was made possible through the sustained help of Harvard librarians Barbara Dames and Maria McEachern; research assistants Anna Catone, Maria Gambale, and Anurima Bhargava; Tom Pixton of Harvard University Publishers; and, of course, our editor at G. K. Hall, Catherine Carter.

–Jennifer Burton

chance for popular appeal to audiences who wanted escape and entertainment. Other intellectuals of this period, particularly Alain Locke and Montgomery Gregory, recognized the limitations of propaganda pieces and encouraged instead the development of folk plays designed to reach a mixed audience. The folk play movement was centered in Washington, DC, at Howard University, where Locke and Gregory directed the Howard Players. Gregory was appointed head of the Department of Speech at Howard in 1919. With the assistance of Marie Moore-Forrest, he established the first professional theater training program for African Americans, offering instruction in playwriting as well as acting and producing and geared toward developing professional productions that would reach white audiences as well as black.[9] Like Du Bois, Gregory and Locke believed that "the Negro has a wonderful opportunity through drama to win a better standing in the community."[10] However, as Gregory said in a 1921 interview, he and Locke favored "win[ning] a broader recognition of our rights and responsibilities as citizens by demonstrating our abilities as artists" rather than "through the production of plays of propaganda."[11] Folk plays were often written in dialect and typically focused on the black culture of lower-class characters, since middle-class black experience was theoretically not substantially different from middle-class white experience.

As Kathy Perkins writes in *Black Female Playwrights*, "Of the many women who would later become well known in the literary field, particularly for their plays, a large percentage either studied under Gregory and Locke or were influenced by the Howard community",[12] including Zora Neale Hurston, Mary P. Burrill, May Miller, Myrtle Athleen Smith Livingston, and Eulalie Spence. Gregory and Locke served as judges for the *Opportunity* and *Crisis* contests and many of the female playwrights included in this volume consulted them as well as Du Bois regarding their work. Several of the periodical plays are in the folk genre, including the work of Spence and Gaines-Shelton. Nevertheless, Du Bois's views are reflected more strongly in many of the periodical plays, due partly to the noncommercial form of the one-act required by the contests, and to the stress on publication rather than professional production.[13]

This volume includes all available prize plays by African-American women (two of which were not published at the time) as well as the extant plays by African-American women writers published in periodicals between 1910 and 1940, with the exception of Georgia Douglas Johnson's prize plays, *Blue Blood* and *Plumes*, which are republished in another volume in this series, edited by Claudia Tate. The following five prize and periodical plays have been lost. *Cooped Up*, by Eloise Bibb Thompson (1878–1928), received an honorable mention in the first *Opportunity* contest of 1925. Although the play was never published, it was produced by the National Ethopian Art Players at the Lafayette Theatre, on October 15, 1924.[14] Zora Neale Hurston's *Spears* was also awarded an honorable mention in the 1925 *Opportunity* contest, but failed to be published. Also never published was May Miller's *The Cuss'd Thing*, which received an honorable mention in the 1926 *Opportunity* contest.[15] Eulalie Spence's *Foreign Mail* won second prize in the *Crisis* competition of 1926, received several productions by the Krigwa Players' Little Negro Theatre of New York City in 1926 and 1927, and was published by Samuel French in 1927. Despite its popularity during the period, no copies have been found. Ottie Graham's *King's Carpenter* was published in *Stylus* in May 1926. As the college magazine for Howard University, *Stylus* is not included in the collections of most libraries, and the issue is not among the collected issues of *Stylus* at Howard's Moorland-Spingarn Research Center. These lost plays illustrate the importance of periodical publications to African-American and theater history. Productions, prizes, and even publication by Samuel French (the major professional play publisher in the United States) did not provide protection against loss, but all of the plays published in major periodicals are still available.

Sixteen of the plays published in this volume were awarded prizes and/or published between 1925 and 1929, with all twenty-two honored or published between 1913 and 1932. This short span demonstrates how black women playwrights were particularly influenced by the energy of the Harlem Renaissance, which included the establishment of black periodicals and literary salons, in addition to the play prizes.

The majority of the plays submitted to the *Opportunity* and *Crisis* play contests were by women and women won most of the prizes.[16] The 1925 *Opportunity* contest attracted a total of sixty-five plays, and four of the seven winners were women.[17] Zora Neale Hurston won the second prize of $35 for *Color Struck*, and May Miller was awarded the third prize of $15 for *The Bog Guide*. Eloise Bibb Thompson's *Cooped Up* and Zora Neale Hurston's *Spears* received honorable mentions. Women fared markedly worse in *Opportunity*'s 1926 contest. First, second, and third prizes all went to men, with all four honorable mentions awarded to women.[18] The honorable mentions were given to Zora Neale Hurston's *Color Struck* (the revised version that is included in this volume), Hurston's *The First One*, May Miller's *The Cuss'd Thing*, and Georgia Douglas Johnson's *Blue Blood*. Female playwrights were awarded three of the five prizes in *Opportunity*'s 1927 contest (by two male and two female judges), including first, second, and one of the third prizes. *Plumes*, by Georgia Douglas Johnson, won first prize, with second prize going to Eulalie Spence's *The Hunch*, and one of the third prizes going to Spence's *The Starter*.

The *Crisis* contest of 1925 attracted only twenty plays (compared with 130 short stories). The three male judges (among them Eugene O'Neill) awarded the second and third prizes to female playwrights: Ruth Ada Gaines-Shelton won the second prize of $40 for *The Church Fight*, and Myrtle Athleen Smith Livingston won the third prize of $10 for *For Unborn Children*.[19] Only one woman was honored in the 1926 contest, which was also judged by three men, including Montgomery Gregory. Eulalie Spence's *Foreign Mail* won the second prize of $50, but first prize and the two honorable mentions went to male playwrights.

Du Bois's support for female playwrights is evident in the results of the *Crisis* contest of 1927, when he was the primary judge.[20] The play and fiction prizes were combined as "Prizes in Literary Art and Expression," and women, particularly female playwrights, fared extraordinarily well. All three major awards went to women, as well as at least two of the seven honorable mentions.[21] Marita Bonner won the first prize of $200 for her plays *The Purple Flower* and *Exit*, along with her short story

"Drab Rambles" and essay "The Young Blood Hungers." Eulalie Spence won the third prize of $50 for her plays *Hot Stuff* and *Undertow*.

Of the plays in this volume, eighteen were published in periodicals during the period, including seven of the eleven prize plays.[22] Seven appeared in *Crisis*, two in *Opportunity*, while three of the plays were printed in *Carolina Magazine*, a publication of the University of North Carolina, which had an active theater program favoring folk drama. Two of the plays (both by Alvira Hazzard) appeared in *The Saturday Evening Quill*, the organ of Boston's literary society, the Saturday Evening Quill Club, which had three annual editions from 1928 to 1930. The literary magazine *Fire!!* (1926), issued only once and co-edited by Zora Neale Hurston, Langston Hughes, and Wallace Thurman, published one of Hurston's plays. One play debuted in *The Liberator*, a small, politically radical magazine founded in 1918. *The Archive* published another of the plays, as did Margaret Sanger's monthly, *Birth Control Review*.

The form of the one-act required by the play contests propelled the development yet limited the scope of these plays. The short length made them easily performable and well suited to performances outside of theaters. However, while making these plays appealing to amateur groups, the one-act form was not commercially viable.[23] As a result playwrights shifted their focus from the performed medium into the published medium, which contributed to the development of a hybrid form of the "play to be read."[24] The mixing of the genres of literary fiction and drama is particularly evident in stage directions, where the narrative voice is often strikingly present. The hybridization is especially powerful in the plays of fiction writers like Marita Bonner, but exists even in the work of performance-oriented playwrights.[25] Ironically, the plays that Bonner specifically labeled as "plays to be read" now seem the most theatrical of the pieces, particularly since they lack the limitations of dramatic realism prevalent during the period.

The plays in this volume explore the range of forms identified by Elizabeth Brown-Guillory in *Their Place on the Stage* (1988),

"(1) protest, (2) genteel school, (3) folk, (4) historical (inter-changeable with race pride and black nationalism), (5) religious, (6) fantasy, and (7) feminist,"[26] with many containing a blend of these elements. Most of the playwrights shared the belief that theater could be used "effectively to break down race prejudice."[27] Many of the periodical plays attempt to instigate social action through unmitigated tragedy, ending the piece with the deterioration or death of a relatively flawless main character. Since the cause of the tragedy is not located in a particular character, the death defies rather than fulfills a vision of higher justice, preventing the release of catharsis within the confines of the theater. If no changeable evil were identified, the injustice of the tragedy would suggest the impossibility of a better world. However, like the mob in *For Unborn Children*, the cause of the tragedy is identified, but remains outside the scene itself. By clearly identifying social causes as the root of the tragedy, this kind of early African-American women's play forces the issues into the world outside the theater walls, implying that only broad societal change will enable alternative, nontragic narratives.

Charlotte Teller Hirsch, the first author considered in this volume, published her short biblical sketch *Hagar and Ishmael* in *Crisis* in 1913. Based on the biblical story of the Egyptian slave Hagar and her son, Ishmael, told in alternative versions in Genesis 16 and 21, Hirsch's play centers on the scene between Hagar and Ishmael in the desert following their expulsion.[28] Although the work opens with a lengthy quotation from Genesis 21, which provides complicated background information, Hirsch's play then not only expands on but diverges from its source. In the two Hebrew Bible versions, the focus of the story is Ishmael's illegitimacy and expulsion from the tribe of Israel. In contrast, much of Hirsch's play is basically a dramatic monologue by Hagar, the character with virtually no voice in the biblical story. Ishmael's periodic interjections serve mainly to promote Hagar's impassioned responses. Furthermore, Hagar credits her salvation in the wilderness to the "Great God of Egypt," not to "Jehovah, God of Abraham," whom she rails against: "You shall breed men to mock [Abraham's] God of Greed" (2), she tells Ishmael. Hagar sees herself as the central agent in her revenge against expulsion by Abraham and Sarah, even though her plans center on pitting "[Ishmael's] seed against young Isaac's from this day!": "If *we* could breed a race to take great vengeance upon Isaac's seed, his son. . . . He has thrust Hagar forth. But *she* shall enter in and lure his sons and work destruction in the midst of them!" (2, italics mine). Hagar's tears of hatred literally save her son, and fuel his conviction that even though he is the "Son of a Slave," he will be "Father to the Free."

Although Hirsch is included in books on African-American playwrights, with the stipulation "racial identity not verified,"[29] she isn't listed under the name "Charlotte Teller Hirsch" in biographical sources of her period, such as *Who's Who in Colored America*. Nevertheless, the combination of a variety of elements in the play supports the possibility of her black racial identity. Not only is *Hagar and Ishmael* a slave narrative, with only the perspectives of the slaves represented, its embellishments on the biblical source reverberate with contemporary antiassimilationist sentiment and the promise of a future revolution against those in power.

In contrast to the hatred-fueled revenge in *Hagar and Ishmael*, Alice Moore Dunbar-Nelson's patriotic play *Mine Eyes Have Seen* specifically denounces answering hate with hate. This play questions whether African Americans have a patriotic duty to their country during war since their country doesn't provide protection from violent acts of racism in their own communities. Dan's final speech acts as the turning point for the main female characters, Lucy and Julia, who had been resisting Chris's draft call: "It is not for us to visit retribution. Nor to wish hatred on others. . . . Can't you be big enough to feel pity for the little crucified French children—for the ravished Polish girls, even as their mothers must have felt sorrow, if they had known, for OUR burned and maimed little ones? Oh, Mothers of Europe, we be of one blood, you and I!"[30] (10).

Mine Eyes Have Seen, published in *Crisis* in 1918, combines the elements of propaganda and black history, common characteristics in many works by early African-American women playwrights. However, unlike most plays of the period, beginning with

Grimké's *Rachel* (1916), *Mine Eyes Have Seen* ends on an upbeat note (literally), harking back to the optimism of black women's writings during the post–Reconstruction period.[31] The title comes from the opening line of "The Battle Hymn of the Republic" and immediately announces the patriotic thrust of the play. However, the title is complicated by its association with the protagonist, Dan, who is described as "eyes wide, as if seeing BEYOND" (4). Dan demonstrates his unblurred vision in the opening scene by systematically countering his sister's nostalgic memories of the South with the grim facts of their experiences of racism. Since his "eyes have seen," his ultimate commitment to "[l]ove of humanity . . . above the small considerations of time or place or race or sect" (10) is presented not as a naïve dream, but as a complex and considered decision to trust the power of justice to combat injustice.

Considered a "precursor of the Harlem Renaissance, as well as a participant in it,"[32] Alice Moore Dunbar-Nelson (1875–1935) was born in New Orleans, Louisiana, where she attended public school and a two-year teaching program at Straight College (now Dillard University). From the time of her 1892 graduation until 1931, she earned her living primarily as a teacher, working in five different cities from New Orleans to Washington, DC. Nevertheless, she was also devoted to her lifelong work as a journalist, author, and social and political activist. Her marriage in 1897 to Paul Laurence Dunbar (the first of her three marriages) helped foster her literary career, which had already begun with the publication of *Violets and Other Tales* in 1895.

Dunbar-Nelson's lifelong interest in drama included acting in amateur theatricals and reviewing dramatic productions. Her distinction as a playwright arises entirely from *Mine Eyes Have Seen*, although she also published a dramatic sketch called *The Author's Evening at Home* in 1900.[33] In addition, her three-act operetta *An Hawaiian Idyll* was produced as a Christmas entertainment in 1916 at Howard High School in Wilmington, Delaware, where she taught. Howard High School was also the location of the only contemporary production of *Mine Eyes Have Seen*.[34]

Mary Burrill's play *Aftermath*, published in *The Liberator* in 1919, reads like a radical response to *Mine Eyes Have Seen*. While Dunbar-Nelson's play explores the extent of black citizens' wartime responsibility to a country where their own rights are violated, *Aftermath* focuses on the need for returning black soldiers to defend their own rights at home.[35] When Burrill's hero, John, victoriously returns from battle, he learns that his father has been lynched during his absence. Unlike Dunbar-Nelson's hero, John chooses to respond to racial hatred not with a continued commitment to virtue, but with a resolve of retribution.[36] Burrill's revolutionary ending arises from a sustained examination of the limit of God's power to combat injustice.[37] Just as faith is maintained but limited by the characters, the structure of the play itself acts to preserve hope despite the explicit and implied tragedy. Unlike most subsequent plays of social protest (including Burrill's own *They That Sit in Darkness*), *Aftermath* does not end in death or tragic despair. By concluding the play with John's defiant exit, the play maintains the possibility that action will lead to positive change.

Burrill's second play, *They That Sit in Darkness*, published in *The Birth Control Review* of September 1919, illustrates the dire consequences of witholding birth control information from the poor. The play does end with a tragic death, but it differs in a crucial way from the plays of racial despair. Unlike plays like *Rachel*, *They That Sit in Darkness* offers a concrete political solution to all the problems of the play. In this way the play resembles the suffrage dramas of the period that suggested that the pervasive problems of gender inequality would be resolved by the passage of the Nineteenth Amendment.[38] *They That Sit in Darkness* suggests that if the poor were given access to birth control information, not only would women and babies avoid death and disfigurement, but education would thrive and arts would even flourish. Burrill's identification of a specific answer to the problems of the play would have contributed to its political efficacy at the time. However, as George Bernard Shaw had earlier observed, "A drama with a social question for the motive cannot outlive the solution of that question."[39] As birth control information became available to the poor, the play became obsolete as a political drama, even though the problems of ignorance, racism, and poverty explored in the play were much too complicated and extensive to be solved by birth control alone.

Thirteen Plays (1935), edited by Richardson and Miller, contains four of her works.[63] Despite her dedication to the idea that drama was one of the most effective ways to teach children black history and racial pride, Miller wrote her last play, *Freedom's Children on the March*,[64] in 1943, and then retired from both teaching and playwriting to dedicate herself to a literary career as a poet. Her poetry was widely published, and she continued to write from her home in Washington, DC, until her death on February 8, 1995.

Color Struck, published in *Fire!!* in November 1926, is one of Zora Neale Hurston's first published works.[65] An earlier version won second prize in the *Opportunity* contest of 1925 (with her play *Spears* given an honorable mention). Hurston revised the play and resubmitted it to the *Opportunity* contest in 1926, where it received an honorable mention (along with her play *The First One*). *Color Struck* is notable as an early use of the Eatonville material that Hurston later reworked into her well-known plays, short stories, and novels.[66] The theatrical premise of the cakewalk contest provides a framework for Hurston's examination of color consciousness within the black community. As with most of Hurston's work, the play focuses on interactions among black characters.[67] The white world is present but remains on the periphery, with the conflict arising from within the black characters themselves rather than from an external, white threat.[68] Further reflecting Hurston's lifelong interests is her use of dialect and black vernacular.[69] The presentation of the dialect lacks the complexity found in her later works, but the content of the dialogue effectively develops the complicated characters and themes in a short amount of space.

While most of the early plays by black women rely predominantly on dialogue, *Color Struck* also utilizes spectacle, music, and dance. However, the play has remained a "play to be read" because it contains a number of dramatic challenges that make staging difficult.[70] Prose stage directions vaguely describe ad-libbed action and dialogue[71]; the main action of the end of Scene Two takes place upstage behind a curtain; all of Scene Three takes place upstage; and Scene Four is supposedly in the dark.[72] Despite the difficulties of production, *Color Struck* succeeds as a cross-genre "play to be read" and provides glimpses of the power of Hurston's later prose.

Hurston's *The First One* won an honorable mention in the *Opportunity* contest of 1926 and was published in Charles S. Johnson's 1927 anthology *Ebony and Topaz, A Collectanea*. This one-act is a satire of the biblical story of Noah's curse on his son Ham and his descendants, told in Genesis 9.[73] In Hurston's version, the original curse of servitude to his brethern, the progenitors of the tribes of Israel, is only a minor part of Ham's punishment. In addition, Hurston has Noah invoke the "curse" of blackness, a fate so horrific to the other characters that they overcome their petty greed and jealousy and bond together in an attempt to "uncurse the curse." Noah's prayers that Ham die if the curse cannot be reversed underscore the negative presentation of blackness in the play, a position tempered but not eradicated by Ham and his wife's[74] ultimate acceptance of his fate.[75]

That there is no record of a performance of *The First One* is not surprising, since the play presents numerous production difficulties, particularly in regard to the intended audience. The satirical humor seems geared toward a black audience, but the cast is nearly entirely white. In production, Eve's whiteness and Ham's new blackness at the end of the play would evoke the issue of miscegnation, which was problematic for both white and black audiences during the period. The politics of the play are too diffuse to be a biting farce, but the play presents virtually imsurmountable obstacles to a realistic production, particularly the difficulty of transforming Ham's color from white to black.[76]

Zora Neale Hurston (1891–1960) was born and reared in the all-black town of Eatonville, Florida, the first black township to be incorporated in the United States. Both Hurston herself as well as critics have linked her strong, independent sense of self with her childhood in Eatonville, where her father was elected mayor three times. After her mother died when she was thirteen, her father remarried and Hurston left home to live with various relatives, attending school only intermittently. She supported herself with a variety of jobs, most notably as a maid to an actress in a traveling theater troupe. In Baltimore she left her job and went back to school, graduating from Morgan Academy in 1918. At the urging of May Miller, Hurston then went to Howard University, where she attended classes sporadically between 1918 and 1924, studying with Georgia Douglas Johnson and Alain Locke. With Locke's encouragement, she submitted her short story "Drenched in Light" to *Opportunity*, where it was published in 1924. She then moved to New York in 1925 and quickly became one of the star writers of the Harlem Renaissance. At the *Opportunity* awards dinner of 1925, she was introduced to novelist Fannie Hurst, who gave her a job as secretary, and to philanthropist Annie Nathan Meyer, who arranged a scholarship to Barnard College. During her last year at Barnard, Hurston began collecting the folklore that would fuel her writing. Graduating in 1928, she went on to graduate work with anthropologist Franz Boas at Columbia University.

Although known primarily for her fiction and folklore, Hurston was involved with the theater throughout much of her professional life. In addition to *Spears* (1925), *Color Struck* (1926), and *The First Ones* (1927), her plays include *Sermon in the Valley* (1931) and *Mule Bone: A Comedy of Negro Life in Three Acts* (1931, with Langston Hughes). She collaborated with eight other writers on a 1931 Broadway musical revue, *Fast and Furious*, in which she made her Broadway acting debut as a cheerleader in one of the sketches. The show was a critical failure, as was the revue she subsequently wrote, *Jungle Scandals*. Nevertheless, Hurston continued to pursue a dramatic career, and from 1931 to 1934 she traveled the country with her own musical revue, *The Great Day* (subsequently revised as *From Sun to Sun* and then *Singing Steel*), achieving critical (although little financial) success. In the fall of 1935 she joined the Federal Theater Project, part of the government-sponsored Works Project Administration (WPA), but left in 1936 to collect folklore in the West Indies on a Guggenheim Fellowship. Her theatrical career resumed in 1939 when she was hired for a year to organize a drama program at the North Carolina College for Negroes in Durham.[77] Her last known theatrical venture was a collaboration with white playwright Dorothy Waring on *Polk County: A Comedy of Negro Life on a Sawmill Camp, With Authentic Negro Music, in Three Acts*, which was never produced, although it was originally scheduled to open on Broadway in 1944. Hurston's theatrical sensibility is evident in her first published anthropological work, "Characteristics of Negro Expression," in which she writes: "The Negro's universal mimicry is not so much a thing in itself as an evidence of something that permeates his entire self. And that thing is drama."[78] Hurston's plays and other writings capture in writing that drama she saw in life.

Like Hurston's plays, Marita Bonner's *The Pot Maker* is written in dialect in the folk genre, although Bonner's work is structured as a morality play. Published in *Opportunity* in February 1927, *The Pot Maker* introduces elements that make Bonner's subsequent plays innovative and powerful, the most striking being the use of the second person, her favored point of view in essays and short stories as well as in plays. The opening stage directions immediately confirm that the work is a cross-genre "play to be read" as the subtitle states: "You know there is a garden because if you listen carefully you can hear a tapping of bushes against the window and a gentle rustling of leaves and grass" (107). In addition to details too subtle for theatrical staging, the stage directions also direct the viewer-reader's focus, making the text not only part play and part short story, but also part film: "As the curtain is drawn, see first MOTHER" (43). After the idiosyncratic opening stage directions, the piece progresses rather traditionally for much of the play. However, near the end the narrator's voice begins to reemerge through the stage directions: "There are no words that can tell you how [Lucinda] looks at her mother-in-law. Words cannot do but so much" (112); "Elias may have thought of a dozen replies. He makes none" (113). By the end, even the dramatic textual form has given way to the powerful narrative voice. Elias's final words are presented in prose rather than in dialogue, culminating the play's shift into a truly hybrid form.

For most of the play Elias appears to be the most sympathetically drawn character, so that his death at the end seems surprising. However, reading the situation from Lucinda's point of view, as Elizabeth Brown-Guillory does in *Wines in the Wilderness*, illuminates the complexity of the piece. After merely presenting Lucinda's mean-spiritedness and duplicity for the bulk of the play, Bonner suddenly has Lucinda reveal the deep-seated motivations for her unfaithfulness and her resistance to Elias's preaching.[79]

Lucinda's revelations show that Elias's "crack" is not only his desire to let Lew and Lucinda die (the flaw he attempts to mend), but also his blindness to Lucinda's needs during the five years of their marriage.

Bonner continues her experimentation with form in *The Purple Flower*, widely considered her masterpiece. The play won first prize in the *Crisis* contest of 1927 (in conjunction with her play *Exit, an Illusion*), and was published by *Crisis* in January 1928. Bonner's surrealistic, revolutionary vision is subtitled "A Phantasy That Had Best Be Read," underscoring the fact that dramatically, it is remarkably ahead of its time.[80] Using her characteristic second person, Bonner not only directs the reader/viewer's focus, but responses as well: "You are amazed at [the white devil's] adroitness" (115).[81] Once the dialogue begins, the play progresses like a politicized *Everyman*, with the various "Us" characters described either in general terms ("An Old Man") or allegorical terms ("Finest Blood"). The Us's first discuss and reject past strategies of racial uplife: manual labor (the philosophy of Booker T. Washington); education (one of W. E. B. Du Bois's strategies); religious faith; and economic advancement. However, the final melting pot ritual credits all these strategies as necessary steps leading toward the inevitable violent revolution.[82]

Bonner's final play, *Exit, an Illusion*, published in *Crisis* in October 1929, masterfully combines a Pirandellian theatrical self-reflexivity with Bonner's unique multigenre style. Although this play lacks the explicit "to be read" directions of Bonner's other plays, it is pointedly literary from its opening line. The initial stage directions are called a "Foreword"; in addition to standard set and character descriptions, it includes assessments of the set (the sagging ragged bottoms of the chairs are "sorry") as well as Bonner's characteristic second-person narration. Theatrical self-consciousness is flagged in the opening dialogue.[83] In addition to gender relations and color consciousness,[84] the play explores the nature of theater itself. As in Pirandello's *Six Characters in Search of an Author* (1921), the dramatic need for a character can make that character materialize onstage: when Dot cries, "He's here!," "Exit Mann" suddenly appears onstage, and "you wonder how he came there. You wonder if perhaps he has not been there all the while"

(131). The ending also resonates with theatrical meaning: by returning to the opening scene, *Exit, an Illusion* evokes the ways plays are rejuvenated with each performance.[85]

Born in Boston, Marita Bonner (1898–1971) attended Brookline High School. From 1918 to 1922 she studied English and comparative literature at Radcliffe College, and was accepted into the exclusive writing seminar of Charles T. Copeland. While he admired her writing, Copeland warned her not to be "bitter," an admonishment Bonner called "a cliché to colored people who write."[86] She began teaching at Cambridge High School during her senior year, and continued her teaching after graduation, working in schools in Bluefield, West Virginia, and then in Washington, DC, where she taught for eight years. In Washington she was inspired to write plays by her interaction with playwrights at Georgia Douglas Johnson's "S Street Salon," including Zora Neale Hurston, May Miller, Willis Richardson, and Jean Toomer,[87] as well as Johnson herself.

Bonner was a member of Washington's Krigwa Players, but fellow members such as Willis Richardson were apparently unaware of her playwriting despite her publications and prizes.[88] None of her three plays were produced during her lifetime, probably in large part because they were so unlike the other African-American plays of her day. In 1930 she married and moved to Chicago, turning away from drama to focus exclusively on fiction. She won recognition for her short stories in the 1930s, but stopped publishing after 1941. Some critics have attributed her abandonment of writing to her devotion to the Christian Science Church and to her teaching and family commitments. Another key factor, as Joyce Flynn suggests in her introduction to *Frye Street and Environs*, was Bonner's "growing despair concerning the city's effect on the individual").[89] Bonner's literary vision tended to be bleak, and she may have tired of waiting for the revolution she foresaw as a young woman in *The Purple Flower.*

One of the rare comedies in this collection is Eulalie Spence's *The Hunch*, which won second prize in the *Opportunity* play contest of 1927 and was published in *Carolina Magazine* in May of the same year. It was produced by the Krigwa Players of Washington, DC, in June 1927. Although Spence was production-oriented as a playwright, the stage directions of *The Hunch* and some of her other plays convey the strong literary voice of a narrator, which is characteristic of "plays to be read." For example, in addition to a straightforward description of the set, Spence includes the unplayable detail that "Mavis rents this room for considerably more than she can afford" (133). *The Hunch* lightheartedly explores the pervasiveness of corruption in the urban environment and introduces elements that recur in many of Spence's plays, including the busybody older female character (Mrs. Reed), the hustler figure (Bert), and the love of Harlem despite its flaws (Steve assures heartbroken Mavis, "Why kid, yuh couldn't stay away from Harlem on a bet" [146]). The play demonstrates Spence's dismissal of propaganda in favor of showing identifiably black characters with problems that are not particularly racial. Unlike most of Spence's other pieces, *The Hunch* ends on an optimistic note regarding male/female relations. Rather than suggesting the impossibility of honest relations between the sexes, the exposure of Mavis's fiancé as a scoundrel actually opens the way for true love between the hero and heroine.

Spence's *The Starter*, which won third prize in the 1927 *Opportunity* contest and was published in Locke and Gregory's *Plays of Negro Life* (1927), is also a romantic comedy set in Harlem.[90] Some elements are remarkably similar to *The Hunch*. The stage directions are literary: "Kelly's face is the most important thing that ever happened to him" (148). *The Hunch*'s affection for Harlem is echoed in *The Starter*'s ending as the hero says, "Harlem sure is great!" (154). Even some lines are nearly identical in the two plays.[91] However, *The Starter* ends on a markedly more ambiguous note than *The Hunch*, with the prospect of a future marriage unlikely. As in many of Spence's darker pieces, the potentially unresolvable conflict is created by a lack of communication between the sexes. Although clearly not a propaganda piece, *The Starter* used the dialogue to introduce some of the problems facing African Americans of the period.[92]

Spence's *Hot Stuff* was awarded the third prize in the 1927 *Crisis* contest (along with her play *Undertow*). The story is a version of *The Hunch* told from a different point of view, with the focus on the Harlem character who cheats in the numbers game, rather than on the characters who are cheated, or who resist the temptation to cheat. The honest lovers, John Cole and Jennie Barbour, only appear as minor characters, used to develop the central story of the amoral Fanny King. Fanny King not only cheats the white establishment by selling stolen dresses and stockings, she steals from her "own people" in the numbers game, and even cheats on her own husband. Still, Spence's multifaceted portrayal prevents Fanny from becoming an unsympathetic villain.[93] Fanny's initial scene with her friend Mary Green demonstrates that she is capable of making connections with others. Her vulnerability is then explicitily represented at the end, and her hardhearted attitude, evident in her final telephone conversation, is revealed to be a way of willfully surviving the harsh realities in her life.

Undertow, awarded third prize in the 1927 *Crisis* contest (with *Hot Stuff*) and published in *Carolina Magazine* in April 1929, is a departure for Spence as a tragic melodrama[94] about the destruction of a marriage through infidelity and the subsequent distrust and anger. As in *Hot Stuff*, Spence presents a female character who appears unsympathetic and even villainous, and then complicates that character. In her character description, the "dark face" of Hattie, the protagonist, is described as "cold and hard." The first scene establishes Hattie's harsh nature as she openly expresses her contempt for her husband, Dan, to their son. However, more than halfway into the play, the primary source of her deep bitterness is revealed to be her husband's infidelity with a friend of hers one year into their marriage, while Hattie was pregnant with their son. Hattie herself recognizes what she has become and tells her husband's lover, "Ah was soft 'nuff when yuh fust stepped on me. Ef Ah's hard now, 'tis yo' fault" (173). Hattie certainly lacks the virtue of forgiveness, but the play subtly suggests that if there is anyone to blame for the tragedy, it is "broken" Dan, whose early weakness destroys his wife's life, and whose later anger ends it.

Episode, published by Spence in *The Archive* in April 1928, is subtitled "A Domestic Comedy," and is certainly lighter than *Undertow*. However, the play is anything but comedic in its exploration of addiction and isolation. Mamie tries to convince her new husband, Jim, not to go out with his friends so that they can "ask friends up an' have some fun" (179). Jim does stop going out, but only trades his physical abandonment of Mamie for emotional abandonment. Jim clearly wants to change his life, and blames his wife for having no ambition. However, his musical aspirations are represented as an unhealthy addiction, since the virtues of diligence and commitment are overshadowed by a lack of connection with others. His character changes to such an extent that Mamie laments that her husband is almost a stranger to her. In this context Mamie's plea for him to go out with his friends is only mildly humorous at best.

Eulalie Spence (1894–1981) was born in Nevis, British West Indies, but immigrated to the United States in 1902 after a hurricane destroyed her family's sugarcane farm. Living first in Harlem, then moving to Brooklyn, Spence attended Wadleigh High School, followed by the Normal Department of the New York Training School for Teachers. In 1914 she began teaching elocution and English at Eastern District High School in Brooklyn, where she continued teaching until her retirement in 1958.[95] During the 1920s she took courses in speech and English at the College of the City of New York (CCNY) and Columbia University, where she worked with Pulitzer Prize-winning playwright Hatcher Hughes. In 1924 she also studied at the short-lived Ethiopian Art Theatre School. She continued her studies during the first part of her teaching career, receiving her B.A. from New York University in 1937 and her M.A. in speech from Columbia in 1939.

Spence won five of the *Crisis* and *Opportunity* play prizes, more than any other playwright, although only a few of her plays were published in the periodicals.[96] She wrote at least twelve plays, and at least seven of them were produced around the time they were written.[97] Spence concentrated on writing playable dramatic comedies, and openly disagreed with Du Bois's stance about the role of propaganda in theater. In a 1973 interview in the Hatch-Billops Collection, she recalls, "I just never believed that you could induce people to come out and see a play about lynching or something that was painful for the writer and it wasn't my background experience anyway."[98] Nevertheless, two of her "comedies" won prizes in the 1926 *Crisis* contest,[99] and Spence became a key figure in the emerging Krigwa Players.[100] In 1926 and 1927 the group produced four of her plays,[101] their production of her comedy *Fool's Errand* winning second prize at the National Little Theatre Tournament at the Frolic Theatre, New York, in 1927.[102] In addition to her playwriting, Spence was a drama critic for *Opportunity* magazine. In 1929 she directed the Dunbar Garden Players at St. Mark's Church in New York. After writing *The Whipping* in 1934,[103] Spence stopped writing plays but continued to be active in theater, acting with the Laboratory Players at Columbia in the late 1930s[104] and directing a number of productions at the high school where she taught. In *Harlem Renaissance and Beyond*, Lorraine Elena Roses and Ruth Elizabeth Randolph attribute Spence's later silence to her aspiration "to write whimsical comedy that could play to both black and white audiences," a goal that "was almost unattainable in the segregated world of the 1920s and 1930s".[105] Still, throughout her life, Spence maintained her commitment to theater "that has universal good and joy and welcome and understanding, [which] opens the door of humanity a little wider."[106] She firmly believed that "hammering at an old illness and old injury, whether it is of eighty years, one hundred years or one thousand, does no good at all. It's defeating."[107]

Alvira Hazzard's *Mother Liked It*, a playful comedy published in *The Saturday Evening Quill* in April 1928, would have satisfied Spence's call for "a little more laughter, please, and fewer spirituals,"[108] if not Spence's professional standards. The play opens with a cast of characters written in a playful literary style, and then proceeds as a sometimes awkward, but nevertheless playable romantic farce. The overt references to theater and to the melodramatic language of the characters would contribute to the humor of an amateur performance.[109] The rather extreme characters are in line with the fantastic coincidences of the plot. True to form, virtue is rewarded and the end finds the kind, charming heroine united with the man of her dreams. The fact that that man turns out not to be an Indian prince but "a husky college half-back and one-hundred-percent American" (198) solves "the problem" of mixed races and cultures before the lovers have even been properly introduced.

In contrast to *Mother Liked It*, Hazzard's other published play, *Little Heads*, centers explicitly on problems of race. Its publication in *The Saturday Evening Quill* in April 1929 includes the subtitle "One-Act Play of Negro Life." For all the characters except the pivotal character, Frances, racial classification seems to be the first and foremost factor in their assessment of whites.[110] Frances's desire to see beyond the color of her Northern classmates is proved naïve by the racism of a white character's party "invitation," proposing that Frances and the one other black guest "help entertain" by dressing "sort of old-fashioned and sing[ing] some of those delightful spirituals" (204). Hazzard also attempts to raise gender issues in the play through criticism of the mother for giving Frances's inheritance to her "spendthrift of a son" (203).

Alvira Hazzard (1899–1953) was born in North Brookfield, Massachusetts, graduated from Worcester Normal School, and then taught in the Boston public schools. She also worked as a clerk at Boston City Hospital (which is listed on her death certificate as her "usual occupation"). In addition to her plays, she published at least four poems and a short story in *The Saturday Evening Quill*, as well as several short stories in the *Boston Post*. She seems to have particularly valued her work as a playwright, since her 1929 autobiographical note for the Saturday Evening Quill Club does not mention the poems or short stories but states that she "has been prolific as a writer on one-act plays, many of which have been acted by amateurs."

Doris Price's *Two Gods: A Minaret*, published in *Opportunity* in December of 1932, explores issues of faith, dramatically raising questions about the power of religion and interestingly leaving them unanswered at the end of the play. Price's sympathetic portrayal of the protagonist, Corrinne Baker, who feels betrayed by God, gives dramatic credit to religious doubt, which is strengthened by the dismissable religious characters, Amy Grey and Reverend Simpson. Nevertheless, several details in the play create a sinister mood and suggest that rejecting God will not go unpunished. The elaborate discussion of the apples in conjunction with Corrinne's husband's grave link the apples to death[111] and to the fruit of knowledge from the Garden of Eden.[112] Corrinne's frequent references to the heat of the kitchen evoke a connection to the fires of Hell. Finally, when the Reverend pulls off Corrinne's headscarf in the final moment to reveal that "her whole head is a sore red spot," his claim that "Der curse of Hebben [is] upon her!" (216) carries some credibility. However, these details do not answer the questions in favor of religion, but serve to maintain the internal and external conflict between blind faith and anger at God's seeming abandonment.[113]

Little is known about the life of Doris Price, not even her dates of birth or death. She wrote at least four plays, including *Two Gods*, while a student of Kenneth Rowe at the University of Michigan in the 1930s. Two of her plays, *The Bright Medallion* and *The Eyes of the Old*, were published in *University of Michigan Plays* in 1932, a compilation of plays from Rowe's class. These two plays, as well as another Price play, *Sokta*, were produced in the University Laboratory Theatre by the Detroit chapter of Delta Sigma Theta. All of her published plays are written in dialect and center on an African-American character who rebels against accepted social mores, suffering greatly as a result of the rebellion.[114]

By writing and publishing their plays, these early playwrights established the foundations for a tradition that became one of the most vital in contemporary American theater. Margaret Wilkerson contends in *9 Plays by Black Women*:

> Women playwrights before 1950 were full partners in the theatre's protest against conditions for blacks, whether in the form of 'race propaganda,' folk plays, or historical dramas. They also made the unique perspective of black women's reality a part of that protest. Not until mid-century, however, would their voices reach beyond their communities into the highly competitive world of professional theatre.[115]

Many of the plays in this volume have appeared in the groundbreaking anthologies of African-American theater published since the early 1970s. However, having them all collected together underscores how the plays were not isolated events but part of a movement. The playwrights met with varying degrees of success in their own time, but all contributed to the dramatic discussion of their day and to the development of voices to follow. It was partly the strength of the early voices represented in this volume that enabled the subsequent work of playwrights like Lorraine Hansberry, Ntozake Shange, Adrienne Kennedy, and Anna Deavere Smith. As May Miller recalled in a 1972 interview:

> [T]he great Krigwa Movement was sponsored by the *Crisis* magazine, and it established all over the country little one-act play groups that performed in churches and schools, and all this was a forerunner to what we're doing now. We would have no Lorraine Hansberry if there had not been behind her those people who were slowly leading up to her great productions.[116]

NOTES

[1]*Opportunity* (August 1924): 228. *Opportunity* (edited by Charles S. Johnson) was founded in 1923 as the organ of the National Urban League.

[2]*Crisis* (November 1924): 24. *Crisis* was founded in 1910 as the magazine of the National Association for the Advancement of Colored People (NAACP). W. E. B. Du Bois edited *Crisis* from its inception until 1934, when he resigned over political differences with the NAACP.

[3]This movement was exemplified by the Krigwa Players' Little Negro Theater, which performed two plays at the first *Crisis* awards dinner on October 25, 1926, including Eulalie Spence's prize play, *Foreign Mail*.

[4]In the same essay, Du Bois set out his four points for the new native drama: it should be "1. About us. . . . 2. By us. . . . 3. For us. . . . 4. Near us. . . ." "'Krigwa Players' Little Negro Theater': The Story of a Little Theatre Movement," *Crisis* (July 1926): 134.

[5]Besides Burrill's *Aftermath*, Richardson cites three plays by white playwright Ridgley Torrence. Willis Richardson, "The Hope of a Negro Drama," *Crisis* (November 1919): 338–9.

[6]*Rachel* was produced by the NAACP's Drama Committee of Washington, DC, which was founded in 1915 to help utilize the power of the stage to promote social justice.

[7]Among the race plays produced on Broadway were those by white playwrights Eugene O'Neill (*All God's Chillun Got Wings*, 1923) and Paul Green (*Abraham's Bosom*, 1924) and black playwrights Willis Richardson (*The Chipwoman's Fortune*, 1923), Garland Anderson (*Appearances*, 1925), and Wallace Thurman (*Harlem*, 1929). *The Chipwoman's Fortune* was the first serious play by a black man produced on Broadway. The first serious play by a black woman was Lorraine Hansberry's *A Raisin in the Sun*, produced thirty-six years later, in 1959.

[8]Richardson, 338.

[9]The majority of the playwriting students at Howard were women.

[10]Montgomery Gregory, quoted in Kathy Perkins, ed., *Black Female Playwrights: An Anthology of Plays Before 1950* (Bloomington: Indiana University Press, 1989), 7.

[11]Quoted in Perkins, 7.

[12]Perkins, 7.

[13]Many of the plays that were produced but never published have yet to be located. Presumably a greater percentage of those plays conform to Spence's performance-oriented views of playwriting: "We go to the theatre for entertainment, not to have old fires and hates rekindled." "A Criticism of the Negro Drama," *Opportunity* (June 28, 1928): 180.

[14]*Cooped Up* was on a double bill with *Being Forty*.

[15]Bernard L. Peterson, Jr. lists the manuscript of *The Cuss'd Thing* as being in May Miller's personal collection. However, Miller's niece, Mrs. Suzanne M. Jefferson, has been unable to locate the manuscript following Miller's death in February 1995. *Early Black American Playwrights and Dramatic Writers: A Biographical Dictionary and Catalog of Plays, Films, and Broadcasting Scripts* (New York: Greenwood, 1990), 145.

[16]However, the top awards and most money usually went to men. The relative performance of the men and women generally corresponded with the gender makeup of the panel of judges. For more details on submissions, judges, and contest winners, see Perkins, 4–5

[17]However, first prize and one of the second prizes, in addition to an honorable mention, were awarded to men. Three of the four judges were men, including Montgomery Gregory.

[18]All four judges were men.

[19]The first prize went to Willis Richardson, for *The Broken Banjo*.

[20]In a *Crisis* editorial in November 1927, Du Bois describes how he was undertaking "to read every single manuscript personally" (312). After he graded and "personally chose the A manuscripts," he wrote that he would "call in expert outside aid to confirm or criticize his decisions." However, these outside "authors, artists and experts" are only vaguely mentioned with the list of prize winners published in December 1927.

[21]The sex of all of the winners cannot be determined because some are listed with initials instead of first names.

[22]Two of the other prize plays were published in anthologies during the period. Of the remaining two prize plays, Spence's *Hot Stuff* was published in Elizabeth Brown-Guillory's 1990 anthology, *Wines in the Wilderness*, and Miller's *The Bog Guide* is being published here for the first time.

[23]As Kenneth Rowe wrote in his 1932 introduction to *University of Michigan Plays* (which featured two plays of Doris Price), one-acts had "little or no chance in the commercial theatre." Quoted in Lorraine Elena Roses and Ruth Elizabeth Randolph, *Harlem Renaissance and Beyond: Literary Biographies of One Hundred Black Women Writers, 1910–1945* (Boston: G. K. Hall, 1990), 275.

[24]This same shift occurred for the suffrage dramatists of the period, who shared the belief with the black female playwrights that performance could be a tactic for social change. As George Middleton argued in a 1914 article entitled "The Publication of Plays," publication could keep the plays alive even if they were not performed well or at all. Furthermore, he contended that published plays had already "raised the standards of amateur performances—and it is in these organs so frequently sneered at, that the taste of the future is being molded." "The Publication of Plays, *Harpers Weekly* (January 24, 1914): 26.

[25]For example, Eulalie Spence's *The Starter* concludes with the poetic directive, "The Moon-man hangs his lantern in the heavens, and we do the only kindly thing we can think of. We draw the Curtain" (154).

[26]Elizabeth Brown-Guillory, *Their Place on the Stage* (New York: Greenwood, 1988), 5.

[27]Esther Fulks Scott, "Negroes as Actors in Serious Plays," *Opportunity* (April 1923): 21.

[28]Isaac is the progenitor of the Egyptian race, and by extension he has also traditionally been considered an ancestor of people of African descent.

[29]See, for example, Peterson, 104.

[30]Dan allies himself with women earlier in the play, albeit in a disparaging way, when he asks his brother, "Have I come to this, that I should be the excuse, the *woman's skirts* for a slacker to hide behind?" (7, italics mine). As a paralyzed veteran, he no longer sees himself as part of the group of "our *men* [who] have always gone" (8, italics mine).

[31]For an in-depth analysis of the shift in strategy in black women's writings from domestic happiness to domestic tragedy, see Claudia Tate's *Domestic Allegories of Political Desire* (New York: Greenwood, 1992).

[32]Ann Allen Shockley, *Afro-American Women Writers 1746–1933: An Anthology and Critical Guide* (Boston: G. K. Hall, 1988), 262.

[33]In *The Smart Set* (September 1900): 105–6.

[34]In an interview in 1973, Dunbar-Nelson's niece, Pauline Young, recalled "she [Dunbar-Nelson] taught us English in the high school. She produced her play and we all took parts. The audience loved it . . . but nobody would publish it." Quoted in James V. Hatch and Ted Shine, eds.,

Black Theater U.S.A.: Forty-Five Plays by Black Americans 1847–1974 (New York: Free Press, 1974), 173.

[35]*Aftermath* echoes an editorial by Du Bois in *Crisis* that encouraged returning soldiers to use the courage and skill they had demonstrated overseas to combat the "forces of hell" at home.

[36]Although *Aftermath* is written in the realistic style characteristic of most plays of the period by black women, the revolutionary thrust (as well as the references to "white devils") foreshadows Marita Bonner's powerful surrealistic play *The Purple Flower* (1926).

[37]Bonner's *The Purple Flower* advocates this same delimited role of God.

[38]For reprints of suffrage plays of the period (all by white suffragists) see Bettina Freidl, ed., *On to Victory: Propaganda Plays of the Woman Suffrage Movement* (Boston: Northeastern University Press, 1987).

[39]George Bernard Shaw, "The Problem Play—A Symposium," *The Humanitarian* 6 (May 1895). Reprinted in *Shaw on Theatre*, ed. E. J. West (New York: Hill & Wang, 1958), 59–60.

[40]In "Under the Days: The Buried Life and Poetry of Angelina Weld Grimké" (1979) Gloria Hull argues that the passionate language demonstrates a "clearly Lesbian relationship," basing her conclusions on several youthful letters. However, Lorraine Elena Roses and Ruth Elizabeth Randolph argue that "Grimké was sixteen years old at the time and Burrill perhaps younger . . . and that Victorian discourse allowed for abstract eroticism in the absence of the physical." See Roses and Randolph, 36–8.

[41]Willis Richardson, the first African American to have a serious play produced on Broadway, was another of Burrill's students.

[42]Little is known about Graham's life, but some further biographical details are provided in her entry in Roses and Randolph, 135–7.

[43]This production, directed by Montgomery Gregory and Marie Morre-Forrest, is described in Gregory's "Chronology of Negro Theatre" in *Plays of Negro Life*, ed. Alain Locke (New York: Harper, 1927), 418.

[44]First prize went to G. D. Lipscomb's *Frances*, a race propaganda play published in *Crisis* in May 1925, which ends in the violent death not only of the villainous white landowner, but also of the Uncle Tom-like character of Frances's uncle.

[45]Hatch, 188.

[46]In addition to Judas, Brother Ananias and Sister Sapphira have biblical counterparts. In the Acts of the Apostles, Ananias and his wife, Sapphira, deceptively lie and withhold money in an attempt to cheat their church.

[47]However, the discursive section of her entry states that she started writing "plays for Clubs, Schools, Churches about 1906 and has written and staged these plays for twenty years" (330). The discrepancy suggests the importance to her of having a continuous professional identity.

[48]Other than *The Church Fight*, none of these plays were ever published and the manuscripts have yet to be discovered. The titles suggest that at least four of them were inspired by her intimate knowledge of the church: her father was a minister of the A.M.E. Church for forty years and the year after graduating from Wilberforce she helped her father direct the building of the Old Bethel A.M.E. Church in Chicago. Her mother died when she was two.

[49]The theatrical tradition of the tragic mulatto, established by Dion Boucucault's *The Octoroon* in 1859 and continuing virtually unimpeded for over a century, invariably involved the death of the mulatto figure, whether the play was written by a black or white author.

[50]Cuban playwright Maria Irene Fornes argues that this prominence of developed female characters is not only the definitive characteristic, but the only common trait in plays by women through history. (Conversation with the playwright, Buffalo, New York, 1994.)

[51]Other examples are *Aftermath* and *Mine Eyes Have Seen*.

[52]With the exception of *Mine Eyes Have Seen*, most of the other plays rely on represented rather than discussed action to develop their arguments.

[53]Since LeRoy has already decided to give up Selma, his death can also be seen as the retribution for his parents' miscegenation.

[54]Quoted in Roses and Randolph, 223.

[55]*The Bog Guide* is one of these plays with white characters in leading roles. Most of the plays are entirely black cast, with minor white characters appearing in Dunbar-Nelson's *Mine Eyes Have Seen*, Burrill's *They That Sit in Darkness*, Graham's *Holiday*, Livingston's *For Unborn Children*, and Spence's *Hot Stuff*, in addition to the "sundry white devils" of Bonner's *The Purple Flower* and the figure of death in Bonner's *Exit, an Illusion*.

[56]The characters who cross racial lines and then die include Chauncey's mother (who was part "Negro"), Chauncey's father, Chauncey, Chauncey's wife (the brown dancer who became an exile from her village because of her relationship with Chauncey), Sabali, and even Masters, who tells Sabali, "I shall be your father" (66).

[57]Dan has already compromised his virtue earlier in the play. Although he repeatedly stresses that it is because he is hungry, he nevertheless

breaks his vow against gambling when he plays Jeff. If his punishment is losing, then it is short-lived.

[58]She is described as "a beautiful tall mulatto," who, "in spite of dissipation, is to the manner born" (69). The color consciousness of the play is strangely uncomplicated: lighter equals more attractive and civilized. In contrast to Abbie as the statuesque mulatto character, "brown" Meldora is not only shorter, but is "overpowdered and heavily rouged" (69). "Dark brown" Stump fares the worst of all, as the hunchback who "swings around" "with apelike movements" (66).

[59]In the 1930s Miller turned to history plays, intended mainly for schools, many of which she published in *Negro History in Thirteen Plays*, which she co-edited with Willis Richardson. See note 63.

[60]Woodson later supported her collaboration with Willis Richardson on *Negro History in Thirteen Plays*.

[61]Among her roles was a part in Georgia Douglas Johnson's *Blue Blood*.

[62]Among the men in the "S Street Salon" who were interested in theater were Langston Hughes, Alain Locke, Carter G. Woodson, Willis Richardson, and Jean Toomer.

[63]The four plays are *Christophe's Daughter*, *Harriet Tubman*, *Samory*, and *Sojourner Truth*. Christine Gray disputes this editorial credit, commenting that "according to an interview with Richardson, May Miller had her name on *Negro History* because her father, Kelly Miller, would not allow the publisher to print her plays unless she received that credit. Richardson said that it didn't matter to him and so he went along with it." Personal correspondence, January 10, 1995.

[64]The play was performed at her last Frederick Douglass commencement as a teacher. The link between her leaving the school, which was her main place of production as a playwright, and her stopping playwriting demonstrates the powerful connection between dramatic productivity and possibilities for production.

[65]Hurston collaborated with other writers, including Langston Hughes and Wallace Thurman, to edit the sole issue of the literary journal *Fire!!*. The title has ironic overtones, since not only were many of the copies of *Fire!!* destroyed in a warehouse fire, but Hurston's own birth and death were clouded by fire. The discrepancies in reportings of Hurston's birth date arose partially because her birth records were destroyed in a courthouse fire and many of her papers were damaged or destroyed when her personal effects were burned after her death at St. Lucie County Welfare Home.

[66]Joe Clarke, "the onliest mayor of de onliest colored town in de state," even appears as a bit player in Scene 2. Clarke resurfaces in a number of

Hurston's later works, most notably her masterpiece, *Their Eyes Were Watching God*.

[67]The character descriptions immediately signal the interracial perspective: Emmaline is described as "a black woman" with her daughter as "a very white girl" (79).

[68]The white father of Emmaline's daughter is discussed, but never brought onstage; although Emmaline's color consciousness certainly was nurtured by societal racism, her inability to accept John's love is represented as self-destructive weakness.

[69]Her anthropological work included collecting slang expressions, such as those listed in "Harlem Slanguage." See *Zora Neale Hurston: The Complete Stories*, ed. Henry Louis Gates, Jr., and Sieglinde Lemke (New York: HarperCollins, 1995), 227–32.

[70]There is no record of the play ever being performed.

[71]John and Emma's winning cakewalk is suggested by "(Seven to nine minutes to curtain.) Fervor of spectators grows until all are taking part in some way—either hand-clapping or singing the words. At curtain they have reached frenzy" (88–9).

[72]Furthermore, the elaborate costumes, stage sets, and dance numbers would require a professional production, but the tremendous number of extra characters would be more suited to an amateur performance.

[73]Ham is traditionally considered to be the father of black-skinned people, and Genesis 9 has been used to support racial prejudice.

[74]By naming Ham's wife Eve, Hurston presents her as the mother of a race.

[75]Ham is developed as a satire of a black stereotype, who is late, lazy, happy-go-lucky, and a talented entertainer. Although some of these characteristics are presented as positive, the actual black color of his skin is consistently presented as a curse that directly elicits revulsion, violence, and ultimately segregation.

[76]Other production problems are the sacrifice on the altar being lit by a torch, and the set, which includes "slopes grassy with grazing herds" and "a plain clad with bright flowers."

[77]There she met playwright Paul Green and discussed the possibility of a collaboration called *John de Conquerer*, which never materialized.

[78]In Nancy Cunard's *Negro: An Anthology—1931–1933* (London: Wishart, 1934).

[79]"Get a job paying good money! Keep it two weeks and jes' when I'm hoping you'll get a little money ahead so's I could live decent like other women—in my house—You had to go and get called of God and quit to preach!" (112–3) she tells Elias.

[80]With *The Purple Flower*, Bonner initiated the revolutionary theater movement, predating playwrights like Amiri Baraka by over three decades.

[81]The world is made up of uniform "Sundry White Devils" and differentiated "Us's," who "can be as white as the White Devils, as brown as the earth, as black as the center of a poppy" (116).

[82]As Hatch points out, "Bonner isn't asking, 'Will there be a revolution?' but, "Is it time?'" (Hatch, 201).

[83]Buddy questions the name of Dot's friend by saying "Exit? Exit! Where'd he get that! off the inside of theayter door?" (128).

[84]In plot, *Exit, an Illusion* is a variation of Hurston's *Color Struck*, with the genders reversed: the darker *man* unable to love the lighter *woman* because he is jealous of the white(r) *man*.

[85]The ending also brings out a contrast between the narrative structure of drama and that of fiction. In traditional fiction the illusion would have been connected with one character's perspective. Since drama presents multiple points of view, it is unclear whether the illusion is Buddy's alone or a vision shared by Dot. However, the final lines do link the vision to Buddy. He explicitly cries out "Exit!! Mann!! Exit!!" (132) in his sleep. In contrast, Dot's line "Say you love me 'fore I go" (132) contradicts the thrust of the illusion that death won't be able to take her if he professes his love.

[86]Quoted in Roses and Randolph, 18.

[87]Like Bonner's plays, Toomer's *Cane* combines dramatic form with fictional elements to make a multigenre text.

[88]See Joyce Flynn's entry on Bonner in *Directory of Literary Biography* 51, 224.

[89]Flynn, *Frye Street*, xxv.

[90]Following its publication, *The Starter* was apparently performed by a number of amateur groups.

[91]Georgia asks Kelly, "Say, yuh doan' hate yuhself, do you?" (150). Mavis's similar line demonstrates the lack of uniformity in the spelling of dialect: "You doan hate yuhself, do yuh?" (145), she asks Steve.

[92]In his work as an elevator operator, T. J. Kelly's education is "being lost" on the customers he serves. Georgia responds that the problem is that he's had too much schooling, but the racism contributing to T. J.'s inability to advance beyond a position as "a starter" is not explicitly explored. Likewise, the class and race dynamics underlying Georgia's work in a sweatshop, with "Eyetalians and Jews and colored—all in tergether" (151), are pushed aside by the flirtatious wordplay about starters and finishers.

[93]In contrast, Goldstein's character is a flat stereotype that borders on the antisemitic, particularly when the stage direction reports that "a well aimed kick sends *the Jew* sprawling" (162–3, italics mine). In the stage directions, other characters are referred to by their names.

[94]Spence's plays, with the exception of *Undertow*, *Her* (drama), and *La Divina Pastora* (drama), are generally considered comedies.

[95]Spence was also the director of the dramatic club. Among her students was director Joseph Papp.

[96]This was partially because some were published elsewhere. *(The Starter* was included in *Plays of Negro Life*, and *Foreign Mail* was published by Samuel French.) However, Peterson suggests that Spence's conflict with W. E. B. Du Bois over the Krigwa Players may have prevented her from having her plays appear in *Crisis* (179).

[97]All her plays were written between 1920 and 1933. In addition to the plays reprinted in this volume, her works include *Brothers and Sisters of the Church Council* (1920); *Being Forty* (1924), a one-act comedy produced by the National Ethiopian Art Players in 1924 and by the Bank Street Players in 1927; *Foreign Mail* (1926), a one-act comedy produced by the Krigwa Players in 1926 and 1927 and published by Samuel French in 1927; *Her* (1927), a one-act drama produced by the Krigwa Players in 1927; *(The) Fool's Errand* (1927) a one-act comedy produced by the Krigwa Players in 1927 and published by Samuel French the same year; *La Divina Pastora* (1929), a one-act drama produced by the Lighthouse Players of the New York Association for the Blind in 1929; and *The Whipping* (1934), a three-act drama. *The Whipping*, Spence's only full-length play, was scheduled for commercial production by the Century Play Company but never opened, and then optioned by Paramount Pictures, but never produced in its original form. For detailed production information on Spence's plays, see Peterson, 178–9.

[98]Later in the interview she adds, "Give a speech. Give any form of presentation. But a play that people are to pay to go and see and have an evening of enjoyment cannot depend on propaganda for success."

[99]Her play *Foreign Mail*, which won second prize in the contest, was published by Samuel French in 1927, but no extant copy has been located.

[100]Spence seems to have played a major role in the organization of Krigwa: in her comments on the group she recalls, "I thought just for fun I'd like to start a little theater group."

[101]*Foreign Mail*, *Her*, *The Fool's Errand*, and *The Hunch*.

[102]When Du Bois claimed the $200 prize money for expenses, the subsequent dispute resulted in the breakup of the theater company after existing only "six or eight months, maybe a year." Spence commented that

"Du Bois was very disappointed. He thought he had established a permanent little theater group and it was all his own meanness really" (Hatch-Billops interview).

[103]According to Spence the $5,000 she made from optioning the play to Paramount was the only money she ever made from playwriting.

[104]"Because I was so thin, I was cast for male parts and old ladies," Spence recalled in the Hatch-Billops interview. In addition to being a member of the players, she used to "alter scripts" for her professor, Estelle Davis Coint, who was the director of the group.

[105]Roses and Randolph, 295.

[106]Hatch-Billops interview.

[107]Hatch-Billops interview.

[108]Spence, "Criticism," 180.

[109]Meena says, "Tess, dear, you mised your calling when you didn't follow the stage" (192).

[110]Joe's abrupt comment that "Miss Perry's white" (199) is then echoed by Mrs. Lee's immediate reaction to the news of the party, "They are all white though, aren't they" (201).

[111]Indeed, the apple tree only started to bloom after Corrinne's husband was buried right under it.

[112]The visitors' interest in the pie is strangely overinvested, with Amy waiting for a piece of pie even after the conversation has turned unpleasant, and the Reverend taking a second piece after Corrinne's direct blasphemy. Furthermore, after one bite he "drops both it and the knife as one who has been burnt," but then "chews the mouthful of pie thoughtfully" (215).

[113]As Roses and Randolph argue, this conflict is symbolized by the house shutter that bangs throughout the play, functioning "as a reminder of past and present hardships in the protagonist's life as well as of the inner struggle she experiences between rejecting Christian religion and adhering to a cult" (276).

[114]While Corrinne in *Two Gods* suffers the pain of lost faith, Carrie Jackson in *The Eyes of the Old* is doomed to repeat her mother's mistakes as an unwed teenage mother and Samuel Hunt of *The Bright Medallion* is actually killed trying to prove his bravery.

[115]Margaret Wilkerson, ed., *9 Plays by Black Women* (New York: New American Library, 1986), xviii–xix.

[116]Interview with Cassandra Willis, quoted in Winifred L. Stoelting, "May Miller," *Directory of Literary Biography* 41, 243.

BIBLIOGRAPHY

Abramson, Doris E. *Negro Playwrights in the American Theatre, 1925–1959.* New York: Columbia University Press, 1969.

Arata, Esther Spring, with Marlene J. Erickson, Sandra Dewitz, and Mary Linse Alexander. *More Black American Playwrights: A Bibliography.* Metuchen, NJ: Scarecrow, 1978.

———, and Nicholas John Rotoli. *Black American Playwrights, 1800 to the Present: A Bibliography.* Metuchen, NJ: Scarecrow, 1976.

Bonner, Marita. *Exit, an Illusion. Crisis* (October 1929): 335–6.

———. *Frye Street & Environs: The Collected Works of Marita Bonner.* Ed. and intr. Joyce Flynn and Joyce Occomy Stricklin. Boston: Beacon, 1987.

———. *The Pot Maker. Opportunity: A Journal of Negro Life* (February 1927: 47–56.

———. *The Purple Flower. Crisis* (January 1928): 9–11, 28, 30.

Brawley, Benjamin. *The Negro Genius: A New Appraisal of the Achievement of the American Negro in Literature and the Fine Arts.* New York: Biblo and Tannen, 1937.

Brown, Sterling A. *Negro Poetry and Drama.* Washington, DC: Associates in Negro Folk Education, 1937.

Brown-Guillory, Elizabeth. *Their Place on the Stage: Black Women Playwrights in America.* New York: Greenwood, 1988.

———, ed. *Wines in the Wilderness: Plays by African American Women from the Harlem Renaissance to the Present.* New York: Greenwood, 1990.

Burrill, Mary P. *Aftermath. Liberator* (April 1919): 55–61.

———. *They That Sit in Darkness. Birth Control Review* (September 1919): 5–8.

Cunard, Nancy. *Negro: An Anthology.* London: Wishart, 1934.

Du Bois, W. E. B. "'Krigwa Players Little Negro Theatre': The Story of the Little Theatre Movement." *Crisis* (July 1926): 134–6.

Dunbar-Nelson, Alice Moore. *Mine Eyes Have Seen. Crisis* (April 1919): 271–5.

Flynn, Joyce. "Marita Bonner Occomy." In *Directory of Literary Biography* 51, 222–8.

Friedl, Bettina, ed. *On to Victory: Propaganda Plays of the Woman Suffrage Movement.* Boston: Northeastern University Press, 1987.

Gaines-Shelton, Ruth. *The Church Fight. Crisis* (May 1926): 17–18, 20–21.

Graham, Ottie. *Holiday*. *Crisis* (May 1923): 12–17.

Hamalian, Leo, and James V. Hatch, eds. *The Roots of African American Drama: An Anthology of Early Plays, 1858–1928*. Detroit: Wayne State University Press, 1991.

Hatch, James V., ed. *Black Theater U.S.A.: Forty-Five Plays by Black Americans, 1847–1974*. New York: Free Press, 1974.

Hazzard, Alvira. *Little Heads*. *Saturday Evening Quill* (1929): 42–4.

———. *Mother Liked It*. *Saturday Evening Quill* (1928): 10–14.

Hill, Errol, ed. *The Theater of Black Americans*. New York: Applause Theatre Book Publishers, 1987.

Hine, Darlene Clark, ed. *Black Women in America: An Historical Encyclopedia*. New York: Carlson, 1993.

Hirsh, Charlotte Teller. *Hagar and Ishmael*. *Crisis* (May 1913): 30–31.

Hurston, Zora Neale. *Color Struck*. *Fire!!* (November 1926): 7–14.

———. *The First One*. In *Ebony and Topaz*, ed. Charles S. Johnson, 53–7. New York: Opportunity/National Urban League, 1927.

———. *Zora Neale Hurston: The Complete Stories*. Ed. Henry Louis Gates Jr. and Sieglinde Lemke. New York: HarperCollins, 1995.

Johnson, Abby Arthur, and Ronald Mayberry Johnson. *Propaganda Aesthetics: The Literary Politics of Afro-American Magazines in the Twentieth Century*. Amherst: University of Massachusetts Press, 1979.

Keyssar, Helene. *The Curtain and the Veil: Strategies in Black Drama*. New York: Burt Franklin, 1981.

———. "Rites and Responsibilities: The Drama of Black American Women." In *Feminine Focus: The New Women Playwrights*, ed. Enoch Brater, 226–40. New York: Oxford University Press, 1989.

Knopf, Marcy, ed. *The Sleeper Wakes: Harlem Renaissance Stories by Women*. New Brunswick, NJ: Rutgers University Press, 1993.

Livingston, Myrtle Smith. *For Unborn Children*. *Crisis* (July 1926): 122–5.

Locke, Alain. *Plays of Negro Life*. New York: Harper, 1927.

McKay, Nellie. "What Were They Saying? Black Women Playwrights of the Harlem Renaissance." In *The Harlem Renaissance Re-Examined*, ed. Victor A. Kramer, 129–47. New York: A. M. S. Press, 1986.

Middleton, George. "The Publication of Plays." *Harpers Weekly* (24 January 1914): 26.

Miller, May. *The Bog Guide*. Typescript. Hatch-Billops Collection, City College of New York.

————. Interview [1972]. Hatch-Billops Oral Black Theatre History Collection, City College of New York.

————. *Scratches. Carolina* (April 1929): 36–44.

Mitchell, Loften. *Black Drama: The Story of the American Negro in the Theatre.* New York: Hawthorn, 1967.

Natalle, Elizabeth J. *Feminist Theatre: A Study in Persuasion.* Metuchen, NJ: Scarecrow, 1985.

Olauson, Judith. *The American Woman Playwright: A View of Criticism and Characterization.* Troy, NY: Whitston, 1981.

Perkins, Kathy A., ed. *Black Female Playwrights: An Anthology of Plays before 1950.* Bloomington: Indiana University Press, 1989.

Peterson, Bernard L., Jr. *Early Black American Playwrights and Dramatic Writers: A Biographical Dictionary and Catalog of Plays, Films, and Broadcasting Scripts.* New York: Greenwood, 1990.

Price, Doris. *Two Gods: A Minaret. Opportunity* (December 1932): 380–83, 389.

Richardson, Willis. "The Hope of Negro Drama." *Crisis* (November 1919): 338–9.

————, ed. *Plays and Pageants from the Life of the Negro.* Introduction by Christine Gray. Jackson: University Press of Mississippi, 1993.

————, and May Miller, eds. *Negro History in Thirteen Plays.* Washington, DC: Associated Publishers, 1935.

Roses, Lorraine Elena, and Ruth Elizabeth Randolph. *Harlem Renaissance and Beyond: Literary Biographies of One Hundred Black Women Writers, 1910–1945.* Boston: G. K. Hall, 1990.

Rush, Theressa Gunnels, Carol Fairbanks Myers, and Esther Spring Arata. *Black American Writers Past and Present: A Biographical and Bibliographical Dictionary.* Metuchen, NJ: Scarecrow, 1975.

Sanders, Leslie Catherine. *The Developmentt of Black Theater in America: From Shadows to Selves.* Baton Rouge: Louisiana State University Press, 1988.

Scott, Esther Fulks. "Negroes as Actors in Serious Plays." *Opportunity* (April 1923): 20–23.

Shaw, George Bernard. "The Problem Play—A Symposium." *The Humanitarian* 6 (May 1885). Reprinted in *Shaw on Theatre*, ed. E. J. West, 58–66. New York: Hill & Wang, 1958.

Shockley, Ann Allen. *Afro-American Women Writers 1946–1933: An Anthology and Critical Guide.* Boston: G. K. Hall, 1988.

Spence, Eulalie. Interview [1973]. Hatch-Billops Oral Black Theatre History Collection, City College of New York.

———. "A Criticism of the Negro Drama." *Opportuntiy* (June 1928): 180.

———. *Episode. The Archive* (April 1928): 3–8, 35–36, 38, 40.

———. *Hot Stuff.* In *Wines in the Wilderness,* ed. Elizabeth Brown-Guillory, 43–50. New York: Greenwood, 1990.

———. *The Hunch. Carolina* (May 1927): 21–30.

———. *The Starter.* In *Plays of Negro Life,* ed. Alain Locke, 205–14. New York: Harper, 1927.

———. *Undertow. Carolina* (April 1929): 5–15.

Stoelting, Winifred L. "May Miller." *Directory of Literary Biography* 41, 241–7.

Stowell, Sheila. *A Stage of Their Own: Feminist Playwrights of the Suffrage Era.* Ann Arbor: University of Michigan Press, 1992.

Tate, Claudia. *Domestic Allegories of Political Desire.* New York: Greenwood, 1990.

Wilkerson, Margaret, ed. *9 Plays by Black Women.* New York: New American Library, 1986.

HAGAR AND ISHMAEL

BY CHARLOTTE TELLER HIRSCH

And Sarah saw the son of Hagar, the Egyptian, which she had borne unto Abraham, mocking. Wherefore she said unto Abraham, Cast out this bondwoman and her son: for the son of this bondwoman shall not be here with my son, even with Isaac. And the thing was very grievous in Abraham's sight because of his son.

"And God said unto Abraham, Let it not be grievous in thy sight because of the lad, and because of thy bondwoman; in all that Sarah hath said unto thee, hearken unto her voice; for in Isaac shall thy seed be called. And also of the son of the bondwoman will I make a nation, because he is thy seed. And Abraham rose up early in the morning, and took bread, and a bottle of water, and gave it unto Hagar, putting it on her shoulder, and the child, and sent her away: and she departed and wandered in the wilderness of Beersheba.

"And the water was spent in the bottle, and she cast the child under one of the shrubs. And she went, and sat her down over against him a good way off, as it were a bow-shot: for she said, Let me not see the death of the child. And she sat over against him, and lifted up her voice and wept."—Genesis 21

(Not far from the tents of Abraham. Hagar stands alone, looking out across the desert. In the shade of low and twisted shrubs lies Ishmael, motionless. There is a barren rock into whose shadow the woman comes slowly, her head averted so that she may not see her son.)

1

HAGAR: How Egypt's God has burned this desert dry! And in the flames of His great wrath my Ishmael dies, because in Abram's tent I yielded me. His cries grow faint, while I afraid to look into his eyes, wait here, apart.

(There comes a moan for answer and she flings herself down upon the sand and reaches up her arms in prayer.)

Great God of Egypt, let Thy Nile flow here that he may drink and live, for am I not a child of Egypt still?

See how my bosom to the burning sands I bend. Draw from it by Thy power that which his new-born lips once drew. Or let my blood slake his youth's thirst for life.

See, now my brow upon the sands, for that I know and understand. But need my son pay for the life I led in Abram's tent? *(Listens and calls.)* Oh, Ishmael!

(This time there is no sound. She rises in terror, her eyes closed, her head lifted in anguish. As she moves toward the bushes her hand touches the rock and she gives a cry, opens her eyes and bends over the crevice, follows it with her gaze and discovers the pool at the base of the rock.)

My cry to Egypt's God has rent these rocks!

(She rushes to Ishmael and drags him back to the pool where she gives him to drink from her own hand. Then she lets him slip from her clasp and stoops to drink.)

My tears! I know the taste of them! And they have saved his life.

ISHMAEL *(weakly):* Jehovah lets me live.

HAGAR *(in horror):* Jehovah, God of Abraham? No! No! He has made mock of us! Did He not promise you should be the father of a race and then let Abram cast you forth with me? *(Stoops.)* You lie so prone upon the sand, child of the desert, flower of my swift advent to the heart of man.

ISHMAEL *(lifting his head):* The father of a race. He promised that?

HAGAR: The lie of God and Man against a woman slave.

ISHMAEL: If we could make it true! *(Lifts himself upon his elbow.)*

HAGAR: If we could breed a race to take great vengeance upon Isaac's seed, his son, who shall have wealth and comfort in his flocks! If we could find upon this fearful plain some child of lust to mother such a race! *(Rises.)* As you have tasted tears from my own breast and live, you shall eat fruit of evil and grow strong! You shall breed men to mock his God of Greed. Your seed against young Isaac's from this day! He has thrust Hagar forth. But she shall enter in and lure his sons and work destruction in the midst of them!

2

ISHMAEL *(rising slowly to his feet):* Your tears were bitter, but I live from them. Your curse upon his tented happiness I hear.

Yet I feel joy! Your tears, his blood are mingled in me now; your hate, his strength. New power, I know!

How great this wilderness in which we are! How small those tents that we have left behind! Not if I could would I go back to tend those flocks that I might have their fleece. Before me lies the way of exiles. See!

My sons, all those who are cast out by men. They shall not march in numbers; but, alone, each one shall wander on to his own truth across the desert's stretch.

Yet every one of them shall find this pool of tears—the exile's bitter drink, by which he lives—Son of a Slave, but Father to the Free.

MINE EYES HAVE SEEN

A PLAY IN ONE ACT

BY ALICE M. DUNBAR-NELSON

CHARACTERS.

DAN: *The Cripple.*
CHRIS: *The Younger Brother.*
LUCY: *The Sister.*
MRS. O'NEILL: *An Irish Neighbor.*
JAKE: *A Jewish Boy.*
JULIA: *Chris' Sweetheart.*
BILL HARVEY: *A Muleteer.*
CORNELIA LEWIS: *A Settlement Worker.*
Time: *Now*
Place: *A manufacturing city in the northern part of the United States.*

SCENE

Kitchen of a tenement. All details of furnishing emphasize sordidness—laundry tubs, range, table covered with oil cloth, pine chairs. Curtain discloses DAN *in a rude imitation of a steamer chair, propped by faded pillows, his feet covered with a patchwork quilt. Practicable window at back.*

Lucy is bustling about the range preparing a meal. During the conversation she moves from range to table, setting latter and making ready the noonday meal.

4

CHRIS: Yes, as slaves. Promised a freedom they never got.

DAN: No, gladly, and saved the day, too, many a time. Ours was the first blood shed on the altar of National liberty. We went in 1812, on land and sea. Our men were through the struggles of 1861—

CHRIS: When the Nation was afraid not to call them. Didn't want 'em at first.

DAN: Never mind; they helped work out their own salvation. And they were there in 1898—

CHRIS: Only to have their valor disputed.

DAN: —And they were at Carrizal, my boy, and now—

MRS. O'NEILL: An' sure, wid a record like that—ah, 'tis me ould man who said at first 'twasn't his quarrel. His Oireland bled an' the work of thim divils to try to make him a traitor nearly broke his heart—but he said he'd go to do his bit—an' here I am.

(There is a sound of noise and bustle without, and with a loud laugh, BILL HARVEY *enters. He is big, muscular, rough, his voice thunderous. He emits cries of joy at seeing the group, shakes hands and claps* CHRIS *and* DAN *on their backs.)*

DAN: And so you weren't torpedoed?

HARVEY: No, I'm here for a while—to get more mules and carry them to the front to kick their bit.

MRS. O'NEILL: You've been—over there?

HARVEY: Yes, over the top, too. Mules, rough-necks, wires, mud, dead bodies, stench, terror!

JULIA *(horrorstricken):* Ah—Chris!

CHRIS: Never, mind, not for mine.

HARVEY: It's a great life—not. But I'm off again, first chance.

MRS. O'NEILL: They're brutes, eh?

HARVEY: Don't remind me.

MRS. O'NEILL *(whispering):* They maimed my man, before he died.

JULIA *(clinging to* CHRIS): Not you, oh, not you!

HARVEY: They crucified children.

DAN: Little children? They crucified little children.

CHRIS: Well, what's that to us? They're little white children. But here, our fellow-countrymen throw our little black babies in the flames—as did the worshippers of Moloch, only they haven't the excuse of a religious rite.

JAKE: *(Slouches out of his chair, in which he has been sitting brooding.)* Say, don't you get tired sitting around grieving because you're colored? I'd be ashamed to be—

DAN: Stop! Who's ashamed of his race? Ours the glorious inheritance; ours the price of achievement. Ashamed! I'm PROUD. And you, too, Chris, smouldering in youthful wrath, you, too, are proud to be numbered with the darker ones, soon to come into their inheritance.

MRS. O'NEILL: Aye, but you've got to fight to keep yer inheritance. Ye can't lay down when someone else has done the work, and expect it to go on. Ye've got to fight.

JAKE: If you're proud, show it. All of your people—well, look at us! Is there a greater race than ours? Have any people had more horrible persecutions—and yet—we're loyal always to the country where we live and serve.

MRS. O'NEILL: And us! Look at us!

DAN: *(Half tears himself from the chair, the upper part of his body writhing, while the lower part is inert, dead.)* Oh, God! If I were but whole and strong! If I could only prove to a doubting world of what stuff my people are made!

JULIA: But why, Dan, it isn't our quarrel? What have we to do with their affairs? These white people, they hate us. Only today I was sneered at when I went to help with some of their relief work. Why should you, my Chris, go to help those who hate you?

(CHRIS clasps her in his arms, and they stand, defying the others.)

HARVEY: If you could have seen the babies and girls—and old women—if you could have—

(Covers his eyes with his hand.)

CHRIS: Well, it's good for things to be evened up somewhere.

DAN: Hush, Chris! It is not for us to visit retribution. Nor to wish hatred on others. Let us rather remember the good that has come to us. Love of humanity is above the small considerations of time or place or race or sect. Can't you be big enough to feel pity for the little crucified French children—for the ravished Polish girls, even as their mothers must have felt sorrow, if they had known, for OUR burned and maimed little ones? Oh, Mothers of Europe, we be of one blood, you and I!

(There is a tense silence. JULIA turns from CHRIS, and drops her hand. He moves slowly to the window and looks out. The door

opens quietly, and CORNELIA LEWIS *comes in. She stands still a moment, as if sensing a difficult situation.)*

CORNELIA: I've heard about it, Chris, your country calls you.

*(*CHRIS *turns from the window and waves hopeless hands at* DAN *and* LUCY.*)* Yes, I understand; they do need you, don't they?

DAN *(fiercely):* No!

LUCY: Yes, we do, Chris, we do need you, but your country needs you more. And, above that, your race is calling you to carry on its good name, and with that, the voice of humanity is calling to us all—we can manage without you, Chris.

CHRIS: You? Poor little crippled Sister. Poor Dan—

DAN: Don't pity me, pity your work, weak self.

CHRIS: *(clenching his fist.)* Brother, you've called me two names today that no man ought to have to take—a slacker and a weakling!

DAN: True. Aren't you both?

(Leans back and looks at CHRIS *speculatively.)*

CHRIS: *(Makes an angry lunge towards the chair, then flings his hands above his head in an impatient gesture.)* Oh, God!

(Turns back to window.)

JULIA: Chris, it's wicked for them to taunt you so—but Chris—it IS our country—our race—

(Outside the strains of music from a passing band are heard. The music comes faintly, gradually growing louder and louder until it reaches a crescendo. The tune is "The Battle Hymn of the Republic," played in stirring march time.)

DAN: *(singing softly.)* "Mine eyes have seen the glory of the coming of the Lord!"

CHRIS: *(Turns from the window and straightens his shoulders.)* And mine!

CORNELIA: "As He died to make men holy, let us die to make them free!"

MRS. O'NEILL: An' ye'll make the sacrifice, me boy, an' ye'll be the happier.

JAKE: Sacrifice! No sacrifice for him, it's those who stay behind. Ah, if they would only call me, and call me soon!

LUCY: We'll get on, never fear. I'm proud! PROUD!

(Her voice breaks a little, but her head is thrown back.)

11

(As the music draws nearer, the group breaks up, and the whole roomful rushes to the window and looks out. CHRIS *remains in the center of the floor, rigidly at attention, a rapt look on his face.* DAN *strains at his chair, as if he would rise, then sinks back, his hand feebly beating time to the music, which swells to a martial crash.)*

CURTAIN.

AFTERMATH

BY MARY BURRILL

Time: *The Present.*
Place: *The Thornton Cabin in South Carolina.*

SCENE

It is late afternoon of a cool day in early spring. A soft afterglow pours in at the little window of the Thornton cabin. The light falls on MILLIE, *a slender brown girl of sixteen, who stands near the window ironing. She wears a black dress and a big gingham apron. A clothes-horse weighted down with freshly ironed garments is nearby. In the rear there is a door leading out to the road. To the left, another door leading into the other room of the cabin. To the right there is a great stone hearth blackened by age. A Bible rests on the mantel over the hearth. An old armchair and a small table on which is a kerosene lamp are near the hearth. In the center of the room sits a well-scrubbed kitchen table and a substantial wooden chair. In front of the hearth, in a low rocking chair drawn close to the smouldering wood fire, sits* MAM SUE *busily sewing. The many colors in the old patchwork quilt that she is mending, together with the faded red of the bandanna on her head, contrast strangely with her black dress.* MAM SUE *is very old. Her ebony face is seamed with wrinkles; and in her bleared, watery eyes there is a world-old sorrow. A service flag containing one star hangs in the little window of the cabin.*

MAM SUE *(crooning the melody).*

> O, yes, yonder comes mah Lawd,
> He is comin' dis way
> Wid his sword in his han'
> O, yes, yonder comes—

13

(A burning log falls apart, and MAM SUE *suddenly stops singing and gazes intently at the fire. She speaks in deep mysterious tones to* MILLIE, *who has finished her task and has come to the hearth to put up her irons.)* See dat log dah, Millie? De one fallin' tuh de side dah wid de big flame lappin' 'round hit? Dat means big doin's 'round heah tonight!

MILLIE *(with a start).* Oh, Mam Sue, don' you go proph'sying no mo'! You seen big doin's in dat fire de night befo' them w'ite devuls come in heah an' tuk'n po' dad out and bu'nt him!

MAM SUE *(calmly).* No, Millie, Ah didn' see no big doin's dat night—Ah see'd *evul* doin's an' Ah tole yo' po' daddy to keep erway f'om town de nex' day wid his cotton. Ah jes knowed dat he wuz gwine to git in a row wid dem w'ite debbils—but he wou'd'n lis'n tuh his ole mammy—De good Lawd sen' me dese warnin's in dis fiah, jes lak He sen' His mesiges in de fiah to Moses. Yo' chillun bettah lis'n to—

MILLIE *(nervously).* Oh, Mam Sue, you skeers me when you talks erbout seein' all them things in de fire—

MAM SUE. Yuh gits skeered cause yuh don' put yo' trus' in de good Lawd! He kin tek keer o' yuh no mattuh whut com'!

MILLIE *(bitterly).* Sometimes I thinks that Gawd's done fu'got us po' cullud people. Gawd didn' tek no keer o' po' dad and *he* put *his* trus' in Him! He uster set evah night by dis fire at dis here table and read his Bible an' pray—but jes look whut happen' to dad! That don' look like Gawd wuz tekin' keer—

MAM SUE *(sharply).* Heish yo' mouf, Millie! Ah ain't a-gwine to 'ave dat sinne-talk 'roun' hyeah! *(Derisively.)* Gawd don't tek no keer o' yuh? Ain't yuh bin prayin' night an' mawnin' fo' Gawd to sen' yo' brudder back f'om de war 'live an' whole? An' ain't yuh git dat lettah no longer'n yistiddy sayin' dat de fightin's all done stopp't an' dat de blessid Lawd's done brung yo' brudder thoo all dem battuls live an' whole? Don' dat look lak de Lawd's done 'membered yuh?

MILLIE *(thoughtfully).* I reckon youse right, Mam Sue. But ef anything had a-happen' to John I wuz'n evah goin' to pray no mo'!

*(*MILLIE *goes to the clothes-horse and folds the garments and lays them carefully into a large basket.* MAM SUE *falls again to her crooning.)*

MAM SUE.

O, yes, yonder comes mah Lawd,
He's comin' dis way-a.

14

MILLIE. Lonnie's so late gittin' home tonight; I guess I'd bettah tek Mis' Hart's wash home tonight myse'f.

MAM SUE. Yas, Lonnie's might late. Ah reckons you'd bettah slip erlon' wid hit.

(MILLIE gets her hat from the adjoining room and is about to leave with the basket when MAM SUE calls significantly.) Millie?

MILLIE. Yas, Mam Sue.

MAM SUE *(firmly)*. Don' yo' fu'git to drap dat lettah fu' John in de Pos' Awfus ez yuh goes by. Whah's de lettah?

MILLIE *(reluctantly)*. But, Mam Sue, please don' lets—

(A knock is heard. MILLIE opens the door and REVEREND LUKE MOSEBY enters. MOSEBY is a wiry little old man with a black, kindly face, and bright, searching eyes; his woolly hair and beard are snow-white. He is dressed in a rusty black suit with a coat of clerical cut that comes to his knees. In one hand he carries a large Bible, and in the other, a stout walking stick.)

MILLIE. Good evenin', Brother Moseby, come right in.

REV. MOSEBY. Good eben', Millie. Good eben', Mam Sue. Ah jes drap't in to see ef you-all is still trus'in' de good Lawd an'—

MAM SUE. Lor', Brudder Moseby, ain't Ah bin trus'n' de good Lawd nigh onter dese eighty yeah! Whut fu' yuh think Ah's gwine to quit w'en Ah'm in sight o' de Promis' Lan'? Millie, fetch Brudder Moseby dat cheer.

MOSEBY *(drawing his chair to the fire)*. Dat's right, Mam Sue, you jes a-keep on trus'n' an' prayin' an evah thing's gwine to come aw-right. *(Observing that Millie is about to leave.)* Don' lemme 'tain yuh, Millie, but whut's all dis good news wese bin heahin' 'bout yo' brudder John? Dey say he's done won some kind o' medal ober dah in France?

MILLIE *(brightening up)*. Oh, yes, we got a lettah day befo' yestiddy f'om John tellin' us all erbout it. He's won de War Cross! He fought off twenty Germuns all erlone an' saved his whole comp'ny an' the gret French Gen'rul come an' pinned de medal on him, *hisse'f!*

MOSEBY. De Lawd bles' his soul! Ah know'd dat boy wud mek good!

MILLIE *(excited by the glory of it all)*. An' he's been to Paris, an' the fines' people stopp't him when they seen his medal, an' shook his han' an' smiled at him—an' he kin go evah-where, an' dey ain't nobody all the time a-lookin' down on him, an' a-sneerin' at him 'cause he's black; but evahwhere they's jes gran' to him! An' he sez it's the firs' time evah in his life he's felt lak a real, shonuf man!

MOSEBY. Well, honey, don't de Holy Book say, "De fust shill be las' and de las' shill be fust"?

MAM SUE (*fervently*). Dat hit do! An' de Holy Book ain't nebber tole no lie!

MOSEBY. Folks ober in Char'ston is sayin' dat some sojers is gwine to lan' dah today or tomorrer. Ah reckons day'll all be comin' 'long soon now dat de war's done stopp't.

millie. I jes hates the thought of John comin' home an' hearin' 'bout dad!

MOSEBY (*in astonishment*). Whut! Yuh mean to say yuh ain't 'rite him 'bout yo' daddy, yit?

MAM SUE. Dat she ain't! Millie mus' 'ave huh way! She 'lowed huh brudder ough'n be tole, an' dat huh could keep on writin' to him jes lak huh dad wuz livin'—Millie allus done de writin'— An' Ah lets huh 'ave huh way—

MOSEBY (*shaking his head in disapproval*). Yuh mean tuh say—

MILLIE (*pleadingly*). But Brother Moseby, I couldn't write John no bad news w'ilst he wuz way over there by hisse'f. He had 'nuf to worry him with death astarin' him in the face evah day!

MAM SUE. Yas, Brudder Moseby, Millie's bin carryin' on dem lies in huh lettahs fu' de las' six months; but today Ah jes sez to huh— Dis war done stopp't now, an' John he gwine to be comin' home soon, an' he ain't agwine to come hyeah an' fin' me wid no lie on mah soul! An' Ah med huh set down an' tell him de whole truf. She's gwine out to pos' dat lettah dis minute.

MOSEBY (*still disapproving*). No good nebber come—

(*The door is pushed violently open, and* LONNIE, *a sturdy black boy of eighteen rushes in breathlessly.*)

LONNIE. Mam Sue! Millie! Whut'da yuh think? John's come home!

MILLIE (*speechless with astonishment*). John? Home? Where's he at?

MAM SUE (*incredulously*). Whut yuh sayin'? John done come home? Bles' de Lawd! Bles' de Lawd! Millie, didn' Ah tell yuh sumpin wuz gwine tuh happen?

LONNIE (*excitedly*). I wuz sweepin' up de sto' jes befo' leavin' an' de phone rung—it wuz John—he wuz at Char'ston—jes landid! His comp'ny's waitin' to git de ten o'clock train fu' Camp Reed, whah dey's goin' to be mustered out.

16

MOSEBY. But how's he gwine to get erway?

LONNIE. Oh, good evenin', Brother Moseby, Ise jes so 'cited I didn' see yuh—Why his Cap'n done give him leave to run over heah 'tell de train's ready. He ought tuh be heah now 'cause it's mos' two hours sence he wuz talkin'—

MAM SUE. Whuffo yuh so long comin' home an' tellin' us?

LONNIE *(hesitatingly)*. I did start right out but when I git to Sherley's corner I seen a whole lot of them w'ite hoodlums hangin' 'round de feed sto'—I jes felt like dey wuz jes waitin' dah to start sumpin, so I dodged 'em waitin' dah to start sumpin, so I dodged 'em by tekin' de long way home.

MILLIE. Po' Lonnie! He's allus dodgin' po' w'ite trash!

LONNIE *(sullenly)*. Well, yuh see whut dad got by not dodgin' 'em.

MOSEBY *(rising to go)*. Ah mus' be steppin' 'long now. Ah got to stop in to see ole man Hawkins; he's mighty sick. Ah'll drap in on mah way back fu' a word o' prayer wid John.

MAM SUE. Lonnie, yu'd bettah run erlon' as Brudder Moseby go an' tote dat wash tuh Mis' Ha't. An' drap in Mis' Hawkins' sto' an' git some soap an' starch; an' Ah reckons yu'd bettah bring me a bottle o' linimint—dis ole pain done come back in mah knee. *(To* MOSEBY.) Good eben, Brudder Moseby.

MOSEBY. Good eben, Mam Sue; Good eben, Millie, an' Gawd bles' yuh.

LONNIE *(as he is leaving)*. Tell John I'll git back fo' he leaves.

*(*LONNIE *and* MOSEBY *leave.* MILLIE *closes the door behind them and then goes to the window and looks out anxiously.)*

MILLIE *(musingly)*. Po' John! Po' John! *(Turning to* MAM SUE.) Mam Sue?

MAM SUE. Yas, Millie.

MILLIE *(hesitatingly)*. Who's goin' to tell John 'bout dad?

MAM SUE *(realizing for the first time that the task must fall to someone)*. Dunno. Ah reckons yu'd bettah.

MILLIE *(going to* MAM SUE *and kneeling softly at her side)*. Mam Sue, don' let's tell him now! He's got only a li'l hour to spen' with us—an' it's the firs' time fu' so long! John loved daddy so! Let 'im be happy jes a li'l longer—we kin tell 'im the truth when he comes back fu' good. Please, Mam Sue!

MAM SUE *(softened by* MILLIE'S *pleading)*. Honey chile, John gwine to be askin' for his daddy fust thing—dey ain't no way—

17

MILLIE *(gaining courage)*. Oh, yes, 'tis! We kin tell 'im dad's gone to town—anything, jes so's he kin spen' these few lil'l minutes in peace! I'll fix the Bible jes like dad's been in an' been a-readin' in it! He won't know no bettah!

(MILLIE takes the Bible from the mantel and opening it at random lays it on the table; she draws the old armchair close to the table as her father had been wont to do every evening when he read his Bible.)

MAM SUE *(shaking her head doubtfully)*. Ah ain't much on actin' dis lie, Millie.

(The soft afterglow fades and the little cabin is filled with shadows. MILLIE goes again to the window and peers out. MAM SUE falls again to her crooning.)

MAM SUE *(crooning)*.

> O, yes, yonder comes mah Lawd,
> He's comin' dis way
> Wid his sword in his han'—

(To MILLIE.) Millie, bettah light de lamp; it's gittin' dark.—

> He's gwine ter hew dem sinners down
> Right lebbal to de groun'
> O, yes, yonder comes mah Lawd—

(As MILLIE is lighting the lamp, whistling is heard in the distance. MILLIE listens intently, then rushes to the window. The whistling comes nearer; it rings out clear and familiar—"Though the boys are far away, they dream of home"!)

MILLIE *(excitedly)*. That's him! That's John, Mam Sue!

(MILLIE rushes out of doors. The voices of JOHN and MILLIE are heard from without in greetings. Presently, JOHN and MILLIE enter the cabin. JOHN is tall and straight—a good soldier and a strong man. He wears the uniform of a private in the American Army. One hand is clasped in both of MILLIE'S. In the other, he carries an old fashioned valise. The War Cross is pinned on his breast. On his sleeve three chevrons tell mutely of wounds suffered in the cause of freedom. His brown face is aglow with life and the joy of homecoming.)

JOHN *(eagerly)*. Where's Dad? Where's Mam Sue?

MAM SUE *(hobbling painfully to meet him)*. Heah's ole Mam Sue!
(JOHN takes her tenderly in his arms.) Bles' yo' heart, chile,

18

bles' yo' heart! Tuh think dat de good Lawd's done lemme live to see dis day!

JOHN. Dear old Mam Sue! Gee, but I'm glad to see you an' Millie again!

MAM SUE. Didn' Ah say dat yuh wuz comin' back hyeah?

JOHN *(smiling)*. Same old Mam Sue with huh faith an' huh prayers! But where's dad? *(He glances toward the open Bible.)* He's been in from de field, ain't he?

MILLIE *(without lifting her eyes)*. Yes, he's come in but he had to go out ag'in—to Sherley's feed sto'.

JOHN *(reaching for his cap that he has tossed upon the table)*. That ain't far. I've jes a few minutes so I'd bettah run down there an' hunt him up. Won't he be surprised!

MILLIE *(confused)*. No—no, John—I fu'got; he ain't gone to Sherley's, he's gont to town.

JOHN *(disappointed)*. To town? I hope he'll git in befo' I'm leavin'. There's no tellin' how long they'll keep me at Camp Reed. Where's Lonnie?

MAM SUE. Lonnie's done gone to Mis' Ha't's wid de wash. He'll be back toreckly.

MILLIE *(admiring the medal on his breast)*. An' this is the medal? Tell us all erbout it, John.

JOHN. Oh, Sis, it's an awful story—wait 'til I git back fu' good. Let's see whut I've got in dis bag fu' you. *(He places the worn valise on the table and opens it. He takes out a bright-colored dress pattern.)* That's fu' you, Millie, and quit wearin' them black clothes.

(MILLIE takes the silk and hugs it eagerly to her breast, suddenly there sweeps into her mind the realization that she cannot wear it, and the silk falls to the floor.)

MILLIE *(trying to be brave)*. Oh, John, it's jes lovely! *(As she shows it to MAM SUE.)*

Look, Mam Sue!

JOHN *(flourishing a bright shawl)*. An' this is fu' Mam Sue. Mam Sue'll be so gay!

MAM SUE *(admiring the gift)*. Who'd evah b'lieved dat yo' ole Mam Sue would live to be wearin' clo'es whut huh gran'chile done brung huh f'om Eu'ope!

JOHN. Never you mind, Mam Sue, one of these days I'm goin' to tek you an' Millie over there, so's you kin breathe free jes once befo' yuh die.

19

MAM SUE. It's got tuh be soon, 'cause dis ole body's mos' wo'e out; an' de good Lawd's gwine to be callin' me to pay mah debt 'fo' long.

JOHN *(showing some handkerchiefs, with gay borders).* These are fu' Lonnie. *(He next takes out a tiny box that might contain a bit of jewelry.)* An' this is fu' Dad. Sum'pin he's been wantin' fu' years. I ain't goin' to open it 'till he comes.

*(*MILLIE *walks into the shadows and furtively wipes a tear from her eyes.*

JOHN *(taking two army pistols from his bag and placing them on the table).* An' these las' are fu' youahs truly.

MILLIE *(looking at them, fearfully).* Oh, John, are them youahs?

JOHN. One of 'em's mine; the other's my Lieutenant's. I've been cleanin' it fu' him. Don' tech 'em—'cause mine's loaded.

MILLIE *(still looking at them in fearful wonder).* Did they learn yuh how to shoot 'em?

JOHN. Yep, an' I kin evah mo' pick 'em off!

MILLIE *(reproachfully).* Oh, John!

JOHN. Nevah you worry, li'l Sis, John's nevah goin' to use 'em 'less it's right fu' him to. *(He places the pistols on the mantel—on the very spot where the Bible has lain.)* My! but it's good to be home! I've been erway only two years but it seems like two cent'ries. All that life ovah there seems like some awful dream!

MAM SUE *(fervently).* Ah know it do! Many's de day yo' ole Mam Sue set in dis cheer an' prayed fu' yuh.

JOHN. Lots of times, too, in the trenches when I wuz dog-tired, an' sick, an' achin' wid the cold I uster say. well, if we're sufferin' all this for the oppressed, like they tell us, then Mam Sue, an' Dad, an' Millie come in on that—they'll git some good ou'n it if I don't! An' I'd shet my eyes an' fu'git the cold, an' the pain, an' them old guns spittin' death all 'round us; an' see you folks set-tin' here by this fire—Mam Sue, noddin, an' singin'; Dad a spellin' out his Bible—*(He glances toward the open book.)* Let's see whut he's been readin'—(JOHN *takes up the Bible and reads the first passage upon which his eye falls.)* "But I say unto you, love your enemies, bless them that curse you, an' do good to them that hate you"—*(He lets the Bible fall to the table.)* That ain't the dope they been feedin' us soljers on! 'Love your enemies!' It's been—git a good aim at 'em, an' let huh go!

MAM SUE *(surprised).* Honey, Ah hates to hyeah yuh talkin' lak dat! It sound lak yuh done fu'git yu Gawd!

20

JOHN. No, Mam Sue, I ain't fu'got God, but I've quit thinkin' that prayers kin do ever'thing. I've seen a whole lot sence I've been erway from here. I've seen some men go into battle with a curse on their lips, and I've seen them same men come back with never a scratch; an' I've seen men whut read their Bibles befo' battle, an' prayed to live, left dead on the field. Yes, Mam Sue, I've seen a heap an' I've done a tall lot o' thinkin' sence I've been erway from here. An' I b'lieve it's jes like this—beyon' a certain point prayers ain't no good! The Lawd does jes so much for you, then it's up to you to do the res' fu' yourse'f. The Lawd's done His part when He's done give me strength an' courage; I got tuh do the res' fu' myse'f!

MAM SUE *(shaking her head).* Ah don' lak dat kin' o' talk—it don' 'bode no good!

(The door opens and LONNIE *enters with packages. He slips the bolt across the door.)*

JOHN *(rushing to* LONNIE *and seizing his hand).* Hello, Lonnie, ole man!

LONNIE. Hello, John. Gee, but Ah'm glad tuh see yuh!

JOHN. Boy, you should 'ave been with me! It would 'ave taken some of the skeeriness out o' yuh, an' done yuh a worl' o' good.

LONNIE *(ignoring* JOHN'S *remark).* Here's the soap an' starch, Millie.

MAM SUE. Has yuh brung mah linimint?

LONNIE. Yassum, it's in de packige.

MILLIE *(unwrapping the package).* No, it ain't, Lonnie.

LONNIE. Mis' Hawkins give it tuh me. Ah mus' a lef' it on de counter. Ah'll git it w'en Ah goes to de train wid John.

MILLIE *(showing him the handkerchief).* See whut John done brought you! An' look on de mantel! *(Pointing to the pistols.)*

LONNIE *(drawing back in fear as he glances at the pistols).* You'd bettah hide them things! No cullud man bettah be seen wid dem things down heah!

JOHN. That's all right, Lonnie, nevah you fear. I'm goin' to keep 'em an' I ain't a-goin' to hide 'em either. See them *(pointing to the wound chevrons on his arm)*, well, when I got them wounds, I let out all the rabbit-blood 'at wuz in me! *(Defiantly.)* Ef I kin be trusted with a gun in France, I kin be trusted with one in South Car'lina.

MAM SUE *(sensing trouble).* Millie, yu'd bettah fix some suppah fu' John.

AFTERMATH

JOHN *(looking at his watch).* I don' want a thing. I've got to be leavin' in a little while. I'm 'fraid I'm goin' to miss dad after all.

(The knob of the door is turned as though someone is trying to enter. Then there is a loud knock on the door.)

JOHN *(excitedly).* That's Dad! Don't tell him I'm here!

*(*JOHN *tips hurriedly into the adjoining room.* LONNIE *unbolts the door and* MRS. SELENA HAWKINS *enters.)*

MRS. HAWKINS. Lonnie fu'got de liniment so I thought I' bettah run ovah wid hit, 'cause when Mam Sue sen' fu' dis stuff she sho' needs hit. Brudder Moseby's been tellin' me dat John's done come home.

JOHN *(coming from his hiding place and trying to conceal his disappointment.)* Yes, I'm here. Good evenin', Mis' Hawkins. Glad to see you.

MRS. HAWKINS *(shaking hands with* JOHN*).* Well, lan' sakes alive! Ef it ain't John sho'nuf! An' ain't he lookin' gran'! Jes look at dat medal -shining' on his coat! Put on yuh cap, boy, an' lemme see how yuh look!

JOHN. Sure! (JOHN *puts on his overseas cap and, smiling, stands at attention a few paces off, while* MAM SUE, LONNIE, *and* MILLIE *form an admiring circle around him.)*

MRS. HAWKINS. Now don' he sholy look gran'! I knows yo' sistah, an' gran'-mammy's proud o' yuh! *(A note of sadness creeps into her voice.)* Ef only yuh po' daddy had a-lived to see dis day!

*(*JOHN *looks at her in amazement.* MILLIE *and* MAM SUE *stand transfixed with terror over the sudden betrayal.)*

JOHN *(looking from one to the other and repeating her words as though he can scarcely realize their meaning).* 'Ef your po' daddy had lived—' *(To* MILLIE.) Whut does this mean?

*(*MILLIE *sinks sobbing into the chair at the table and buries her face in her hands.)*

MRS. HAWKINS. Lor', Millie, I thought you'd tole him!

(Bewildered by the catastrophe that she has precipitated, SELENA HAWKINS *slips out of the cabin.)*

JOHN *(shaking* MILLIE *almost roughly).* Come, Millie, have you been lyin' to me? Is Dad gone?

MILLIE *(through her sobs).* I jes hated to tell you—you wuz so far erway—

JOHN *(nervously).* Come, Millie, for God's sake don' keep me in this su'pense! I'm a brave soldier—I kin stan' it—did he suffer much? Wuz he sick long?

22

MILLIE. He wuzn't sick no time—them w'ite devuls come in heah an' dragged him—

JOHN *(desperately)*. My God! You mean they lynched dad?

MILLIE *(sobbing piteously)*. They burnt him down by the big gum tree!

JOHN *(desperately)*. Whut fu,' Millie? What fu'?

MILLIE. He got in a row wid ole Mister Withrow 'bout the price of cotton—an' he called dad a liar an' struck him—an' dad he up an' struck him back—

JOHN *(brokenly)*. Didn' they try him? Didn' they give him a chance? Whut'd the Sheriff do? An' the Govnur?

MILLIE *(through her sobs)*. They didn't do nothin'.

JOHN. Oh, God! Oh, God! *(Then recovering from the first bitter anguish and speaking.)* So they've come into ouah home, have they! *(He strides over to LONNIE and seizes him by the collar.)* An' whut wuz you doin' when them hounds come in here after dad?

LONNIE *(hopelessly)*. They wuz so many of 'em come an' git 'im—whut could Ah do?

JOHN. Do? You could 'ave fought 'em like a man!

MAM SUE *(pleadingly)*. Don't be too hard on 'im, John, wese ain't got no gun 'round heah!

JOHN. Then he should 'ave burnt their damn kennels ovah their heads! Who was it leadin' em?

MILLIE. Old man Withrow and the Sherley boys, they started it all.

(Gradually assuming the look of a man who has determined to do some terrible work that must be done, JOHN *walks deliberately toward the mantel where the revolvers are lying.)*

JOHN *(bitterly)*. I've been helpin' the w'ite man git his freedom, I reckon I'd bettah try now to get my own!

MAM SUE *(terrified)*. Whut yuh gwine ter do?

JOHN *(with bitterness growing in his voice)*. I'm sick o' these w'ite folks doin's—we're 'fine, trus'worthy feller citizuns' when they're handin' us out guns, an' Liberty Bonds, an' chuckin' us off to die; but we ain't a damn thing when it comes to handin' us the rights we done fought an' bled fu'! I'm sick o' this sort o' life—an' I'm goin' to put an' end to it!

MILLIE *(rushing to the mantel, and covering the revolvers with her hands)*. Oh, no, no, John! Mam Sue, John's gwine to kill hisse'f!

MAM SUE *(piteously)*. Oh, mah honey, don' yuh go do nothin' to bring sin on yo' soul! Pray to de good Lawd to tek all dis fiery feelin' out'n yo' heart! Wait 'tel Brudder Moseby come back— he's gwine to pray—

JOHN *(his speech growing more impassioned and bitter)*. This ain't no time fu' preachers or prayers! You mean to tell me I mus' let them w'ite devuls send me miles erway to suffer an' be shot up fu' the freedom of people I ain't nevah seen, while they're burnin' an' killin' my folks here at home! To Hell with 'em!

(He pushes MILLIE *aside, and seizing the revolvers, thrusts the loaded one into his pocket and begins deliberately to load the other.)*

MILLIE *(throwing her arms about his neck)*. Oh, John, they'll kill yuh!

JOHN *(defiantly)*. Whut ef they do! I ain't skeered o' none of 'em! I've faced worse guns than any sneakin' hounds kin show me! To Hell with 'em! *(He thrusts the revolver that he has just loaded into* LONNIE's *hand.)* Take this, an' come on here, boy, an' we'll see what Withrow an' his gang have got to say!

(Followed by LONNIE, *who is bewildered and speechless,* JOHN *rushes out of the cabin and disappears in the gathering darkness.)*

CURTAIN

THEY THAT SIT IN DARKNESS

A ONE-ACT PLAY OF NEGRO LIFE

BY MARY BURRILL

CHARACTERS

MALINDA JASPER: *the mother*

LINDY, MILES, ALOYSIUS, MARY ELLEN, JIM-
MIE, JOHN HENRY, A WEEK-OLD INFANT: *her
children*

ELIZABETH SHAW: *a visiting nurse*

*The action passes in a small country
town in the South in our own day.*

SCENE

*It is late afternoon of a day in September. The room which does a
three-fold duty as kitchen, dining room, and living room for the
Jasper family is dingy and disorderly. Great black patches as
though from smoke are on the low ceilings and the walls. To the
right is a door leading into a bedroom. In the opposite wall another door leads into a somewhat larger room that serves as bedroom
for six Jasper children. In the rear wall a door opens into a large
yard. A window is placed to the left of the door while against the
wall to the right there stands an old, battered cow-hide trunk. The
furniture which is poor and dilapidated, consists of a table in the
center of the room, a cupboard containing a few broken cups and
plates, a rocker, and two or three plain chairs with broken backs
and uncertain legs. Against the wall to the left there is a kitchen
stove on which sit a tea-kettle and a wash-boiler. Near the window placed upon stools are two large laundry tubs. Through open
window and door one gets a glimpse of snowy garments waving
and glistening in the sun. Malinda Jasper, a frail, tired-looking*

25

woman of thirty-eight, and Lindy, her seventeen year-old daughter, are bending over the tubs swirling their hands in the water to make sure that their task is completed. From the yard come the constant cries of children at play.

MRS. JASPER: *(Straightening up painfully from the tubs.)* Lor', Lindy, how my side do hurt! But thank goodnis, dis job's done! *(She sinks exhausted into the rocker.)* Run git me one them tablits de doctor lef' fo' dis pain!

(Lindy hurries into the adjoining room and returns with the medicine.)

MRS. JASPER: *(Shaking her head mournfully.)* Dis ole pain goin' be takin' me 'way f'om heah one o' dese days!

LINDY: *(Looking at her in concern.)* See, Ma, I tole yuh not to be doin' all this wuk! Whut's Miss 'Liz'beth goin' er say when she comes heah this evenin' an' fine out you done all this wuk after she tole yuh pertic'lar yestiddy that she wuz'n goin' let yuh out'n bed 'fo' three weeks—an' here 't'ain't been a week sence baby wuz bawn!

MRS. JASPER: Ah ain't keerin' 'bout whut Mis' 'Liz'beth say! Easy nuf, Lindy, fo' dese nurses to give dey advice—dey ain't got no seben chillern to clothe an' feed—but when dis washin' git back Ah kin nevah ketch up!

LINDY: *(Reprovingly.)* But I could 'a done it all mys'f.

MRS. JASPER: An' been all day an' night doin' it—an' miss gittin' you'se'f off in de mawnin' tuh Tuskegee—no indeedy!

LINDY: *(Hesitatingly.)* P'rhaps I oughtn' be goin' erway an' leavin' yuh wid all dis washin' to do ever' week, an' de chillern to look after—an' the baby an' all. Daddy he gits home so late he cain't be no help.

MRS. JASPER: *(Wearily.)* Nebber you mind, Lindy, Ah'm going be gittin' aw-right bime-by. Ah ain't a-goin' be stan'in' in de way yo' gittin' dis edicashun. Yo' chance don' come, Lindy, an' Ah wants ter see yuh tek it! Yuh been a good chile, Lindy, an' Ah wants ter see yuh git mo'e out'n life dan Ah gits. Dem three yeah at Tuskegee warn't seem long.

LINDY: *(Her face brightening up.)* Yassum, an' ef Mister Huff, the sup'inten'ent meks me county teacher lak he sez he'll do when I git back, I kin do lots mo'e fo' you an' the chillern!

(The cry of a week-old infant comes from the adjoining room.)

MRS. JASPER: Dar now! Ah'm mighty glad he didn' wake up 'tel we git dis washin' done! Ah reckon he's hongry. Ain't Miles come back wid de milk yet? He's been gawn mos' 'en hour—see ef he's took dat guitar wid 'im.

LINDY: *(Going to the door and looking out.)* I doan see it nowheres so I reckon he's got it.

MRS. JASPER: Den Gawd knows when we'll see 'im! Lak es not he's some'airs settin' by de road thumpin' dem strings—dat boy 'ud play ef me or you wuz dyin'! Ah doan know whut's goin' come o' 'im—he's just so lazy en shif'lis!

LINDY: Doan yuh go werrin' 'bout Miles, Ma. He'll be aw-right ef he kin only learn music an' do whut he likes. *(The cry of the infant becomes insistent.)* No, Ma, you set still—I'll git his bottle an' 'tend to him. *(She goes into the bedroom.)*

(The shrieks of the children in the yard grow louder. A shrill cry of anger and pain rises above the other voices, and Mary Ellen, age six, appears crying at the door.)

MARY ELLEN: *(Holding her head.)* Ma! Ma! Mek Aloysius b'have hisse'f! He hit me on de haid wid all his might!

MRS. JASPER: *(Rushing to the door.)* Aloysius! Yuh Aloysius! It warn't do yuh no good ef Ah 'ave to come out'n dere to yuh! John Henry, git down f'om dat tree, 'fo yuh have dem clo'es in de durt! Yo' chillern 'nuf to werry me to death!

(As Lindy returns with the baby's empty bottle, Miles enters the rear door. He is a good-natured but shiftless looking boy of sixteen. A milk pail is swinging on his arm, leaving his hands free to strum a guitar.)

LINDY: Have yuh brought the milk, Miles? An' the bread?

MILES: *(Setting down the milk pail.)* Nup! Mister Jackson say yuh cain't have no milk, an' no nothin' 'tel de bill's paid.

MRS. JASPER: Den Gawd knows we'll starve, 'cause Ah see'd yo' daddy give de doctor ebery cent o' his wages las' week. An' dey warn't be no mo'e money comin' in 'tel Ah kin git dis wash out to de Redmon's.

LINDY: Well, baby's gawn back to sleep now, and p'rhaps Miss 'Liz'beth will bring some milk fo' de baby when she come in lak she did yestiddy—but they ain't nothing heah fo' de other chillern.

(The shrieks of the children at play in the yard grow louder.)

ALOYSIUS: *(Calling from without.)* Ma! Ma! John Henry done pull' down de clo'es line!

MRS. JASPER: *(Rushing again to the door.)* Come in heah! Ever' single one o' yuh! Miles, run fix 'em up an' see ef any o' 'em got in de durt!

(The Jasper children, four in number, a crest-falleen, pathetic looking little group—heads unkempt, ragged, undersized, under fed, file in terrified.)

JOHN HENRY: *(Terror-stricken.)* It warn't me, Ma, it was Aloysius!

MRS. JASPER: Heish yo' mouf'! March yo'se'f ever' one o' yuh an' go to baid!

MARY ELLEN: *(Timidly.)* We's ain't had no suppah.

MRS. JASPER: An' whut's mo'e, yuh ain't goin' git no suppah 'tel yuh larns to b'have yo'se'f!

ALOYSIUS: *(In a grumbling tone.)* Cain't fool me—Ah heerd Lindy say dey ain't no suppah fo' us!

(Calling to the children as they disappear in the room to the left.)

MRS. JASPER: Ef Ah heahs one soun' Ah'm comin' in dere an' slap yuh into de middle o' nex' week! *(As she sinks again exhausted into the rocker.)* Them chillern's goan ter be de death o' me yit!

MILES: *(Appearing at the door.)* De clo'es ain't dirty. I fo'git to tell yuh—I stopp't by Sam Jones an' he say he'll be 'round fo' Lindy's trunk 'bout sundown.

MRS. JASPER: Ah reckons yu'd bettah git yo' clo'es an' pack up 'cause it warn't be long fo' sundown.

LINDY: *(Dragging the old trunk to the center of the room.)* I ain't a goin' less'n you git bettah, Ma. Yuh look right sick to me!

(As Lindy is speaking Miss Elizabeth Shaw in the regulation dress of a visiting nurse, and carry a small black bag, appears at the rear door.)

MISS SHAW: *(Looking in consternation at Mrs. Jasper.)* Malinda Jasper! What are you doing out of bed! You don't mean to say that you have washed all those clothes that I see in the yard?

MRS. JASPER: Yassum, me an' Lindy done 'em.

MISS SHAW: *(Provoked.)* And you look completely exhaused! Come you must get right to bed!

MRS. JASPER: *(Leaning her head wearily against the back of the rocker.)* Lemme res' myse'f jes a minute—Ah'll be goin' 'long torectly.

MISS SHAW: It's a wonder in your condition that you didn't die standing right at those tubs! I don't mean to scare you but—

MRS. JASPER: *(With extreme weariness.)* Lor', Mis' 'Liz'beth, it ain't *dyin'* Ah'm skeer't o', its *livin'*—wid all dese chillern to look out fo'. We ain't no Elijahs, Mis' 'Lis'beth, dey ain't no ravens flyin' 'roun' heah drappin' us food. All we gits, we has to git by wukin' hard! But thanks be to Gawd a light's dawnin'! My Lindy's gittin' off to Tuskegee to school tomorrer, Mis' 'Liz'beth!

MISS SHAW: *(Surprised.)* I didn't know that Lindy was thinking about going away to school.

MRS. JASPER: Thinkin' 'bout it! Lindy ain't been thinkin' an' dreamin' 'bout nothin' else sence Booker Washin'ton talked to de farmers down youder at Shady Grove some ten yeah ergo. Did yo' know Booker Washin'ton, Mis' 'Liz'beth?

MISS SHAW: I saw him once a long time ago in my home town in Massachusetts. He was a great man.

MRS. JASPER: Dat he wuz! Ah kin see him now—him an' Lindy, jes a teeny slip o' gal—after de speakin' wuz ovah down dere at Shady Grove, a-standin' under de magnolias wid de sun a-pou'in' through de trees on 'em—an' he wid his hand on my li'l Linly's haid lak he wuz givin' huh a blessin', an' a-sayin': "When yuh gits big, li'l gal, yuh mus' come to Tuskegee an' larn, so's yuh kin come back heah an' he'p dese po' folks!" He's daid an' in his grave but Lindy ain't nevah fo'git dem words.

MISS SHAW: Just think of it! And ten years ago! How glad I am that her dream is coming true. Won't it cost you quite a bit?

MRS. JASPER: Lor', Lindy 'ud nevah git dere ef we had to sen' huh! Some dem rich folks up yonder in yo' part de world is sen'in' huh.

LINDY: *(Entering with her arms laden with things for her trunk.)* Good evenin', Mis' 'Liz'beth.

MISS SHAW: Well, Lindy, I've just heard of your good fortune. How splendid it is! But what will the baby do without you! How is he this afternoon?

LINDY: He's right smart, Mis' 'Liz'beth. I been rubbing his leg lack you showed me. Do yuh think it'll evah grow er long ez the other'n?

MISS SHAW: I fear, Lindy, those little withered limbs seldom do; but with care it will grow much stronger. I have brought him some milk—there in my bag. Be careful to modify it exactly as I showed you, and give what is left to the other children.

LINDY: *(Preparing to fix the milk.)* Yes Mis' 'Liz'beth.

MISS SHAW: *(Nodding at Lindy.)* What *will you do,* Malinda, when she goes? You will have to stop working so hard. Just see how exhausted you are from this heavy work!

MRS. JASPER: Lor', Mis' 'Liz'beth, Ah'll be awright to-reckly. Ah did de same thing after my li'l Tom was bawn, an' when Aloysius wuz bawn Ah git up de nex' day—de wuk had to be done.

MISS SHAW: *(Very gravely.)* But you must not think that you are as strong now as you were then. I heard the doctor tell you very definitely that this baby had left your heart *weaker than ever,* and that you *must* give up this laundry work.

MRS. JASPER: *(Pleadingly.)* 'Deed, Mis' 'Liz'beth, we needs dis money whut wid all dese chillern, an' de sicknis' an' fune'ul 'spenses of li'l Tom an' Selena—dem's de chillern whut come 'tween John Henry an' dis las' baby. At'er dem bills wuz paid heah come Pinkie's trouble.

MISS SHAW: Pinkie?

MRS. JASPER: *(Sadly.)* Yuh nevah seed Pinkie 'cause she lef' 'fo' yuh come heah. She come 'tween Miles an' Aloysius—she warn't right in de haid—she wuked ovah tuh Bu'nett's place—Ah aint nevah been much on my gals wukin' round dese white men but Pinkie *mus' go;* an' fus thing we know Bu'nett got huh in trouble.

MISS SHAW: Poor, poor girl! What did you do to the Burnett man?

MRS. JASPER: *(With deep feeling.)* Lor', Mis' 'Liz'beth, cullud folks cain't do nothin' to white folks down heah! Huh Dad went on sumpin awful wid huh ever' day, an' one mawnin' we woked up and Pinkie an' huh baby wuz gawn! We ain't nevah heerd f'om huh tuh dis day—*(she closes her eyes as if to shut out the memory of Pinkie's sorrow.)* Me an' Jim 'as allus put ouah tru's in de Lawd, an' we wants tuh raise up dese chillern to be good, hones' men an' women but we has tuh wuk so hard to give 'em de li'l de gits dat we ain't got no time tuh look at'er dey sperrits. When Jim go out to wuk—chillern's sleepin'; when he comes in late at night—chillern's sleepin'. When Ah git through scrubbin' at dem tubs all Ah kindo is set in dis cheer an' nod—Ah doan wants tuh see no chillern! Ef it warn't fo' Lindy—huh got a mighty nice way wid 'em—Gawd he'p 'em!

MISS SHAW: Well, Malinda, you have certainly your share of trouble!

MRS. JASPER: *(Shaking her head wearily.)* Ah wonder whut sin we done that Gawd punish me an' Jim lak dis!

MISS SHAW: *(Gently.)* God is not punishing you, Malinda, you are punishing yourselves by having children every year. Take this last baby—you knew that with your weak heart that you should never have had it and yet—

MRS. JASPER: But whut kin Ah do—de chillern *come!*

MISS SHAW: You must be careful!

MRS. JASPER: *Be keerful!* Dat's all you nu'ses say! You an' de one whut come when Tom wuz bawn, an' Selena! Ah been keerful all Ah knows how but whut's it got me—ten chillern, eight livin' an' two daid! You got'a be tellin' me sumpin' better'n dat, Mis' 'Liz'beth!

MISS SHAW: *(Fervently.)* I wish to God it were lawful for me to do so! My heart goes out to you poor people that sit in darkness, having, year after year, children that you are physically too weak to bring into the world—children that you are unable not only to educate but even to clothe and feed. Malinda, when I took my oath as nurse, I swore to abide by the laws of the State, and the law forbids my telling you what you have a right to know!

MRS. JASPER: *(With the tears trickling from her closed eyes.)* Ah ain't blamin' you, Mis' 'Liz'beth, but—

MISS SHAW: Come, come, Malinda, you must not give away like this. You are worn out—come, you must get to bed.

LINDY: *(Entering with more things for her trunk.)* I'm glad yuh gittin' huh to bed, Mis' 'Liz'beth, I been tryin' to all day.

MRS. JASPER: *(As she walks unsteadily toward her room.)* Lindy, honey, git yo' trunk pack't. Thank Gawd yo' chance done come! Give dat *(Nodding toward the partially filled bottle of milk.)* to de chillern. Mis' 'Liz'beth say dey kin have it.

LINDY: All right, Ma. Mis' 'Liz'beth, ef you needs me jes call.

(Malinda and the nurse enter the bedroom. Lindy is left packing her trunk. Miles can be heard from without strumming upon his guitar.)

MARY ELLEN: *(Poking her head out of the door to the children's room.)* Lindy, Lindy, whut wuz dat Ma say we all kin have?

LINDY: Some milk—it ain't much.

(The children. bound into the room. Mary Ellen, first at the table, seizes the bottle and lifts it to her lips.)

ALOYSIUS: *(Snatching the bottle from Mary Ellen.)* Yuh got 'a be las', 'cause Mis' 'Liz'beth say we mus'n' nebber eat or drink at'er yuh! Did'n' she, Lindy?

LINDY: *(As Mary Ellen begins to cry.)* Ef yo' all git to fussin' I ain't goan to bring yuh nothin' when I comes back!

MARY ELLEN: *(As the children crowd about Lindy.)* Whut yuh goan 'a bring us, Lindy?

LINDY: *(As she puts her things carefully into her trunk.)* When I comes back I'm goan to bring yuh all some pretty readin' books, an' some clo'es so I kin tek yuh to school ever'day where yuh kin learn to read 'em!

JOHN HENRY: *(Clapping his hands.)* Is we all goin', Lindy? Miles too?

LINDY: Yes indeedy! An' whut's mo'e I'm goan 'a git Miles a fine new guitar an' let him learn music. An' some day ever' body'll be playin' an' singin' his songs!

ALOYSIUS: *(Glowing with excitement.)* Some day he might have his own band! Might'n' he, Lindy? Lak dat big white one whut come fru heah f'om 'Lanta! Ole Miles'll come struttin' down de road.

(Aloysius seizes the broom, and in spite of the handicap of bow legs, gives a superb imitation of a drummajor leading his band.)

LINDY: *(Watching Ayolsius' antics.)* An' I'm goin' tuh have Aloysius' li'l legs straightened. *(As the children roll in merriment.)* 'Sh! 'sh! Mus'n' mek no noise 'cause Ma ain't well! An' in de evenin' we'll have a real set-down-to-de table suppah—Dad he won't have to wuk so hard so he kin git home early—an' after suppah we all kin set 'round de fiah lak dey do ovah to Lawyer Hope's an' tell stories an' play games—

(The children, radiant as though these dreams were all realities, huddle closer about Lindy who, packing done, now sits enthroned upon her battered trunk.)

LINDY: 'Sh—sh! Wuz that Mis' 'Liz'beth callin'? *(They listen intently but can hear nothing save the sweet, plaintive notes of an old Spiritual that Miles is playing upon his guitar.)* Then we'll git some fine Sunday clo'es, an' a hoss an' wagun, an' when Sunday come we'll all climb in an' ride to Shady Grove to Meetin'—an' we'll set under de trees in de shade an' learn 'bout li'l Joseph an' his many-cullud coat; an' li'l Samu'l whut de Lawd called while he wuz sleepin'; an' de li'l baby whut wuz bawn in de stable an' wuz lots poor'n me an' you. An' on Sunday evenin' we'll—

MISS SHAW: *(Appearing at the bedroom door and speaking hurriedly.)* Send the children to bed quickly, Lindy, I need you.

(The children run into their room.)

ALOYSIUS: *(Wistfully, at the door.)* Ef we's good, Lindy, let us git up when Sam Jones come an' see de trunk go?

tall, slender girl, wrapped in a cape, comes in. She is colored and very comely. She hesitates within the entrance, panting and convulsive. The maid, Bertie, starts to her, but waits to see what Madame will do. Margot is dazed as she rises and stands staring at the visitor. For a moment the three stand gazing, none seeming to know what to do. The girl is Claire Meade.)

CLAIRE—*(Trying to be calm and to announce herself)*—I—I am—*(She is overcome with tears. Standing with outstretched arms in the doorway, she makes a silent appeal.)*

CLAIRE—Please! Please! *(She drops to the floor in a little heap. Margot nods dismissal to the maid, who leaves reluctantly, not hiding her curiosity.)*

(The sobbing girl jumps up from the floor upon the approach of Madame, and forcing back her tears, stands erect. Margot starts as though she would caress her, but holds back. Claire sees this and speaks.)

CLAIRE—Ah, Madame, you *will* come and do so when I have told you; when you know how lonely I am you will take me in your arms as though I were your child. My life is so queer, everything for me is so dull; this day is so dark.—Whoever saw a morning in summer so black—so chilly! It *frightened* me because I was so lonely! *(Margot unable to withstand the sobbing voice of the pathetic little figure, takes her almost madly into her arms and leads her to the chaise-longue, soothing her tears.)*

MARGOT—Poor, poor little girl! There, there, don't be sad. I know, you were lonely—*lonely—I know, I know. (After a moment of comforting)*—Tell me child, what under heaven's sun made you come to me? People seldom are real in my presence because—because I am—Madame Cotell.—Oh, I *hate* it now. Child, why did you come?

CLAIRE—Because I knew you were—I—I used to know you when you lived across from my uncle and me in Mersville. *(Margot starts slightly, but listens intently.)* You lived in that pretty yellow stone house. I used to watch you come and go from my play room window, and when you had gone down the street I would try so hard to walk like you. You were the wife of every fine prince in my fairy-tale books; when you came over to see uncle I tried to talk like you. Oh, I remember so well—when you took me for walks and held me on your knee—I—I thought I was in paradise.—Then you went away. You came over to talk with uncle one night in a hard storm. Uncle would not let me stay that night; I was sent off to bed, and I never saw you any more. It was all like a child's pretty dream. I used to call you Miss

Marjorie. Oh, it's been so long a time, I'm sure you must have forgotten.

MARGOT—(*Looking steadily at the girl*)—No, I remember quite well.

CLAIRE—It—It must be that I remember you so well all the time because you were the only lovely woman I ever knew in my home.

MARGOT—Ah, you have been frightfully lonesome, child.

CLAIRE—Madame, I am sick of it here! School was far better, even though I was always anxious to get away. I believe there is not another colored person around here except your maid. Since uncle died I have lived with a great-aunt. I don't know anything about her. I never saw her before his death. And—and—somehow I—I do not believe she is any kin to me at all. She never talks at the right time, and, oh it's terrible! This is a summer resort—a place for a good time, and everybody has it but me. They're all white—I don't want to go with them—but I am absolutely alone!

MARGOT—Why did you come here, Claire?

CLAIRE—Oh—you—remember my name?

MARGOT—To be sure I do! Why did you choose this place for the summer?

CLAIRE—(*Bursting into sobs*)—Oh, I didn't choose it! I did not choose it! I tell you I don't believe she's any kin to me—Miss Jenson! She acts all the time as though she were being directed, still there's no one to direct her. She made the doctor say I must come here for the climate, and I'm not ill! I'm just lonely.—I want Uncle. He's the only mother I ever knew.—And—and this morning was so black—it *is* getting lighter now—I just could not stay in that big cottage and hear the ocean all by myself. I knew you were here. I saw you play in "Crinoline" the other night—and—I—I—

MARGOT—You came because you knew—that—I—was—

CLAIRE—Colored.

(*Margot had expected this and so is not surprised. She sits thinking for a moment.*)

MARGOT—(*Calmly*)—It's really good to hear someone say it. This masquerading, once entered into, is not so easily put aside. I took a big chance when it came to me, and circumstances swept me on.—Once started I had to—go on. I pleased the people and they gave me this fame. I lost old ties and friends for it—this fame; but I could not go back—I needed the money for—I needed the money.

BERTIE—(*Entering*)—Will you have the table prepared for lunch, madame?

MARGOT—No, Bertie, I shall not. It is time for them to arrive, but there will be no need for lunch. (*Bertie looks surprised.*) That will be all right, Bertie. You may go.

(*Bertie starts out to the next room, but the bell rings and she turns back to answer it.*)

CLAIRE—(*Rising to leave*)—Madame Cotell, you have been so kind. I shall go now. Perhaps some other—

BERTIE—(*Reëntering with cards on a tray*)—The guests, Madame.

MARGOT—(*Pushing Claire gently upon the seat from which she has just arisen*) Have them enter, Bertie.—You're not going now, Claire, child. Sit there and be perfectly at home.

(*The maid ushers in the distinguished-looking party of five,— three men and two women. They exchange greetings with Margot.*)

ONE OF THE WOMEN—Ah, the weather is wretched today. So dark!

MARGOT—Yes. I thought perhaps it would prevent your coming.

FIRST MAN—Now, now, Margot, weather never keeps one from a *luncheon* engagement! (*The others laugh.*)

BARTER—You're not Margot Cotell today. What's wrong?

MARGOT—Oh, fatigue I suppose. It's the day—and the ocean. I'm so glad it's growing more like daytime. Goodness! Everytime the ocean roars it drowns me. (*The women are busy pretending to listen to the conversation and taking in Claire at the same time. The girl, seeing this, becomes interested in a book.*)

BARTER—Ha, ha, ha, that is the way these grey days get on the nerves sometimes. But let me say what—

SECOND MAN—(*Turning from other conversation*)—I say, Barter, spring the news on Madame.

FIRST MAN—Yes, yes—she'll like to hear it.

MARGOT—Pardon if I am abrupt. I shall not entertain you to-day, Mr. Barter. I shall not even ask you to sit. I am sorry, but—

BARTER—Oh, then we'll just charge it to Dame Temperament and lunch out. (*They laugh.*) But first hear the new proposition. Margot Cotell's fame will be doubled! Now folks!

(*The others stand around ready to chime in, but Margot stands very still, half defiant, half frightened, yet very composed withal.*)

39

MARGOT—It will be of no use, Mr. Barter I am breaking my contract tonight—now.

(There is quite a little commotion at this, but it does not seem to affect Margot. She still stands quietly. Mr. Barter is quite alarmed, yet he does not believe her.)

BARTER—Ye gods, this *is* temperament, Madame! Just what's the trouble may I ask?

MARGOT—(*With a short cynical laugh, and slowly*)—You will *want* me no longer, sir. You, nor any of them. Ah, you conceive in a flash a vital idea.

(This as his keen eyes search her then shift to Claire upon the chaise-longue. Claire has been watching the whole procedure from over her book.)

BARTER—(*With pointed shrewdness*)—Who is our interesting little friend?

MARGOT—(*In what is almost a retort*)—She will prove more interesting than you might imagine. She is Claire Meade, my daughter, who is with me now from school, for good.

(This produces a shock. There is no word spoken for the space of a half minute. Then Margot, shaking her head gently, goes to Claire, who sits rigid, staring at the woman, her book dropped to the floor, her lips parted but dumb.)

MARGOT—(*Forgetting everyone else and talking only to Claire*)—I know—I know—it was—you'll understand Claire, you'll understand! No, you will not! You *must*, Claire, child, you must understand! Your father died; you were too precious not to have the best; there was no one to get it for you but me! (*Calming herself*) Your father died and I went to the stage. Why? Because it fascinated me and I was young enough to yield to fascination. It was vaudeville, and I made enough with what my husband had left, to keep a woman for baby and the home. Then I went to a stock company for bigger pay, and let a neighbor, a dear old friend, take you. He was a widower and he loved children. I *had* to make the money, and to do so I left you with him.—Yes, you do remember me, child. I came whenever I could to be with you. We kept putting off telling you until I came home for good. I know it sounds incredible—I *know*—but it was the only way to manage. There was no trade for me, no other profession. The company was white, so they took it for granted—they never asked me my race, I never told them. I worked hard and they liked me; a big producer starred me. It meant the loss of my people and old ties, but—it also meant the very best for you. Still it did not mean *having* you,

40

but I kept putting off just a little longer. Your old guardian loved you dearly. When he died I was sure that I would come immediately to take you, but just then, came this contract for the summer. I swore I would not make it, but I let myself be persuaded, declaring it would be the last time. *I* sent this woman who is with you; she seemed gentle and kind. Oh Claire, God knows I'm sorry! I had you come here from school because I wanted you near me. Oh, I was coming for you,—to tell you,—to bring you home with me to have a holiday—a real holiday—more than a vacation. I've planned for it *so* long. My heart has ached, has done nothing but ache. Fame is nothing, child, I only—

CLAIRE—Hush! Don't tell me any more. You have let me live in cold luxury with a poor old man pitifully trying to mother me, when I should have had some kind of woman-mother. I should have loved her, had we had to dig in a ditch together. You—

MARGOT—But Claire, child, do listen—

CLAIRE—No! All this time I've wanted you and never, never knew. It was your selfish ambition that made you leave me behind. What harm could there have been if you had let me know that I had a mother? As *I* know myself, I sprang from some comforting myth told by a soothing old man.—Heartaches! Longing! I've had just a thumping pain where my heart ought to be. You didn't care—you—

(The visitors are spellbound and they stand watching, touched in spite of themselves.)

MARGOT—Claire, Claire, child you're young—you can't see! You *still* want me, child you do!

CLAIRE—No! Look at them there, waiting for you to say it isn't so— to say it's just a whim or something. You're used to being one of them. What are you going to change for? How—how do I know you are my mother? I'm still lonesome—I'm going!

(At this the girl turns and runs out by the way she entered, knocking over a chair in her mad flight. Margot drops to her knees catching the chair in her arms as she does so. She has held herself somewhat in restraint up to this point, but the doubt in her child is more than she can stand. Hysterical, she clutches the chair, screaming until it is taken from her.)

MARGOT—Don't let her say that—don't! Don't!—Oh, Claire, my baby! Claire! Claire!

(The guests all move slowly to the door with the exception of Mr. Barter, who lays down his hat and cane and starts with the maid

41

who has come in, to the crazed woman. The curtain descends as her calls rend the air.)

SCENE 2.

Same room at dusk. There is still the sound of the ocean. The window curtains are partly drawn. Margot is lying on the chaise-longue in negligée. A small stand bearing medicines and glasses is near by.

In the center of the room Mr. Barter is talking in whispers to a group of seamen in oil skins. The maid is attending the woman. As the seamen start out, their coats rattle, and Margot starts up wildly.

MARGOT—Go back to the ocean! Why are you here? The *ocean!* The *ocean!* Don't you hear it laughing, blustering, crashing out there! *Why* are you here? *Ah*—

BARTER—It is all right, Madame, it is all right. They will find her. You must be quiet.

BERTIE—Oh, Madame, you must be calm. The doctor said you must be quiet or—Oh, Madame you will be quiet?

MARGOT—You have not brought Claire. Why?

SEAMAN—Our men are searching steadily, ma'am. The water is rough today. We've sighted a drifting skiff and we're trying to reach it. We think—

SECOND SEAMAN—Don't worry ma'am we'll reach it.

THIRD SEAMAN—(*Looking through window*)—The water's getting rougher.

BARTER—All right, men, let's go. Reach that skiff! (*Turning to maid*) I'll run over to the theatre, then I'll come back. Take care.

BERTIE—Yes sir.

(She returns from seeing the men out to Margot who has sat staring hard since she last spoke. Bertie gets her to lie down then sits by her side. The ocean grows louder.)

MARGOT—(*Sitting up*)—Listen, Claire, listen!

BERTIE—Yes, yes, Madame, it is the ocean. Do lie down. Don't listen to it.

MARGOT—No, no, child, it is applause. Hear how they call for me. More! I must get back into my part. (*Bertie looks on, frightened, while Margot goes into acting.*) Ah, sir, and here's a rose; it has a symbol. Know you it? 'Twas mine, 'tis yours. No go, sir, and ponder o'er the symbol. (*She waits for an imagined cue, pantomiming all the while.*) Ah, but if you stay our secret is given away! It is not yet time for that. Ah, you *will* go! Here comes my cousin Clara. (*Changing from acting at the sound of the name she has spoken.*) Clara—Clara—Claire! *Claire! Claire!*

BERTIE—(*Running to her*)—Madame Cotell! Please! Come!

MARGOT COTELL—Madame Cotell! Why, I am Marjorie Meade, you know, but of course I shall take another name for my work. Go, Claire, darling, sit there and hear my new lines.

BERTIE—Now, now, Madame, do come. I am Bertie. Come, lie down before the doctor returns.

MARGOT—There now, they're applauding again. I must get back into the part. (*Acting again*)

Rush on, my brain—I cannot comprehend things infinitesimal!

I cannot grasp the things that sweep me on.

I cannot leave the cloudrealms,—yet

The abstract drowns me—utterly, utterly.

Poor despairing mortal, I. This is madness!

(*Hearing the waves again*) Why do they applaud in the midst of my lines! Why do they not—Ah, they have gone, and left the ocean in their place! And it is laughing—shouting at me! *Stop it!*—Oh, my baby! Claire!—Baby! Bring her back! (*She falls screaming to the floor.*)

BERTIE—(*Running to her*)—Oh, poor, poor Madame If you had just kept quiet. Oh—oh—I can't do a thing! (*Wringing her hands and running to the window and opening it.*) Hey! Mister! Please come in here at once. Yes! To the front; I'll let you in! (*Over the woman*) You poor, poor darling. Anyhow you've showed 'em you could be great. I know you suffered. (*Goes to let the man in. He is one of the seamen.*)

BERTIE—Just help me get her on the *chaise longue.*

SEAMAN—Right! There y'are. Now what're you gonna do? Give'er some more medicine? Too much dope in this here.

BERTIE—Thank you I can manage now. She's coming to. If she just didn't hear those waves! They *do* sound awful.—Poor Madame (*tending her*). (*To seaman*) Are people stirring much?

SEAMAN—Wa'al, they ain't just up on what's happened. They know we're searching for someone. We don't know awrsef whether the miss is out there or whether she run away. They're nearin' that skiff though.

BERTIE—Do they know Madame Cotell is connected with the affair?

SEAMAN—Oh, well, I guess it's 'bout sneaked around now that she's—she's colored. Course this here's a kind of swellish neighborhood, whole place is in fact, and I guess—

BERTIE—(*Flaring up*)—Well, what'n the devil's that got to do with it! She didn't bother a darned soul unless *they* came after *her*. She never told nobody what she was because nobody asked her. I'd like to tell these white guys something around here. I may not be so doggoned high-up, but I certainly know the real stuff when I see it. Margot Cotell's got in her what a lot o' folks around here need, and need bad! She took the chance that came to her, and she's let 'em know what she is.

SEAMAN—(*Noticing Margot stirring*)—Hey! Yer wakin' her up! (*He goes out while he can.*)

BERTIE—(*Turning quickly to Margot*)—Oh, I'm sorry! I didn't go to make all that fuss, Madame.

MARGOT—What is the trouble Bertie? Shouldn't I be at the—What is it?—Why—

BERTIE—(*Giving her something to quiet her*)—Now, Madame, you must be very still.

(*The bell rings sharply. Bertie answers and returns with Mr. Barter who is a bit excited.*)

BARTER—How do you feel now Madame? Fine, fine! I'll just tell you this right now. The people screamed for Margot Cotell! The understudy can't hold them. Madame must return regardless.

MARGOT—(*As though it were all just dawning on her*) Did you tell them Margot Cotell is colored?

BARTER—It is never to be mentioned again.

MARGOT—Has my child been found?

BERTIE—(*She has been looking out of the window.*) Pardon, Madame, but the—the—the men are—are coming.

(*Barter and Margot both turn, asking the same question with their eyes.*)

BERTIE—Yes—yes—they—they have something! It's—it's the wrap she wore—and—a shoe—and—Oh! (*Hiding her face in her hands*)

(*Margot sits very still. She is strangely calm.*)

MARGOT—(*Motioning to Mr. Barter*)—Go meet them, Mr. Barter. (*He leaves the room hesitating*) I am all right.

(This calm surprises Bertie, but as soon as the man has left the room Margot changes.)

MARGOT—*(Rising)*—Come here, Bertie, quick! Away from the window! Now sit here! Stay! If you follow me I'll strangle you. *(She is wild again and talking in loud whispers. She flings the long window open.)* You dare! *(This as Bertie starts after her. The girl is too frightened to start again.)* Old waves, you have not called in vain! You led her through this door and out again. Now I'm coming, and we'll have our holiday together. *(Her wild laughter floats back as she dashes away. Mr. Barter and the other men come as she vanishes. They and the maid run to the long window. The men go after her. Bertie stands on the stoop outside the long window, staring after them. A final, wild, victorious scream comes back, and Bertie falls, fainting where she stands. The men do not overtake Margot. Only the roar of the ocean is heard as the curtain falls.)*

THE CHURCH FIGHT

A PRIZE PLAY

BY RUTH A. GAINES-SHELTON

This play took the second prize of *$40.00* in our contest of *1925*. For rights of reproduction please write *The Crisis*.

Mrs. Shelton is 53 years old and has three children and two grandsons. She was born in Missouri, educated at Wilberforce and lives in St. Louis. She has written and staged a number of successful amateur plays. One of her daughters, a kindergarten teacher, is studying dramatic art at Emerson during her summers.

CHARACTERS

The Brethren
    Ananias
    Investigator
    Judas
    Parson Procrastinator
The Sisters
    Sapphira
    Instigator
    Meddler
    Experience
    Take-it-Back
    Two-Face

SCENE.—*In the kitchen of Sister Sapphira's home. A small kitchen table with red table cloth on it and breakfast dishes for two; kitchen chair; cupboard with dishes in it; pans and skillets hanging up.*

THE CHURCH FIGHT

TIME.—7:30 *in the morning.*

Brother Ananias and Sister Sapphira have just finished their breakfast. Ananias has on overalls and jumper ready for day's work. Sapphira is in neat house dress, gingham apron, with dust cap on.

BROTHER ANANIAS. (*Lighting pipe.*).—Well wife, I must go, it's 7:30 and I'll have to skip along; but I want you to remember if that committee meets here today tell them that we ain't going to pay another cent into the Church unil Parson Procrastinator leaves. Tell them Parson Shoot, from Rocky-town, says he'll come and take our Church any time.

SISTER SAPPHIRA.—Don't you worry, Ananias, I ain't going to pay no more money to that man. Why he has plumb robbed the treasury. Why it's just a shame for a preacher to stay at a Church until he kills it plumb dead. Here honey, take your dinner bucket. (*Ananias takes his bucket, says goodbye as he goes out the door.*)

SISTER SAPPHIRA. (*Cleaning up table.*).—I do hope they can git brother Procrastinator moved by night. I've got so much work today it looks like I just ain't got time to fool with all them people acoming here. But we've got to attend to God's work first.

(*Knock at door; opens door.*)—Why, you all are here before I've got my house cleaned up; but come right in. I'm so glad you all mean business.

(*Enter Sister Instigator with glasses on, looking over them; Sister Meddler, chewing gum. Sister Experience with book and pencil looking very important. Sister Take-it-Back, with head down as if afraid of being discovered. Sister Two-Face, smiling sweetly with pretty hat and veil on; Brother Investigator, with Bible; Brother Judas, leaning on cane.*

All ladies are dressed in house dresses except Sister Two-Face, who has a street dress on. Sister Sapphira shakes hands with each one calling the name as she does so.)—Just sit right down and let us see what can be done. I'm just all on fire about it.

BROTHER INVESTIGATOR. (*Sits down at table, takes off glasses and wipes them.*).—Well, Sister Sapphira, I'll tell you in the beginning, it's no easy task to move a Minister. You see, in the first place, we got to have a "charge" against him; now what charge have we aginst Parson Procrastinator?

SISTER INSTIGATOR.—Well Brother Investigator, we ain't got no particular charge agin him, only he's been here thirteen years and we are tired looking at him.

BROTHER INVESTIGATOR.—That won't do, Sister Instigator; you must have sufficient evidence and proof that he has broken the law, or lived unrighteously.

SISTER MEDDLER.—Couldn't we make up some kind of a charge agin him?

SISTER EXPERIENCE.—Better not do that sisters, you'll get into trouble!

SISTER SAPPHIRA.—There's no danger of that; we could just simply say that Brother Procrastinator has not walked in the straight and narrow path since he's been here.

BROTHER INVESTIGATOR.—Well, Sister Sapphira, you can't say that unless you tell just *wherein* he failed to walk in the path.

BROTHER JUDAS.—Well, I'll just tell you the truth, Brother Investigator; you know I know him. He and I have been arm and arm ever since he's been here. He's a pretty crooked sort of a fellow. Of course I wouldn't like for him to know I squealed on him.

SISTER TAKE-IT-BACK.—Well I know one thing, and I saw this with my own eyes: I saw him hold on to Sister Holy's hand so long one night at prayer meeting until Brother Two-Face had to speak to him about it!

SISTER SAPPHIRA.—There now! Do you hear that? I've been watching them two, for some time. You know Sister Holy was the one what gave him that gold pencil.

SISTER EXPERIENCE.—Sisters you all had better listen to me; you know I've been in one church fight, and I promised God that I'd never be in another. Now in the first place, no church fight can be built on a lie. It's better to let the preacher stay, than damn our souls trying to get rid of him.

BROTHER JUDAS. (*Singing.*).—"We want no cowards in our band."

SISTER EXPERIENCE.—If there's anybody here, that's afraid to come out and fight in the open, let them get out at once.

SISTER TAKE-IT-BACK.—Well I'm one that's not afraid; you all know me. You know what I say first, I say last; and I started out to move Brother Procrastinator and I don't expect to stop until he's gone.

BROTHER JUDAS.—That's the way to win out; Sisters, you got to have that fighting spirit.

SISTER INSTIGATOR.—I tell you, we just must git rid of this man. Why none of the young people will come to Church because he can't read so anybody can understand him. If he don't go, this Church is going to destruction and ruin.

BROTHER INVESTIGATOR.—Now sisters and brothers, I have listened careful to every word you said and I ain't yet had sufficient evidence to ask Parson Procrastinator to go.

SISTER EXPERIENCE.—Brother Investigator, I wish to drop this word of warning. When I was in the fight aginst Parson Hard-head, some of the sisters told so many stories that the Bishop had to turn them out of the Church for lying. Now I don't think we ought to tear the Church all to pieces just to git the Minister to go. If he ain't doing right, let the officers see that he does do right; if he ain't a good man, let the Church get together and pray for God to touch his sinful heart, and convert him. For after all, we are serving God, not man. Men may come and men may go, but God stays forever.

SISTER INSTIGATOR.—I see Sister Experience ain't with us in this fight. Of course I ain't never been in a church fight before, but I am in this one heart and hand.

SISTER MEDDLER.—I think we ought to find out where Brother Procrastinator got his money from to buy that $7,000 house on 6th Street.

SISTER SAPPHIRA.—Oh yes! I forgot that. That does seem funny when we poor creatures can't hardly get a crust of bread to eat; now, there's a charge agin him right there.

SISTER MEDDLER.—That's so, I never thought of that. That is a good charge agin him.

BROTHER INVESTIGATOR.—What's that, Sister Meddler?

SISTER SAPPHIRA.—Why he bought a big house on 6th Street and paid a whole lot of money spot cash for it.

BROTHER INVESTIGATOR.—Well what can you do about it? That was his own affair so long as he does not infringe on ours.

SISTER INSTIGATOR.—I don't know why it ain't a charge against him. It gives our Church a bad name to have the Parson flashing money around like he was a rich man and then agin where did he git all that money anyway? I know Morning Glory Baptist Church didn't give it to him, because we only pay him $10 a week.

SISTER MEDDLER.—He don't deserve but $5 a week.

BROTHER JUDAS. (*Looks out window.*).—Sisters, here comes Brother Procrastinator now.

BROTHER INVESTIGATOR. (*Goes to door.*)—Come in Parson Procrastinator, I am glad you came.

(Parson Procrastinator enters with long Prince Albert coat, stove-pipe hat and gold-headed cane; a big gold watch chain is prominent.)

PARSON PROCRASTINATOR.—Yes, Brother Investigator, I just got back from Conference, and heard a church fight was on agin me and that they didn't want me to come back again another year. Now I am here; what charge have you all agin me? (*Silence*).

BROTHER INVESTIGATOR.—I just told them, Brother Procrastinator, that they would have to have some charge agin you.

PARSON PROCRASTINATOR.—That's correct; now let me see who's here. (*Puts on glasses; looks around.*) Why here's my old friend who will die by me I know. Ain't that so Brother Judas?

BROTHER JUDAS.—Oh yes, Parson, you can always depend on me.

SISTER EXPERIENCE.—Parson Procrastinator you know I am your friend; I told them there was no charge agin you, but some of them said they had a charge.

BROTHER PROCRASTINATOR.—Had a charge aginst me? Now who was it who said so?

SISTER TAKE-IT-BACK.—It wasn't me, Brother Procrastinator, I've never seen nothing wrong out of you.

SISTER SAPPHIRA.—I never said it, Parson.

PARSON PROCRASTINATOR.—Well, somebody *must* have said it. Look it up in the minutes, Brother Investigator.

SISTER MEDDLER.—I know who said it, cause I was looking right in their mouth when they said it.

SISTER SAPPHIRA.—I know I never had no charge agin Brother Procrastinator 'cause I don't know nothing about him only something good.

SISTER TWO-FACE.—Parson Procrastinator you do look so fine since you came back from Conference, and we is all just crazy about you.

BROTHER INVESTIGATOR (*who has been searching minutes*).—It says here in the minutes that you bought a $7,000 house on 6th Street, but I failed to put down who said it.

PARSON PROCRASTINATOR.—So that's it, is it? Well, I wants the one who said it, to git right up and tell me why they call it a "charge" agin me.

SISTER EXPERIENCE.—Well I never said it but I know who did say it. But it's none of my business.

PARSON PROCRASTINATOR.—Yes it is your business, Sister Experience, you know from your past experience what it means to have a church fight. Now I want the one what said that charge to own it.

SISTER MEDDLER.—I think it was sister,—

PARSON PROCRASTINATOR.—That will do, Sister Meddler. We want the sister what said it to speak for herself and if she can't say last what she said first, she is a prevaricator by the law. Now Brother Investigator since nobody will own the charge agin me, just scratch it out, and I wants all them what's for me to stand, and Brother Investigator you count 'em.

BROTHER INVESTIGATOR.—All what's in the favor of Parson Procrastinator staying with us this year, stand. (*All stand except Sister Experience.*) What's your objection Sister Experience?

SISTER EXPERIENCE.—I was just sitting here counting the liars.

PARSON PROCRASTINATOR.—Well that will do. That vote is carried. If it is carried by liars, just put it down, Brother Investigator; and I will meet you all at prayer meeting Friday night. (*Goes out.*)

SISTER TWO-FACE.—Ain't he a wonderful man. I don't think we could ever get another one like him.

SISTER INSTIGATOR.—Well I had intended to tell him just what I thought of him if he had stayed.

BROTHER JUDAS.—Well, he's a good man, and we can't afford to let him go.

SISTER SAPPHIRA.—I said that in the first place. The trouble with our people is they never stop to think.

SISTER TAKE-IT-BACK.—That's just it, Sister Sapphira. Now I thank God I've never said a harmful word agin the man in my life.

SISTER MEDDLER. (*Who has been standing serenely all the time with a look of disgust on her face.*).—You all ought to be ashamed of yourselves after starting all this fuss and then denying it. Never mind I'm going to tell Parson Procrastinator.

SISTER TWO-FACE.—I'm glad I didn't say a word agin him. You all know I always did love Parson Procrastinator. I was the one what gave him that gold pencil, but I didn't want everybody to know it.

SISTER EXPERIENCE.—Sisters, do let us go home, before we defy the law any longer.

BROTHER INVESTIGATOR. Yes, all stand please, (*with uplifted hands*)—Lord, smile down in tender mercies upon those who have lied, and those who have not lied; close their lips with the seal of forgiveness, stiffen their tongues with the rod of obedience, fill their ears with the gospel of truth, and direct Parson Procrastinator's feet toward the railroad track.

BROTHER JUDAS. (*In hard voice.*).—"Amen."

(*All break up in confusion each saying that Parson Procrastinator should be moved and they weren't going to put up with him.*)

CURTAIN

FOR UNBORN CHILDREN

A PLAY IN ONE ACT

MYRTLE A. SMITH LIVINGSTON

This play won the third prize of *$10* in *The Crisis* Contest of *1925*. It cannot be reproduced without permission. Persons interested may write *The Crisis*.

"I was born in Holly Grove, Arkansas, on May 8, 1902, but have lived in Denver, Colorado, since I was eight years old, receiving a part of my education in the public schools there. I attended Howard University, Washington, D. C., for two years, where I was a member of the Rho Psi Phi Medical Sorority. I am now a senior student at Colorado Teachers College, Greeley, Colo., where I was a partner in the organization and presentation of a dance rhythm, and am a member of a writers' association, 'The Modern Wills'. I married in June, 1925."

The scene of the play is "Somewhere in the South"; the characters are all of Negro descent except the "young white girl" and the members of the mob. The time is the present.

CHARACTERS:

LEROY CARLSON: *a young lawyer*
MARION CARLSON: *his sister*
GRANDMA CARLSON: *his grandmother*
SELMA FRAZIER: *a young white girl*
A mob.

Scene

A living room is tastefully, though not richly, furnished, denoting the occupancy of a refined family, evidently of the middle class. There is a sofa to one side, a table in the center, and a leather comfort-chair in the corner; another leather chair sits in the upper part of the room. A window is in the rear. There are two entrances, one right and one left. Marion is seen sitting on the sofa reading the evening paper as the curtain rises. After perusing it quietly for a minute, she throws it down and goes to the window, peering out into the night.

Her grandmother, a gentle, well-bred, old lady enters.

GRANDMA CARLSON—Hasn't Roy come yet, Marion?

MARION—No, he hasn't, grandmother; and I'm beginning to get worried; it's almost 9 o'clock now and he said he'd be here by 6.

GRANDMA CARLSON—Did you telephone the office for him?

MARION—Yes; he left about 5:30, they said.

GRANDMA CARLSON—(*with a sigh sits in the comfort-chair*) I suppose he's somewhere with that girl again.

MARION—Oh! If he would only let her alone! He knows what it will mean if they find it out; it's awful for him to keep us in this terrible suspense!

GRANDMA CARLSON—Do you suppose talking to her would do any good? Do you know her?

MARION—Yes, by sight; as far as I know she's a nice enough girl all right, but then she's white and she ought to stay in her own race; she hasn't any right to be running around after our men. I know it wouldn't be of any use to talk to her; and Roy—!

GRANDMA CARLSON—Yes, dear, I know; we hardly dare to say anything to him about it; but, Marion, we've got to do something!

MARION—But, grandmother, what? I'm at my wit's end! Since they can't be married here, they're going to run away and go north someplace where they can, and (*despairingly*) I don't see anything we can do to stop them!

GRANDMA CARLSON—(*sadly and preoccupied*) I suppose I'll have to tell him;—well, if it will stop him—

MARION—Tell him what?

GRANDMA CARLSON—(*with a start as she realizes she has said something she didn't intend to*) Oh, nothing, child; look again; don't you see him yet?

MARION—No. Oh! It's terrible not knowing whether he's all right or if some mob has—(*buries her face in her hands*).

GRANDMA CARLSON—(*wincing*) No,—no—don't say that!

MARION—But you know that's what will happen if it's found out before they get away!

GRANDMA CARLSON—(*moaning*) Oh, my child! I don't know which would be the hardest to bear! I'd almost rather that he should die now than to marry a white woman, but O! Dear Lord! Not such a death as that!

(*The noise of a door being unlocked is heard outside; it is opened and then shut.*)

MARION—(*relieved*) Here he is now; well, thank goodness, it hasn't happened yet. (*Her nervous tension relaxes and her anger rises throughout the following scene.*)

LeRoy enters.

LEROY—(*throws cap on table*) Hello; (*smiles sheepishly*) been giving me "Hail Columbia", I guess, haven't you?

MARION—(*sarcastically*) This is what you call 6 o'clock, I suppose, is it?

LEROY—I'm sorry, sis; I had an engagement and I couldn't make it here by then; I meant to call you and let you know, but,—well, I'm sorry.

GRANDMA CARLSON—We were just worried; you know we can't feel very easy these days, Roy, when we don't know where you are; you know the sentiment down here.

MARION—(*bitterly*) What does he care about how we feel? His family and his career too, for that matter, mean nothing to him now; and his whole heart and soul are wrapped up in his girl,— a white girl! I guess your engagement this evening was with her; I know it was!

LEROY—(*trying to control his temper*) Yes, it was; I still have the liberty of making an engagement with anyone I choose, Marion.

GRANDMA CARLSON—But you haven't the right, son, to cause us unnecessary worry and pain. You know how much your sister and I both care about you, and it wouldn't be much to just let us know where you are.

LEROY—(*contritely*) I didn't mean to worry, you, Granny; I was on my way home when—her note was brought to me, and I didn't have time to call you then. But you won't have to worry about me much longer now, anyway; we've decided to leave tomorrow night.

MARION—(*shocked*) Tomorrow night? Good Heavens, Roy! You can't go through with it! Have you lost all your manhood?

GRANDMA CARLSON—(*her voice throbs with pain*) Ah, boy, you've forgotten us! Don't you love us at all anymore since she came into your life?

LEROY—O, Granny, I hate to leave you and sis; but you know we can't stay here and marry, confound these laws! It will be better for us to go some place where we aren't know, anyway. I wish you and Marion could go with us.

MARION—(*almost hysterical*) I wouldn't go a step with you and your white woman if I was going to be killed for it! If you've lost your self-respect, I still have mine! I wouldn't spit on a woman like her! There must be something terribly wrong with her, for white women don't marry colored men when they can get anybody else! You poor fool! If it's color you want, why couldn't you stay in your own race? We have women who are as white as any white person could be! My God! What is to become of us when our own men throw us down? Even if you do love her can't you find your backbone to conquer it for the sake of your race? I know they're as much to blame as we are, but intermarriage doesn't hurt them as much as it does us; laws would never have been passed against it if the states could have believed white women would turn Negro men down, but they knew they wouldn't; they can make fools out of them too easily, and you're too much of a dupe to see it! Well, if you marry her, may God help me never to breathe your name again! (*runs from the room sobbing*).

LEROY—(*sorrowfully and pleadingly*) Oh, Granny, you don't feel that way too, do you? Selma and I can't help it because we don't belong to the same race, and we have the right to be happy together if we love each other, haven't we?

GRANDMA CARLSON—(*sadly*) We have the right to be happy, child, only when our happiness doesn't hurt anybody else; and when a colored man marries a white woman, he hurts every member of the Negro race!

LEROY—(*perplexed*) But,—I don't understand;—how?

GRANDMA CARLSON—He adds another link to the chain that binds them; before we can gain that perfect Freedom to which we have every right, we've got to prove that we're better than they! And we can't do it when our men place white women above their own!

LEROY—(*imploringly*) But, Grandmother, I love her so much! Not because she's white, but just for herself alone; I'd love her just the same if she were black! And she loves me too! Oh! I can't believe it would be wrong for us to marry!

GRANDMA—Sometimes we best prove our love by giving up the object of it. You can't make her happy, Roy; she'll be satisfied for a while, but after that the call of her blood will be stronger than her love for you, and you'll both be miserable; she'll long for her own people; you won't be enough.

LEROY—(*miserably*) What shall I do? Oh, Lord, have mercy! Granny, I can't give her up! I couldn't live without her!

GRANDMA—(*with tears in her eyes*) Think of the unborn children that you sin against by marrying her, baby! Oh, you can't know the misery that awaits them if you give them a white mother! Every child has a right to a mother who will love it better than life itself; and a white woman cannot mother a Negro baby!

LEROY—But, Granny—

GRANDMA—(*pathetically*) I know, Honey! I've never told you this,—I didn't want you to know,—but your mother was a white woman, and she made your father's life miserable as long as he lived. She never could stand the sight of you and Marion; she hated you because you weren't white! I was there to care for you, but I'm getting old, Honey, and I couldn't go through it again! Boy, you can't make the same mistake your father did!

LEROY—(*in repugnance*) Oh, Granny, why didn't you tell me before? My mother, white! I've wondered why you never spoke of her! And she hated us! My God! That makes it different!

(*Grandma rises and kisses him on the forehead, holding his face between her hands, and looking deep into his eyes.*)

GRANDMA—I'll leave you alone with God and your conscience, and whatever you decide, I'll be satisfied (*goes out*).

(*LeRoy sits with his head bowed in his hands; presently a light tapping is heard at the window, which finally attracts his attention; he crosses to it, and seeing who is there, motions toward the door, going to open it; Selma enters, almost exhausted.*)

SELMA—(*breathless and terrorized*) A mob!—Hurry!—They're—coming—here—after—you.—You—must—go!—Hurry!

LEROY—(*in amazement*) A mob—after me?

SELMA—Hurry and go!—They're coming now! (*a rumble of voices is heard in the distance*) (*despairingly*) Oh! It's too late! (*sobs*) What shall I do? Oh, they'll—they'll—kill you!

FOR UNBORN CHILDREN

(The rumble grows louder as it nears the house; cries of "Lynch him!" "The dirty nigger!" "We'll show him how to fool around a white woman!" are heard.)

(Grandma Carlson and Marion enter, fearfully apprehensive.)

MARION—*(seeing Selma)* What's the matter? What's that noise?

GRANDMA—*(as realization dawns upon her; clutches her heart)* Oh! It can't be! *(falls on her knees and prays)* Dear God! have mercy! Oh, Father in Heaven! Do not desert us now! Hear my prayer and save my boy!

LEROY—*(a light breaks over his face and he is transfigured; a gleam of holiness comes into his eyes; looking heavenward he says)*: Thy will be done, O Lord! *(he turns and takes Selma's hands in his)* It has to be, sweetheart, and it is the better way; even though we love each other we couldn't have found happiness together. Forget me, and mary a man of your own race; you'll be happier, and I will too, up there. Goodbye. *(He turns to Marion)* Forgive me, sis, if you can.

MARION—*(sobs heartbrokenly)* There isn't anything to forgive, Roy! It's I you should forgive! I'm sorry for everything I said! Oh, God! I can't stand this!

LEROY—*(soothingly)* Don't cry, sis; what you said was right; and I want you to know that even if this hadn't happened, I was going to give her up *(kisses her tenderly)*.

(Picks his grandmother up from the floor and holds her close in his arms)

It's better this way, Granny; don't grieve so; just think of it as a sacrifice for UNBORN CHILDREN!

A VOICE IS HEARD OUTSIDE:—Come out, you damned nigger, or we'll burn the house down!

MARION—*(clings to him, sobbing)* Don't go, Roy! We'll all die together!

LEROY—*(puts her from him gently)* No. *(Loud and clear)* I'm coming, gentlemen!

(With a last, long, loving look at the three of them he walks out to his death victorious and unafraid.)

CURTAIN.

THE BOG GUIDE

MAY MILLER

1925

CHARACTERS

RUPERT MASTER
ELWOOD BEALER } *English tourists.*
SABALI: *The bog guide.*
Place: *The great dark continent.*

SCENE: *Back stage and to the side up stage the narled trunks of trees twist as if to bend over a stretch of marsh-land that begins about center stage and extends off to the left. A rotting stump on the margin of the swamp adds to the atmosphere of decay. The rest of the stage is covered with vivid green moss and vines which seem to reach out from the quagmire.*

It is near the end of day. A heavy gray mist hangs over the tree-tops. The wild life of the forest is stilled except for an occasional cry from afar.

THE PLAY

Masters and Bealer enter from the right. They are stalwart men of about forty. Their costumes are the customary kaki outfit of the English tourist. They walk cautiously, peering on all sides as if expecting to meet someone.

BEALER: (*hesitating and looking around*) "I think it is the damned silence of the thing that I can't stand."

MASTERS: "So it's the silence tonight? Last night it was the noise."

BEALER: "I am sick of the whole mess. First it's those black creatures in their stinking villages beating their bally heads off on those infernal tomtoms."

MASTERS: "African civilization, old chap."

BEALER: "Confound this nigger civilization. I wish you would stop mouthing and get back to a bathtub and a pavement."

MASTERS: (*in a light bantering tone*) "When you could be communing with nature?"

BEALER: (*bitterly*) "Of course, with beautiful nature which spreads a quarter mile bog before you, a damned black waste with hell like suckholes."

MASTERS: "And what did the natives say?"

BEALER: "Yes consolation it was truly. They blubber down there in the village about this quarter mile of mud and slime where if you make one misstep, you'll be so completely lost that there'll not even be a gap to tell where you sank."

MASTERS: "But you forget there will be a guide."

BEALER: "O! to be sure. Some half-wild creature who haunts the bog to guide tourists over, probably more dangerous than the bog itself."

MASTERS: "Nevertheless I'd be rather glad to meet even that wild creature."

BEALER: "Somehow I believe that for all your assurance you are as weak about this thing as I."

(*A silence falls between the two and for the first time Masters drops his care-free attitude. Bealer takes out his case and selects a cigarette. He lights his cigarette. Masters prepares to do likewise*).

BEALER: "Light, old man? You'd better save them, no telling when there will be need in this Godforsaken place."

(*Masters approaches Bealer and lights his cigarette*).

MASTERS: "Do you know, Elwood, in all my year of travel this bog is about the first thing that has got me. There's something about that waste-land that has gripped me. The thing is positively creepy. I can almost feel it stretch out to catch me. There is that lost feeling that no matter how far I go it will eventually reach me."

BEALER: "Then why go on? We haven't got to cross this bog. Let's turn back now. We can make the village to-night and the coast in a few days. One month and we shall be in old London Town. What say you, old man?"

MASTERS: (*slowly*) "No, I am afraid not."

BEALER: "Well, why not? You admit that this beastly hole has got your nerve and I've said all along I was sick of the plagued expedition."

MASTERS: "I am too, but I can't turn back now."

BEALER: "You can't! Why? There is something about this thing that I don't understand. We leave England on a sporting expedition through Africa. The pleasure goes from the trip for both of us, yet you stand here and blubber that you can't turn back now. A pleasure trip!" (*he laughs, ironically*).

MASTERS: (*slowly*) "Well no, not exactly." (*Masters seats himself on a stump but Bealer starts off stage*).

MASTERS: (*rising hastily*) "And where are you going?"

BEALER: "Back. I might overtake the guides."

(*Bealer goes off. Masters rushes out after him. They return together*).

MASTERS: "Don't be stupid, Elwood. Stop your infernal capering and listen to me. I want to talk to you."

BEALER: (*pacing restlessly to and fro*) "Don't waste time talking. Let's get away from here."

MASTERS: God alone knows why I should select this time and place—a quagmire, at the end of day. I guess it's that bog again. It has torn me to pieces."

BEALER: "You were sufficiently warned and why in Heaven's name did you insist on making the next village without the guides?"

MASTERS: "I guess that did seem queer to you, but the whole thing is uncanny."

BEALER: (*dryly*) "Including us." (*ignoring the invitation of Masters, to share the stump with him*). "Now look here, old man, if you insist on waiting for this little barbarian guide, you sit and talk, I'll watch."

(*Bealer continues his nervous walking to and fro. Silence falls for a moment, broken only by some animal's faraway call to his mate in the dusky twilight*).

MASTERS: (*breaking the prolonged silence*) "Do you remember Chauncey Bayne?"

BEALER: (*halting suddenly as if surprised at mention of the name*). "Your cousin, a dreamer with wild poetic ideas! Who in our set has ever forgot Chauncey Bayne?"

MASTERS: "Do you remember he disappeared on the eve of his marriage to Audrian Waylon?"

BEALER: "How could I forget? You know we fellows often wondered what happened."

MASTERS: "Well let me tell you."

BEALER: "No. I didn't mean to intrude. It was only curiosity. In fact I'd rather not hear now. I am sure that story will be more interesting when told in a hotelroom on the coast."

MASTERS: (*rising excitedly*) "I must tell you. Do you hear, I must tell you."

BEALER: (*standing as if resigned to the outcome*) "Forgive me, old chap, of course."

MASTERS: "Elwood, it's an ugly story. I loved Audrian. God, how I loved her! And she loved Chauncey. Two days before their proposed wedding I went to her—Now don't judge too harshly what I did—O! the torture of seeing the girl you love about to marry another." (*he pauses in his reverie*).

BEALER: (*becoming interested in spite of his surroundings*) "Yes, yes and—"

MASTERS: Lord Bayne had two children, a son and a daughter. When still young, they married and sons were born to both."

BEALER: "Yes, I know Chauncey was the child of the son and you of the daughter. But did the old man ever care much for these matches?"

MASTERS: "No and there's the story. Chauncey's mother, the son's wife was too reserved. However, her unnatural attitude was explained when she was dying in childbirth with Chauncey. She called her husband, my mother, and grandfather to her and told them that she thought they ought to know before she died that she was a Negro."

BEALER: "You mean Chauncey's mother was a Negro? It is unbelievable."

MASTERS: "Further investigation proved it true."

BEALER: "And who told you all this?"

MASTERS: "My mother, always a little jealous that Chauncey, her brother's child, a nigger she called him, should carry on the title, told me the story."

BEALER: "But I thought you and Chauncey were both left orphans to your grandfather's care."

MASTERS: "That's true; but young as I was, I never forgot the story. And that's the story I told Audrian. The next day she dismissed Chauncey telling him what I had told her."

BEALER: "But just imagine it, man, to hear from the lips of the girl you love that you're a nigger when you've never even suspected it!"

MASTERS: "And don't you think I have not realized since what a horrible thing I had done. I think I shall always see Chauncey as he stood before grandfather on that last day. With his shoulders unbent and his head high, I can remember his words even now. 'Sir,' he said, 'since you can not deny that which Rupert has said, I now know it to be true. Unfortunately in your mind it does make a difference or why else would you have hidden it all these years? To Audrian it is the one unforgivable.'"

BEALER: "Man, how he must have suffered! You know it's so easy to read about Negroes and sympathize with them—but somehow none of that is quite like being one of them."

MASTERS: "That's what Chauncey said but he added that he would never stop until he found the place where there is no difference. We never saw him again, and the next year I married Audrian. The following year grandfather died, a broken old man: Chauncey was his heart."

BEALER: "My God, this is like a message from the dead." (*he pauses listening to a stir of leaves*).

MASTERS: "That's probably our guide."

BEALER: (*returning from side stage where he has been peering as if to discover someone*) "Guide or no guide, I am convinced that this is decidedly not the place for that weird story of yours. Why select a quagmire to talk of men who disappeared?"

MASTERS: "But he did not disappear altogether. Carter made an expedition in this part of Africa last year. On his return, he told me that he had seen Chauncey and that he was living somewhere between those two villages near this bog. Now do you understand my trip? I have come to find him. He shall go back and men shall not make a difference. I tell you, Elwood, we must find him."

BEALER: "Surely we shall. Let's go back a little. There's an English trader about half mile away—maybe he can help us."

MASTERS: "No. You stay here. We don't want to run the chance of missing the guide over the bog. You wait here. I'll go."

(*Masters goes off stage to the right leaving Bealer, who paces back and forth nervously. He is peering up stage when a halfclad beautiful brown girl of about fourteen enters from left. Bealer wheels around facing her*).

BEALER: (*stammering*) "Who are you? Where did you come from?"

SABALI: (*pointing to her naked breast*) "I am Sabali. I sprang from the dreams of Flotsam and the music of the dancer. Their passionate love gave me body."

BEALER: (*unable to conceal his surprise*) "You look like a savage and speak like an English lady. Child, what are you?"

SABALI: "Flotsam said I was just a solid little strip of land on which he was cast at last, the dancer said I was the music that made her beautiful [???] for to come. Flotsam ordered before he lay down to his slumber that Sabali should continue to be solid land for bits of humanity drifting this way, so you see her the only safe path across this bog where only evil should perish."

BEALER: "Ah! so you're the bog guide: but, child, who taught you that language?"

SABALI: "My words with man are these of Flotsam. He brought them with him from Faraway Land, where men build structures to hide their wickedness and clothe their bodies to cover black souls—a land inhabited by vices masquerading under fair names. The language that the people in Faraway Land use to their faraway God—all that Flotsam taught me. But the words I use to answer my God's murmur in the water and his whisper in the trees—those are the dancer's and I use them because my God knows them."

BEALER: (*speaking as if thinking aloud*) "And they call you a savage! Child, I understand your jargon less and less, but tell me who are Flotsam and the dancer?"

SABALI: "Flotsam? O! Flotsam was just a bit of humanity tossed on the ocean of discontent by a storm of prejudice. Restless and disillusioned he floated on seas and seas on his way to nowhere. For ah so short a time he was cast on the Island of Love. He saw the beautiful black body of the dancer away and bend as graceful as the flames by whose light she was dancing. He loved her beauty and they came out here a little away from the others. But the love of one from Faraway Land and a dancer of a tribe has its hours of soul torture. There were times when even a wonderful love failed, and Flotsam suffered! T'is not so easy to forget the structures, the clothes, and even the masqueraders of Faraway Land. But then I came. The dancer named me Sabali, her music, but Flotsam called me solid land, his haven at last."

BEALER: "And you say this Flotsam taught you all these things?"

SABALI: "Ah yes! Oft at night when the dancer had curled up to sleep and forget the tom-toms and the dancers down there in the village—you know she never could go back—then Flotsam and I sat alone with only those distant noises to disturb us and talked far into the night. Sometimes in the darkness he would hold me close, calling me his little anchorage, the one barrier between him and his endless journey. He warned me that even after he slept, some might come and try to lure me away, and he made me promise to stay here. Sometimes we knelt together under the guarding stars and he prayed God to keep me away from that land where beautiful souls are snatched and shells are left in their places—shells where only bitterness and hatred can hide."

BEALER: (*approaching Sabali and grasping her arm in his eagerness*) "And where—where are the dancer and Flotsam?"

SABALI: (*wistfully*) "O they're sleeping now. Only to-day the villagers, who never stopped when the dancer wanted them, came and laid them away. Listen! Can't you hear their farewell tom-toms?"

BEALER: (*apparently disappointed*) "You mean they are dead."

SABALI: "Is that what they call it in your land? Well soon Sabali shall sleep too. Already the dreaded tse-tse has sent her the same drowsy warning. And, oh man, I shall be glad to sleep."

BEALER: (*horrified*): You mean you too will die soon?"

SABALI: "Sabali is not afraid to sleep. 'Tis only pain that is horrid and men brought that too from faraway Land, but Sabali shall throw that in the bog and then she can sleep—O! I am so tired. You are probably the last one whom I shall lead over the bog. But come, it grows late."

BEALER: (*hesitating*) "But I have a companion."

SABALI: (*starting through the bog*) "I shall see your companion when you are safely over. Place your hand in mine."

BEALER: (*giving Sabali his hand reluctantly and following her off*) "I wonder—"

MASTERS: (*entering from right calling eagerly*) "Bealer! Bealer! Maybe he is reconnoitering a little for himself, but there's no use in my moving now. I know enough—too much. What that trader has just told me leaves me room for doubt. I must see this bogguide, I must."

(*Masters seats himself on the stump and lights his pipe. The faint echo of distant tom-toms is hoard. He is about to put his pipe in his mouth, but stops midway*)

MASTERS: "O my God! and they tell me those are the funeral cele-
brations for Chauncey. Chauncey is dead and all he has left is a
beautiful brown savage, who speaks his language and does his
bidding, guiding souls over the bog. I must see her—Chauncey's
child and maybe—I shall—I shall." *(Masters rises as if he has
arrived at a decision. He raises his hands as if to pray)* "O
God! I swear it. Give me the chance. I'll take her back and fight
her battles. Chauncey's child shall be Lady Bayne—please
God!" *(he drops his head on his arm. Sabali returns on the
path through the bog. Masters looks up to see her. He rises hurriedly, dropping the lighted pipe).*

MASTERS: "O! O! and you're—

SABALI: "I am Sabali, the bog guide."

MASTERS: "You're beautiful and you're Chauncey's child. I hear
him when you speak; I trace him in your features, in your car-
riage. It shall be easy."

SABALI: "I am only Sabali and I do not understand. What shall be
easy?"

MASTERS: "Listen, child. I was your father's friend and I have come
to take you away with me. You're going to England and I shall
be your father. You're going back to the land that your father
left. Now do you understand?"

SABALI: *(slowly)* "Yes, I think I do. Your other name is Ruport and
you're the one Flotsam feared would come."

MASTERS: "Flotsam?"

SABALI: "Yes, Chauncey was his masquerade name, but he was just
Flotsam."

MASTERS: "Now I do not understand."

SABALI: "It grows late, come."

MASTERS: "But my companion?"

SABALI: "He awaits in vain on the other side. Place your hand in
mine."

MASTERS: *(stopping with Sabali into the bog)* "Very well, we stay
in the village to-night. To-morrow across the bog, down to the
coast, and then we sail for England."

SABALI: "No Sabali shall not go to Faraway Land. Though Flotsam
sleeps, he has the promise. Nor shall you go back. You see I
know you; you're Prejudice. Already Faraway Land has too
many masqueraders and Prejudice must not go back."

MASTERS: *(hesitating)* "You mean—"

66

SABALI: "I mean we soon shall sleep with the others. Feel how gradually we sink."

(they are clearly sinking now. Masters struggles and starts to scream. Sabali gently places her hand over his mouth).

SABALI: "Sh! you will awake the birds, and we all want to sleep."

(as the curtain falls, the echo of distant tom-toms is heard).

END

SCRATCHES

BY MAY MILLER

PERSONS OF THE PLAY

DANIEL BROADUS

JEFFERSON MEEKS

STUMP

ABBIE

MELDORA

Time: *1915.*

Place: *Poodle Dog Pool Parlor, LeDroit Park,*
Washington, D.C.

Scene: *The room is the typical pool room of pre-war days. In the rear wall are two large windows, suggestive of a shop, and between them a door opens on the street. In the middle of the left side wall a door leads into a hallway. On both sides of the door are short rails with hooks for hanging wraps. On the right wall two cue stick racks are hung and above these a cheap gas fixture extends. Along this wall several chairs, with cuspidors close by their legs, are primly placed. Cheap prints and advertisements decorate all the available spaces. Well out in the room from the left down-stage is a large egg stove behind which in the corner a chair is almost hidden from view. Four pool tables are ranged in the middle of the room.*

It is about five o'clock on a blustry winter day. The shadows of dusk are gathering. The brisk pace of the stooped figures that pass by the windows indicate the severity of the weather. (When the curtain rises the room is vacant save for Stump, a dark brown hunchback of uncertain age, who is asleep on the chair behind the stove. He awakes with a start and with apelike movements goes to the stove. He opens the door of the stove and peers in anxiously. From the box at his feet he scoops two shovels of coal which he throws on the fire. Closing the door he nods and humming lazily goes to the rack for the triangle. With this in hand, he swings around the tables racking the balls.)

STUMP: *(Singing softly)*

> What a wurl! What a wurl!
>
> Tuh be bad, yuh musta been good;
>
> An' tuh be good, yuh musta been bad
>
> What a wurl! What a wurl!

(The door is flung open with a flourish and Abbie and Meldora enter. Abbie, a beautiful tall mulatto of about twenty-five years, is swathed in a long black fur coat and a dark toque fits snugly over her dark hair. Her companion, an overpowdered and heavily rouged brown woman, is shorter in stature. She wears a coat of lighter fur, though plainly one of cheaper skins, and a brightly colored toque. The contrast between the two women is marked. Meldora is clearly a cheap imitation, whereas one indefinably feels that Abbie, in spite of dissipation, is to the manner born.)

MELDORA: *(Rushing to the stove)* Gawd! It's colder'n hell out there.

ABBIE: *(With a musical drawl)* You surely ain't expectin' no summer heat in January.

MELDORA: Foh Jesus sake, shut that door tight an' come on here an' git warm foh a minute.

ABBIE: *(Closing the door and turning to Stump)* Hello, Stump!

STUMP: Evenin', Mis' Abbie. What brung yuh out a day lak dis?

MELDORA: Even us lil' daughters of the rich need air.

ABBIE: You know good an' well I wouldn't of come if you hadn't dogged me to go to the theater with you.

MELDORA: Well not 'xactly dogged; but seein' I ain't goin' to be here nex' week, I did think as you might go wid your poor workin' friend to see huh lil' act.

STUMP: But from all I kin heah, it ain't no lil' act. All de men stops dere games tuh talk 'bout it.

MELDORA: Well you know them that's poor jus' natur'ly got to do. Now if all of us could be pretty an' grab a nice fella like Jeff.

ABBIE: Ah, Mel, quit that! *(Turning to Stump)* You ain't seen nothin' of Jeff lately; has you?

STUMP: No, I ain't. Jeff don' come heah 'til mos' nigh six o'clock. Fact, nobody much come 'til den.

ABBIE: That's the time I'm supposed to come back foh Jeff.

STUMP: *(Hesitantly)* Mis' Abbie, yuh think yuh mought be heah foh 'bout five minutes?

MELDORA: *(Quickly)* We sure do; it'll take me ten to thaw out.

STUMP: *(Apologetically)* Well, I was jus' athinkin' beings dere ain't nobody comin' no time soon dat I'd jus' step 'cross de street foh a minute.

ABBIE: To the chapel, eh?

MELDORA: An' he'll come back drunker 'n a biled owl.

STUMP: No, Mis' Abbie, honest. . . .

MELDORA: Oh, foh Gawd's sake stop your chinnin' an' git your coat. You could of been back, all the time you're mouthin'.

STUMP: Yes'm an' I'll be right back. *(Stump hurriedly slings down the rack and grabs from a hook a rather shabby coat, which is much too big for him. He hastily goes out not daring to look back, as if afraid the women will change their minds.)*

ABBIE: *(Approaching the stove)* You know, Mel, I ain't so much on stayin' in this Poodle Dog. Jeff'd raise the devil if he knew I come by here when he's away; but my feet jus' wouldn't carry me a step farther 'til they got warm.

MELDORA: Don' say nothin' 'bout feet! I'll be scared to take my shoes off. There ain't no tellin' whether my toes would be on or off.

(Meldora extends first one foot and then the other to the heat. Abbie stamps her feet alternately and spreads her hands to the heat, then restlessly strolls over to the window.)

ABBIE: *(Impatiently)* I know Stump ain't comin' back here no time soon, an' you ought to be gittin' to the theater. What time does your act go on?

MELDORA: Don' go talkin' 'bout that damn'd act. Ada Overton herself couldn't dance on these feet.

ABBIE: *(Glancing restlessly out the window.)* I wish that—. *(She stops suddenly, then continues as if speaking to herself.)* There's somethin' awfully familiar 'bout that beggar's back. — — — Oh, no, it can't be though.

MELDORA: Are you talkin' to yourself or me? Remember please I hates riddles.

ABBIE: *(Not heeding Meldora's words)* My gawd, it is! *(She peers once more, then recoils. She rushes back to the stove and grasps Meldora's arm.)*

70

ABBIE: *(Whispering)* Mel, Mel, I saw him!

MELDORA: *(Starting)* Who?

ABBIE: *(Breathlessly)* My husband!

MELDORA: Gawd! you scared me. How kin that be your husban'? Didn't you say you lef' him in Philly?

ABBIE: *(A little reassured)* Uh-huh, I did. *(Stepping back to the window and again peering cautiously)* Oh, Mel, it is him. It don't matter where I lef' him, he's out there. Nobody don't forget Dan Broadus in a hurry—leastways I wouldn't.

MELDORA: *(Cautiously approaching the window to see)* Well, if that's him, he ain't none too prosp'rous.

ABBIE: *(Turning rather defiantly on Meldora)* Don't joke 'bout him, 'cause there ain't nothin' funny 'bout bein' cold out there in that blizzard an' you know it. *(Abbie looks out the window as if drawn toward the man in the street.)* Mel, look, he's beggin'!

MELDORA: Now what'cha got to go in mournin' 'bout that foh?

ABBIE: But he mus' be hungry an' cold to be beggin'. I know Dan well 'nough to know he wouldn't be if. . . . .

MELDORA: That's his lil' load an' let him tote it. Ain't you full an' warm wid the best lookin' coat Jeff could buy on your back?

ABBIE: I know all that too, but. . . .

MELDORA: I ain't got nothin' to say myself. You had him an' it seems to me if you'd wanted him you'd have kept him while you had him. Nobody stole you; you yourself ran away from Philly an' him.

ABBIE: It wasn't 'cause I wanted to so much; I jus' had to.

MELDORA: Don' go tellin' nobody that lie.

ABBIE: Well I mean I liked Dan, but things didn't go right. It was jus' fine till he went to that church. 'Course Dan was a gambler, but he was such a good gambler. He didn't think nothin' of winnin' a hundred dollars at one haul. We ate well, we dressed well, an' we was happy. Then he went to that dam'd church an' come away vowin' that he'd got religion an' wasn't never goin' to touch a card nor no dice again; swore he'd starve first.

MELDORA: An' that's jus' what you started to do; eh?

ABBIE: Jus' 'bout. There wasn't much to eat an' nothin' to wear.

MELDORA: Ain't nobody blamin' you.

ABBIE: Nobody 'ceptin' Dan; an' I think he mus' hate me. Somehow he couldn't understan' why I wanted him to go back to gamblin'. He ustah say all the time, 'Lil' lady, you jus' wait. I'm goin' to make it yet at somethin' hones' an' respectable.' *(Rather regretfully)* But I couldn't wait.

MELDORA: No, an' he don' seem to have gone up in the world none.

ABBIE: I don't know so much 'bout that.

MELDORA: 'Course I don't know neither, but I was jus' judgin' by 'pearences.

ABBIE: You can't never tell. You know there's some folks that scratches in life jus' like the men does at that table. They aims at one thing an' hits two. Wid Jeff, bein' respectable has to mean bein' poor, too.

MELDORA: An' some folks I know ain't got no better sense 'n to leave good providers foh them that scratches.

ABBIE: Don't be no fool, I ain't leavin' Jeff an' his money foh no beggar.

MELDORA: I knows good an' well you ain't.

ABBIE: *(Insinuatingly)* I guess you knows someone who'd take him right up, eh?

MELDORA: Now don't go slurrin' none 'cause two of us kin do that. Maybe there'd be them as wouldn't want Jeff an' his money, 'cause lot of them say, an' more believes, that it ain't all good money.

ABBIE: *(Quickly)* What 'cha mean?

MELDORA: *(Lightly)* Nothin'. Only Jeff's got gangs of money and gangs of time.

ABBIE: Well, what of it?

MELDORA: Nothin'. Oh, Abbie, let's quit this. What's the use in us fussin' 'bout that?

ABBIE: You're right, Mel; but seein' Dan out there kinda got to me. Fact, anybody beggin' a day like this gits to me. I wonder could I give him some money?

MELDORA: Now there you go again. 'Course you can't. He mus' never see you. As jealous as Jeff is, if he found out who he was he'd kill him in a hurry.

ABBIE: No tellin' what he'd do. 'Course, he swears I'll always love Dan an' that someday he's goin' to send me back to him.

MELDORA: An' you—how you feel 'bout it?

ABBIE: That ain't the question. The point is we got to get out of this place sometime. Then he'll see me, an' what's more he'd know me if I was draped like the Virgin Mary.

MELDORA: Ain't there no back door?

ABBIE: Yes, but Stump's got the keys. He'd have to open it.

MELDORA: *(Going back to window)* An' that onery nigger ain't come yit. *(Looking more closely)* I believe that's him now. Jumping Jerusalem! he has stopped to talk to your husban'.

ABBIE: *(Drawing near the door which leads to the hallway)* He ain't—he ain't bringin' him in here?

MELDORA: Wait—uh-huh—yes, he is. No, un-un, Stump's comin' alone.

(Abbie, who had gone into the hall when Meldora was talking, returns to the room just as Stump enters from the street.)

MELDORA: You tried to stay a lifetime.

STUMP: Ah! now, I didn't stay so long neither, but a old beggar stopped me.

ABBIE: *(Over eagerly)* An' what did he say?

STUMP: *(Looking at her in surprise)* What beggars allus says.

ABBIE: Yes, yes, but what did you say?

STUMP: Who me? I tol' him de Gawd's truf—dat I'd jus' spent mah las' penny foh a drink. But I tol' him as how Jeff mought be in an' I knew he'd give him de price of a dinner.

(Abbie and Meldora start perceptibly.)

MELDORA: *(Recovering first)* Say, Stump, ain't there no way we kin git into the alley from this place?

STUMP: What 'cha wan' tuh git in de alley foh?

MELDORA: The theater ain't far an' I was jus' wanderin' if we couldn't find a sheltered way. I hates to go out on that windy street. In the alley we could keep right warm close to the fence.

ABBIE: Sure, Stump can open that back door foh us. Can't you, Stump? *(Abbie tucks a coin in Stump's hand.)* An' you needn't say nothin' to Jeff 'bout me stoppin'.

STUMP: *(Pocketing the coin and bringing out a bunch of keys)* Sho! sho! Miss Abbie.

(Stump goes out into the hall and Abbie follows. Meldora goes near the stove for a final warming.)

ABBIE: *(Calling from the hall)* Come on, Mel, the door's open.

(Meldora exits. The street door opens and a rather heavy set brown man of about thirty-five enters. He is shabbily dressed and in spite of the cold wears no overcoat. When he enters his shoulders are badly stooped, but under the influence of the heat he

straightens up and is surprisingly impressive. He nears the stove as Stump enters from the hall.)

DANIEL BROADUS: Do you mind me comin' in to wait?

STUMP: Naw.

DAN: I jus' couldn't stan' that cold no longer. It wasn't only this part of me that got cold. *(He repeatedly flaps his arms across his chest to increase circulation.)* Man, I was froze clean through, even down to my heart.

STUMP: Oh! Come on now, yo' heart can't freeze.

DAN: No, I guess it can't, but I jus' had that feelin' that there wasn't nothin' there. I looked at them folks passin' me by wrapped in warm coats an' I hated 'em. I looked at the lights burnin' in warm houses an' I wanted to break in an' bust 'em up.

STUMP: Uh! you mus' have been feelin' right bad. *(Eyeing Daniel suspiciously)* Yuh ain't got no such feelin' now; has yuh?

DAN: No. It's kinda funny what a fire kin do to a man. A minute ago I was hatin' everyone, but I ain't got no such feelin' now. This fire's done warmed me clean through.

(He nears the fire and sinks contentedly in a chair half hidden on the farther side of the stove. He sits smiling to himself with hands stretched out to the heat.)

STUMP: I ain't understandin' what 'cha sayin' but I guess it's awright.

DAN: You kin understan' when a man says he's hungry; can't you?

STUMP: Now, if you had jus' said thirsty!

DAN: If you was talkin' 'bout licker you don't know what I mean, 'cause no man can't be as thirsty foh licker as I am hungry foh food. I ain't had nothin' to eat since yistiddy.

STUMP: Uh! dat is right bad, but yuh jus' set dere an' wait 'til Jeff come. Jeff's got long dough. *(Stump returns to his task of racking the balls, singing as he works. The street door opens and Jefferson Meeks enters. He is of the same stature as Dan, but there is a decided air of prosperity about him. He is well dressed and walks with ease. He does not notice the stranger in the corner nor does Dan immediately come forward.)*

JEFF: Hey, Stump! How's things?

STUMP: Awright, Jeff, but de folks ain't started tuh come in yit.

JEFF: Oh, dey'll be comin' along now. Kinda hard tuh tear yo'self 'way from a fire dis evenin', even if dat fire is at home.

STUMP: I feels right sorry foh dem as ain't got no home an 'no fire dis evenin'.

JEFF: Well, I don't. I passed a beggar on de street dis aftahnoon an' I wouldn't give 'im a cent. *(Dan who has been listening starts as if struck but remains where he is.)* Dey ain't got no bus'ness bein' cold an' hungry. If dey had two cents wurth of guts, dey wouldn't be lak dat. *(Jeff walks to the window and looks up and down the street.)*

STUMP: How yuh mean?

JEFF: *(Still looking out the window)* Well, foh instance dey ain't willin' tuh chance nothin'. Look at me. I got a pocket full of yaller money an' what's mo' I got a yaller gal comin' tuh meet me in a haf hour. How I come by either ain't nobody's bus'ness but I guess I kin stan' foh what I got. More 'n dat I can't say; but I ain't hungry an' cold, an' what's bes' I ain't alone.

(Dan moves slowly from behind the stove and comes to the front facing Jeff who wheels around nervously and looks in surprise at him and then furtively out the window.)

JEFF: *(Harshly)* Who're yuh?

DAN: I'm that beggar you wouldn't give a cent this afternoon.

JEFF: *(Regaining his composure)* Well, what 'cha want now?

DAN: Nothin', only I wants to tell you here's one beggar what's got guts an' if there's a chance of food I takes that chance.

JEFF: Aw! dey all talks dat way. Talk's so easy.

DAN: Maybe 'tis, but all I got to say is more better not come my way. I'd chance a trip to hell if it meant a good square meal.

JEFF: Yuh would, eh?

DAN: Sure. Any man what's hones' to God hungry will do anything.

JEFF: An' yuh says yuh is hones' tuh Gawd hungry, huh? You hear him, Stump?

STUMP: *(Dropping the rack and approaching with interest)* I sho do.

DAN: You talk like you got somethin' in mind.

JEFF: I has.

DAN: Well, what is it? I'm game.

JEFF: Yeah, dey all is 'til payin' time.

DAN: We ain't those kind of men where I comes from.

JEFF: An' where does yuh come from?

DAN: Philly.

JEFF: *(Talking slowly)* Philly—Philly—I knows some folks from Philly. Did yuh know a . . . .

STUMP: *(In disgust)* Huh, dis is goin' be a recollectin' party. I thought I was goin' tuh heah somethin' wurth while.

JEFF: An' yuh is, too, *(Pointing to Dan)* if he's still game.

DAN: Let's hear it.

JEFF: Heah it is. We shoots a snappy game of pool, fo' out of seben. *(He extracts a yellow bill from a large roll of money.)* If yuh wins, yuh gits dis yaller bill—money 'nough fo' gangs of dinners.

DAN: But I ain't got nothin' to put up.

JEFF: Yuh got yo'self, ain't yuh?

DAN: You mean me myself. But what 'cha want of me.

JEFF: An' heah's de man what'd chance dat hell journey! *(He laughs in scorn.)*

DAN: Hold that laff, I ain't backin' out of nothin'. An if I loses—.

JEFF: Yuh got tuh swap places wid me—me, money, gal an' all. Yuh'll be Jeff'son Meeks an' I'll be—. *(He points to Dan.)*

DAN: Daniel Broadus.

JEFF: *(Starting in surprise and looking intently at Dan. He opens his mouth as if to speak. He pauses and then speaks very slowly.)* An' I'll be Daniel Broadus.

DAN: But both ways you'se the loser.

JEFF: I ain't kickin' none, is yuh game?

DAN: I said once I ain't changin' my mind. *(To Stump)* Here give me a stick; I ain't had one in my hand foh a year.

JEFF: 'Scuse, eh? 'Cause I guess yuh knows I'm 'bout de bes' in dese parts.

DAN: 'Scuse nothin'. Let's play.

JEFF: Stump, rack up seben.

(Stump goes willingly to the table. Dan turns the cue stick over and over in his hand as if trying to get accustomed to it. Jeff goes to the window and looks up and down the street, then carefully takes off his hat and coat and hangs them on a hook. He listens in the hallway for a minute, then cautiously closes the door. He takes a cue stick from the rack and approaches the table.)

JEFF: I guess Stump kin be our ref'ree, eh?

DAN: Sure.

JEFF: Befo' we begins, Stump, take one look up dat street.

STUMP: *(Going to the window and peering out)* I don' see nobody.

JEFF: Sho' dere ain't no one up or down, parked nowheres near.

STUMP: Naw, I tole yuh once; why?

JEFF: Come on let's play den. Stranger, yuh break 'em. *(Dan shoots.)*

STUMP: Dat ain't so bad! One in de corner.

DAN: Five in the side. *(He shoots and misses.)*

STUMP: Awright, Jeff.

JEFF: Nation on de fo' in de side.

STUMP: Damned good shot! Once again.

JEFF: Five in de side. *(Jeff shoots and misses)* Hell! dat English didn't work.

STUMP: Not so good, buddy. Awright, stranger.

DAN: Nation in the two in the corner.

(Dan shoots and succeeds in pocketing two balls.)

STUMP: An' yuh says yuh ain't had a cue in yo' han' foh a yeah! Yuh're good. Once again an' dis is de money.

DAN: Six ball cross corner! *(He shoots and scratches. Stump spots up two.)*

STUMP: Tough luck, stranger. Nobody don' want no scratches right through heah. Awright, Jeff, call 'em.

JEFF: Pretty spot shot on de six. *(He shoots.)* Look at dat perfect English on de cue.

DAN: Couldn't of been better; worthy of Willie himself.

STUMP: Go on, Jeff.

JEFF: Two in de side. *(He shoots and succeeds.)*

STUMP: Jeff's goin' good. Call 'em again.

JEFF: Three in de corner. *(He shoots, succeeds, and lays down the cue stick.)*

STUMP: Easy out, ol' man!

DAN: *(Laying down his stick)* You surely plays a damned good game.

JEFF: Thanks. Not so worse, yo'self.

DAN: An' now that I've lost, what next?

JEFF: Dere ain't no next, only from now on I'm Daniel Broadus an' yuh're Jeff'son Meeks, de wanted one.

DAN: *(In surprise.)* Wanted? Wanted foh what?

JEFF: Foh a lil' transaction an' dis roll I'm carryin'. De coppers is hot on de trail, too.

STUMP: Lawd! Jeff, dey ain't goin' pull de place. *(Stump goes to the window and peers up and down the street.)*

STUMP: I sees two of 'em standin' down de street a lil' ways.

JEFF: I knowed dey had me spotted. An' what's mo' dere's two in de back, what's been dere.

DAN: I can't see that I kin help none.

JEFF: Yes, yuh kin. De onliest clue dey got is dat gray hat an' coat on de wall, dat's your'n from now on. Dey're goin' grab de one dat wears it out of dis room, an' yuh're jus' 'bout my size. All niggers look alak tuh 'em, an' dey'd jus' as soon have yuh as me.

DAN: You mean as Jeff'son Meeks I'm guilty, too.

JEFF: I means jus' dat. Now whine an' say dat ain't fair an' yuh didn't mean it.

DAN: It's too late to whine; ain't it? All dat was settled befo' the game.

STUMP: *(Nervously from his stand by the window)* I believes dey're comin' a lil' closer.

DAN: *(Going to the rack and taking down the hat and coat)* I guess I'll be gittin' along an' have this over with. There ain't no use havin' no messy scene. *(He starts toward the door.)*

JEFF: *(Blocking the way and grabbing the hat and coat from Dan)* Dat's my hat an' coat, Daniel Broadus. Yuh're too damned a good sport tuh rot in jail.

DAN: *(In surprise)* It's a chance I won't an' it's up to me to take it.

JEFF: *(Gently pushing Dan back)* Git out de way. Dis is my job an' I'se goin'a see it through. Remember de gal's part of de bargain. She'll be by heah in a lil while aftah me. Look out foh her. *(He takes a large roll of money from his pocket and thrusts it into the hand of the astonished Dan.)* Yuh'd bettah keep dat 'cause dat woman sho has needs.

(Dan starts to remonstrate as Jeff nears the door.)

STUMP: Jeff, don' go walkin' right into 'em.

JEFF: *(Unheeding)* Jus' don' yuh go followin' me into de street. Dere's still a chance I mought make it. So long boys. *(Jeff goes out and closes the door behind him. Stump remains at the window staring down the street while Dan stands in the middle of the floor looking stupidly at the roll of bills as the curtain falls.)*

(THE END)

COLOR STRUCK

A PLAY IN FOUR SCENES

BY ZORA NEALE HURSTON

Time: *Twenty years ago and present.*   Place: *A Southern City.*

PERSONS

JOHN: *A light brown-skinned man*
EMMALINE: *A black woman*
WESLEY: *A boy who plays an accordion*
EMMALINE'S DAUGHTER: *A very white girl*
EFFIE: *A mulatto girl*
A RAILWAY CONDUCTOR
A DOCTOR
Several who play mouth organs, guitars, banjos.
Dancers, passengers, etc.

SETTING.—*Early night. The inside of a "Jim Crow" railway coach. The car is parallel to the footlights. The seats on the down stage side of the coach are omitted. There are the luggage racks above the seats. The windows are all open. They are exits in each end of the car—right and left.*

ACTION.—*Before the curtain goes up there is the sound of a locomotive whistle and stopping engine, loud laughter, many people speaking at once, good-natured shrieks, strumming of stringed instruments, etc. The ascending curtain discovers a happy lot of Negroes boarding the train dressed in the gaudy, tawdry best of 1900. They are mostly in couples—each couple bearing a covered over market basket which the men hastily deposit in the racks as they scramble for seats. There is a litle friendly pushing and shoving. One pair just miss a seat three times, much to the enjoyment of the crowd. Many "plug" silk hats are in evidence, also sunflowers in button holes. The women are showily dressed in the manner of the time, and quite conscious of their finery. A few seats remain unoccupied.*

Enter Effie (left) above, with a basket.

ONE OF THE MEN (*standing, lifting his "plug" in a grand manner*). Howdy do, Miss Effie, you'se lookin' jes lak a rose. (*Effie blushes and is confused. She looks up and down for a seat.*) Fack is, if you wuzn't walkin' long, ah'd think you *wuz* a rose—(*he looks timidly behind her and the others laugh*). Looka here, where's Sam at?

EFFIE (*tossing her head haughtily*). I don't know an' I don't keer.

THE MAN (*visibly relieved*). Then lemme scorch you to a seat. (*He takes her basket and leads her to a seat center of the car, puts the basket in the rack and seats himself beside her with his hat at a rakish angle.*)

MAN (*sliding his arm along the back of the seat*). How come Sam ain't heah—y'll on a bust?

EFFIE (*angrily*). A man dat don't buy me nothin tuh put in *mah* basket, ain't goin' wid *me* tuh no cake walk. (*The hand on the seat touches her shoulder and she thrusts it away*). Take yo' arms from 'round me, Dinky! Gwan hug yo' Ada!

MAN (*in mock indignation*). Do you think I'd look at Ada when Ah got a chance tuh be wid you? Ah always wuz sweet on you, but you let ole Mullethead Sam cut me out.

ANOTHER MAN (*with head out of the window*). Just look at de darkies coming! (*With head inside coach.*) Hey, Dinky! Heah come Ada wid a great big basket.

(*Dinky jumps up from beside Effie and rushes to exit right. In a moment they re-enter and take a seat near entrance. Everyone in coach laughs. Dinky's girl turns and calls back to Effie.*)

GIRL. Where's Sam, Effie?

EFFIE. Lawd knows, Ada.

GIRL. Lawd a mussy! Who you gointer walk de cake wid?

EFFIE. Nobody, Ah reckon. John and Emma gointer win it nohow. They's the bestest cakewalkers in dis state.

ADA. You'se better than Emma any day in de week. Cose Sam cain't walk lake John. (*She stands up and scans the coach.*) Looka heah, ain't John an' Emma going? They ain't on heah!

(*The locomotive bell begins to ring.*)

EFFIE. Mah Gawd, s'pose dey got left!

MAN (*with head out of window*). Heah they come, nip and tuck—whoo-ee! They'se gonna make it! (*He waves excitedly.*) Come on Jawn! (*Everybody crowds the windows, encouraging them by gesture and calls. As the whistle blows twice, and the train begins to move, they enter panting and laughing at left. The only seat left is the one directly in front of Effie.*)

DINKY (*standing*). Don't y'all skeer us no mo' lake dat! There couldn't be no cake walk thout y'all. Dem shad-mouf St. Augustine coons would win dat cake and we would have tuh kill 'em all bodaciously.

JOHN. It was Emmaline nearly made us get left. She says I wuz smiling at Effie on the street car and she had to get off and wait for another one.

EMMA (*removing the hatpins from her hat, turns furiously upon him*). You wuz grinning at her and she wuz grinning back jes lake a ole chessy cat!

JOHN (*positively*). I wuzn't.

EMMA (*about to place her hat in rack*). You wuz. I seen you looking jes lake a possum.

JOHN. I wuzn't. I never gits a chance tuh smile at nobody—you won't let me.

EMMA. Jes the same every time you sees a yaller face, you *takes* a chance. (*They sit down in peeved silence for a minute.*)

DINKY. Ada, les we all sample de basket. I bet you got huckleberry pie.

ADA. No I aint, I got peach an' tater pies, but we aint gonna tetch a thing tell we gits tuh de hall.

DINKY (*mock alarm*). Naw, don't do dat! It's all right tuh save the fried chicken, but pies is *always* et on trains.

ADA. Aw shet up! (*He struggles with her for a kiss. She slaps him but finally yields.*)

JOHN (*looking behind him*). Hellow, Effie, where's Sam?

EFFIE. Deed, I don't know.

JOHN. Y'all on a bust?

EMMA. None ah yo' bizness, you got enough tuh mind yo' own self. Turn 'round!

(*She puts up a pouting mouth and he snatches a kiss. She laughs just as he kisses her again and there is a resounding smack which causes the crowd to laugh. And cries of "Oh you kid!" "Salty dog!"*)

(Enter conductor left calling tickets cheerfully and laughing at the general merriment.)

CONDUCTOR. I hope somebody from Jacksonville wins this cake.

JOHN. You live in the "Big Jack?"

CONDUCTOR. Sure do. And I wanta taste a piece of that cake on the way back tonight.

JOHN. Jes rest easy—them Augustiners aint gonna smell it. *(Turns to Emma.)* Is they, baby?

EMMA Not if Ah kin help it.

Somebody with a guitar sings. "Ho babe, mah honey taint no lie."
(The conductor takes up tickets, passes on and exits right.)

WESLEY. Look heah, you cake walkers—y'all oughter git up and limber up yo' joints. I heard them folks over to St. Augustine been oiling up wid goose-grease, and over to Ocala they been rubbing down in snake oil.

A WOMAN'S VOICE. You better shut up, Wesley, you just joined de church last month. Somebody's going to tell the pastor on you.

WESLEY. Tell it, tell it, take it up and smell it. Come on out you John and Emma and Effie, and limber up.

JOHN. Naw, we don't wanta do our walking steps—nobody won't wanta see them when we step out at the hall. But we kin do something else just to warm ourselves up.

(Wesley begins to play "Goo Goo Eyes" on his accordian, the other instruments come in one by one and John and Emma step into the aisle and "parade" up and down the aisle—Emma holding up her skirt, showing the lace on her petticoats. They two-step back to their seat amid much applause.)

WESLEY. Come on out, Effie! Sam aint heah so you got to hold up his side too. Step on out. *(There is a murmur of applause as she steps into the aisle. Wesley strikes up "I'm gointer live anyhow till I die." It is played quite spiritedly as Effie swings into the pas-me-la—)*

WESLEY *(in ecstasy).* Hot stuff I reckon! Hot stuff I reckon! *(The musicians are stamping. Great enthusiasm. Some clap time with hands and feet. She hurls herself into a modified Hoochy Koochy, and finishes up with an ecstatic yell.)*

There is a babble of talk and laughter and exultation.

JOHN *(applauding loudly).* If dat Effie can't step nobody can.

EMMA. Course you'd say so cause it's her. Everything she do is pretty to you.

JOHN (*caressing her*). Now don't say that, Honey. Dancing is dancing no matter who is doing it. But nobody can hold a candle to you in nothing.

(*Some men are heard tuning up—getting pitch to sing. Four of them crowd together in one seat and begin the chorus of "Daisies Won't Tell." John and Emma grow quite affectionate.*)

JOHN (*kisses her*). Emma, what makes you always picking a fuss with me over some yaller girl. What makes you so jealous, nohow ? I don't do nothing.

(*She clings to him, but he turns slightly away. The train whistle blows, there is a slackening of speed. Passengers begin to take down baskets from their racks.*)

EMMA. John! John, don't you want me to love you, honey?

JOHN (*turns and kisses her slowly*). Yes, I want you to love me, you know I do. But I don't like to be accused o' ever light colored girl in the world. It hurts my feeling. I don't want to be jealous like you are.

(*Enter at right Conductor, crying "St. Augustine, St. Augustine." He exits left. The crowd has congregated at the two exits, pushing goodnaturedly and joking. All except John and Emma. They are still seated with their arms about each other.*)

EMMA (*sadly*). Then you don't want my love, John, cause I can't help mahself from being jealous. I loves you so hard, John, and jealous love is the only kind I got.

(*John kisses her very feelingly.*)

EMMA. Just for myself alone is the only way I knows how to love.

(*They are standing in the aisle with their arms about each other as the curtain falls.*)

SCENE II

SETTING.—*A weather-board hall. A large room with the joists bare. The place has been divided by a curtain of sheets stretched and a rope across from left to right. From behind the curtain there are occasional sounds of laughter, a note or two on a stringed instrument or accordion. General stir. That is the dance hall. The front is the ante-room where the refreshments are being served. A "plank" seat runs all around the hall, along the walls. The lights are kerosene lamps with reflectors. They are fixed to the wall. The lunch-baskets are under the seat. There is a table on either side upstage with a woman behind each. At one, ice cream is sold, at the other, roasted peanuts and large red-and-white sticks of peppermint candy.*

People come in by twos and three, laughing, joking, horse-plays, gauchily flowered dresses, small waists, bulging hips and busts, hats worn far back on the head, etc. People from Ocala greet others from Palatka, Jacksonville, St. Augustine, etc.

Some find seats in the ante-room, others pass on into the main hall.

Enter the Jacksonville delegation, laughing, pushing proudly.

DINKY. Here we is, folks—here we *is*. Gointer take dat cake on back tuh Jacksonville where it belongs.

MAN. Gwan! Whut wid you mullet-head Jacksonville Coons know whut to do wid a cake. It's gointer stay right here in Augustine where de *good* cake walkers grow.

DINKY. Taint no 'Walkers' never walked till John and Emmaline prance out—you mighty come a tootin'.

Great laughing and joshing as more people come in. John and Emma are encouraged, urged on to win.

EMMA. Let's we git a seat, John, and set down.

JOHN. Sho will—nice one right over there.

(They push over to wall seat, place basket underneath, and sit. Newcomers shake hands with them and urge them on to win.)

(Enter Joe Clarke and a small group. He is a rotund, expansive man with a liberal watch chain and charm.)

DINKY *(slapping Clarke on the back)*. If you don't go 'way from here! Lawdy, if it aint Joe.

CLARKE *(jovially)*. Ah thought you had done forgot us people in Eatonville since you been living up here in Jacksonville.

DINKY. Course Ah aint. *(Turning.)* Looka heah folks! Joe Clarke oughta be made chairman uh dis meetin'—Ah mean Past Great Grand Master of Ceremonies, him being the onliest mayor of de onliest colored town in de state.

GENERAL CHORUS. Yeah, let him be—thass fine, etc.

DINKY *(setting his hat at a new angle and throwing out his chest)*. And *Ah'll* scorch him to de platform. Ahem!

(Sprinkling of laughter as Joe Clarke is escorted into next room by Dinky.)

(The musicians are arriving one by one during this time. A guitar, accordian, mouth organ, banjo, etc. Soon there is a rapping for order heard inside and the voice of Joe Clarke.)

JOE CLARKE. Git yo' partners one an' all for de gran' march! Git yo' partners, gentmens!

A MAN. *(drawing basket from under bench)*. Let's we all eat first.

(John and Emma go buy ice-cream. They coquettishly eat from each other's spoons. Old Man Lizzimore crosses to Effie and removes his hat and bows with a great flourish.)

LIZZIMORE. Sam ain't here t'night, is he, Effie.

EFFIE *(embarrassed)*. Naw suh, he aint.

LIZZ. Well, you like chicken? *(Extends arm to her.)* Take a wing!

(He struts her up to the table amid the laughter of the house. He wears no collar.)

JOHN. *(squeezes Emma's hand)*. You certainly is a ever loving mamma—when you aint mad.

EMMA. *(smiles sheepishly)*. You oughtn't to make me mad then.

JOHN. Ah don't make you! You makes yo'self mad, den blame it on me. Ah keep on tellin' you Ah don't love nobody but you. Ah knows heaps uh half-white girls Ah could git ef Ah wanted to. But *(he squeezes her hard again)* Ah jus' wants *you!* You know what they say! De darker de berry, de sweeter de taste!

EMMA *(pretending to pout)*. Oh, you tries to run over me an' keep it under de cover, but Ah won't let yuh. *(Both laugh.)* Les' we eat our basket!

JOHN. Alright. *(He pulls the basket out and she removes the table cloth. They set the basket on their knees and begin to eat fried chicken.)*

MALE VOICE. Les' everybody eat—motion's done carried. *(Everybody begins to open baskets. All have fried chicken. Very good humor prevails. Delicacies are swapped from one basket to the other. John and Emma offer the man next them some supper. He takes a chicken leg. Effie crosses to John and Emma with two pieces of pie on a plate.*

EFFIE. Y'll have a piece uh mah blueberry pie—it's mighty nice! *(She proffers it with a timid smile to Emma who "freezes" up instantly.)*

EMMA. Naw! We don't want no pie. We got cocoanut layercake.

JOHN. Ah—Ah think ah'd choose a piece uh pie, Effie. *(He takes it.)* Will you set down an' have a snack wid us? *(He slides over to make room.)*

EFFIE. *(nervously)*. Ah, naw, Ah got to run on back to mah basket, but Ah thought maybe y'll mout' want tuh taste mah pie. *(She turns to go.)*

JOHN. Thank you, Effie. It's mighty good, too. *(He eats it. Effie crosses to her seat. Emma glares at her for a minute, then*

*turns disgustedly away from the basket. John catches her
shoulder and faces her around.*)

JOHN (*pleadingly*). Honey, be nice. Don't act lak dat!

EMMA (*jerking free*). Naw, you done ruint mah appetite now, carryin' on wid dat punkincolored ole gal.

JOHN. Whut kin Ah do? If you had a acted polite Ah wouldn't a
had nothin' to say.

EMMA. Naw, youse jus' hog-wile ovah her cause she's half-white!
No matter whut Ah say, you keep carryin' on wid her. Act
polite? Naw Ah aint gonna be deceitful an' bust mah gizzard
fuh nobody! Let her keep her dirty ole pie ovah there where she
is!

JOHN (*looking around to see if they are overheard*). Sh-sh! Honey,
you mustn't talk so loud.

EMMA (*louder*). Ah-Ah aint gonna bite mah tongue! If she don't
like it she can lump it. Mah back is broad—(*John tries to cover
her mouth with his hand*). She calls herself a big cigar, but *I*
kin smoke her!

(*The people are laughing and talking for the most part and pay
no attention. Effie is laughing and talking to those around her
and does not hear the tirade. The eating is over and everyone is
going behind the curtain. John and Emma put away their basket
like the others, and sit glum. Voice of Master-of-ceremonies can
be heard from beyond curtain announcing the pas-me-la contest.
The contestants, mostly girls, take the floor. There is no music
except the clapping of hands and the shouts of "Parse-me-lah" in
time with the hand-clapping. At the end Master announces winner. Shadows seen on curtain.*)

MASTER. Mathilda Clarke is winner—if she will step forward she
will receive a beautiful wook fascinator. (*The girl goes up and
receives it with great hand-clapping and good humor.*) And
now since the roosters is crowin' foah midnight, an' most of us
got to git up an' go to work tomorrow, The Great Cake Walk
will begin. Ah wants de floor cleared, cause de representatives
of de several cities will be announced an' we wants 'em to take
de floor as their names is called. Den we wants 'em to do a
gran' promenade roun' de hall. An' they will then commence to
walk fuh de biggest cake ever baked in dis state. Ten dozen
eggs—ten pounds of flour—ten pounds of butter, and so on and
so forth. Now then—(*he strikes a pose*) for St. Augustine—

Miss Lucy Taylor, Mr. Ned Coles.

(*They step out amid applause and stand before stage.*)

For Daytona—

Miss Janie Bradley, Enoch Nixon

(Same business.)

For Ocala—

Miss Docia Boger, Mr. Oscar Clarke

(Same business.)

For Palatka—

Miss Maggie Lemmons, Mr. Senator Lewis

(Same business.)

And for Jacksonville the most popular "walkers" in de state—

Miss Emmaline Beazeby, Mr. John Turner.

(Tremendous applause. John rises and offers his arm grandiloquently to Emma.)

EMMA *(pleadingly, and clutching his coat)*. John let's we all don't go in there with all them. Let's we all go on home.

JOHN *(amazed)*. Why, Emma?

EMMA. Cause, cause all them girls is going to pulling and hauling on you, and—

JOHN *(impatiently)*. Shucks! Come on. Don't you hear the people clapping for us and calling our names? Come on!

(He tries to pull her up—she tries to drag him back.)

Come on, Emma! Taint no sense in your acting like this. The band is playing for us. Hear 'em? *(He moves feet in a dance step.)*

EMMA. Naw, John, Ah'm skeered. I loves you—I—.

(He tries to break away from her. She is holding on fiercely.)

JOHN. I got to go! I been practising almost a year—I—we done come all the way down here. I can walk the cake, Emma—we got to—I got to go in! *(He looks into her face and sees her tremendous fear.)* What you skeered about?

EMMA *(hopefully)*. You won't go it—You'll come on go home with me all by ourselves. Come on John. I can't, I just can't go in there and see all them girls—Effie hanging after you—.

JOHN. I got to go in—*(he removes her hand from his coat)*— whether you come with me or not.

EMMA. Oh—them yaller wenches! How I hate 'em! They gets everything they wants—.

VOICE INSIDE. We are waiting for the couple from Jacksonville— Jacksonville! Where is the couple from—.

(Wesley parts the curtain and looks out.)

WESLEY. Here they is out here spooning! You all can't even hear your names called. Come on John and Emma.

JOHN. Coming. (*He dashes inside. Wesley stands looking at Emma in surprise.*)

WESLEY. What's the matter, Emma? You and John spatting again? (*He goes back inside.*)

EMMA (*calmly bitter*). He went and left me. If we is spatting we done had our last one. (*She stands and clenches her fists.*) Ah, mah God! He's in there with her—Oh, them half whites, they gets everything, they gets everything everybody else wants! The men, the jobs—everything! The whole world is got a sign on it. Wanted: Light colored. Us blacks was made for cobble stones. (*She muffles a cry and sinks limp upon the seat.*)

VOICE INSIDE. Miss Effie Jones will walk for Jacksonville with Mr. John Turner in place of Miss Emmaline Beazeley.

SCENE III—*DANCE HALL*

Emma springs to her feet and flings the curtains wide open. She stands staring at the gay scene for a moment defiantly, then creeps over to a seat along the wall and shrinks into the Spanish Moss, motionless.

Dance hall decorated with palmetto leaves and Spanish Moss—a flag or two. Orchestra consists of guitar, mandolin, banjo, accordian, church organ and drum.

MASTER (*on platform*). Couples take yo' places! When de music starts, gentlemen parade yo' ladies once round de hall, den de walk begins. (*The music begins. Four men come out from behind the platform bearing a huge chocolate cake. The couples are "prancing" in their tracks. The men lead off the procession with the cake—the contestants make a grand slam around the hall.*)

MASTER. Couples to de floor! Stan' back, ladies an' gentlemen— give 'em plenty room.

(*Music changes to "Way Down in Georgia." Orchestra sings. Effie takes the arm that John offers her and they parade to the other end of the hall. She takes her place. John goes back upstage to the platform, takes off his silk hat in a graceful sweep as he bows deeply to Effie. She lifts her skirts and curtsies to the floor. Both smile broadly. They advance toward each other, meet midway, then, arm in arm, begin to "strut." John falters as he faces her, but recovers promptly and is perfection in his style. (Seven to nine minutes to curtain.) Fervor of spectators grows until all are taking part in some way—either hand-clapping or singing the words. At curtain they have reached frenzy.)*

QUICK CURTAIN

(It stays down a few seconds to indicate ending of contest and goes up again on John and Effie being declared winners by Judges.)

MASTER *(on platform, with John and Effie on the floor before him)*: By unanimous decision de cake goes to de couple from Jacksonville! *(Great enthusiasm. The cake is set down in the center of the floor and the winning couple parade around it arm in arm. John and Effie circle the cake happily and triumphantly. The other contestants, and then the entire assembly fall in behind and circle the cake, singing and clapping. The festivities continue. The Jacksonville quartet step upon the platform and sing a verse and chorus of "Daisies won't tell." Cries of "Hurrah for Jacksonville! Glory for the big town," "Hurrah for Big Jack.")*

A MAN *(seeing Emma)*. You're from Jacksonville, aint you? *(He whirls her around and around.)* Aint you happy? Whoopee! *(He releases her and she drops upon a seat. She buries her face in the moss.)*

(Quartet begins on chorus again. People are departing, laughing, humming, with quartet cheering. John, the cake, and Effie being borne away in triumph.)

SCENE IV

TIME—*present. The interior of a one-room shack in an alley. There is a small window in the rear wall upstage left. There is an enlarged crayon drawing of a man and woman—man sitting cross-legged, woman standing with her hand on his shoulder. A center table, red cover, a low, cheap rocker, two straight chairs, a small kitchen stove at left with a wood-box beside it, a water-bucket on a stand close by. A hand towel and a wash basin. A shelf of dishes above this. There is an ordinary oil lamp on the center table but it is not lighted when the curtain goes up. Some light enters through the window and falls on the woman seated in the low rocker. The door is center right. A cheap bed is against the upstage wall. Someone is on the bed but is lying so that the back is toward the audience.*

ACTION—*As the curtain rises, the woman is seen rocking to and fro in the low rocker. A dead silence except for the sound of the rocker and an occasional groan from the bed. Once a faint voice says "water" and the woman in the rocker arises and carries the tin dipper to the bed.*

WOMAN. No mo' right away—Doctor says not too much. *(Returns dipper to pail.—Pause.)* You got right much fever—I better go git the doctor agin.

(There comes a knocking at the door and she stands still for a moment, listening. It comes again and she goes to door but does not open it.)

WOMAN. Who's that?

VOICE OUTSIDE. Does Emma Beasely live here?

EMMA. Yeah—*(pause)*—who is it?

VOICE. It's me—John Turner.

EMMA *(puts hands eagerly on the fastening)*. John? did you say John Turner?

VOICE. Yes, Emma, it's me.

(The door is opened and the man steps inside.)

EMMA. John! Your hand *(she feels for it and touches it)*. John flesh and blood.

JOHN *(laughing awkwardly)*. It's me alright, old girl. Just as bright as a basket of chips. Make a light quick so I can see how you look. I'm crazy to see you. Twenty years is a long time to wait, Emma.

EMMA *(nervously)*. Oh, let's we all just sit in the dark awhile. *(Apologetically.)* I wasn't expecting nobody and my house aint picked up. Sit down. *(She draws up the chair. She sits in rocker.)*

JOHN. Just to think! Emma! Me and Emma sitting down side by each. Know how I found you?

EMMA *(dully)*. Naw. How?

JOHN *(brightly)*. Soon's I got in town I hunted up Wesley and he told me how to find you. That's who I come to see, you!

EMMA. Where you been all these years, up North somewheres? Nobody round here could find out where you got to.

JOHN. Yes, up North. Philadelphia.

EMMA. Married yet?

JOHN. Oh yes, seventeen years ago. But my wife is dead now and so I came as soon as it was decent to find *you*. I wants to marry you. I couldn't die happy if I didn't. Couldn't get over you— couldn't forget. Forget me, Emma?

EMMA. Naw, John. How could I?

JOHN (*leans over impulsively to catch her hand*). Oh, Emma, I love you so much. Strike a light honey so I can see you—see if you changed much. You was such a handsome girl!

EMMA. We don't exactly need no light, do we, John, tuh jus' set an' talk?

JOHN. Yes, we do, Honey. Gwan, make a light. Ah wanna see you. (*There is a silence.*)

EMMA. Bet you' wife wuz some highyaller dicktydoo.

JOHN. Naw she wasn't neither. She was jus' as much like you as Ah could get her. Make a light an' Ah'll show you her pictcher. Shucks, ah gotta look at mah old sweetheart. (*He strikes a match and holds it up between their faces and they look intently at each other over it until it burns out.*) You aint changed none atall, Emma, jus' as pretty as a speckled pup yet.

EMMA (*lighter*). Go long, John! (*Short pause*) 'member how you useter bring me magnolias?

JOHN. Do I? Gee, you was sweet! 'Member how Ah useter pull mah necktie loose so you could tie it back for me? Emma, Ah can't see to mah soul how we lived all this time, way from one another. 'Member how you useter make out mah ears had done run down and you useter screw 'em up agin for me? (*They laugh.*)

EMMA. Yeah, Ah useter think you wuz gointer be mah husban' then—but you let dat ole—.

JOHN. Ah aint gonna let you alibi on me lak dat. Light dat lamp! You cain't look me in de eye and say no such. (*He strikes another match and lights the lamp.*) Course, Ah don't wanta look too bossy, but Ah b'lieve you got to marry me tuh git rid of me. That is, if you aint married.

EMMA. Naw, Ah aint. (*She turns the lamp down.*)

JOHN (*looking about the room*). Not so good, Emma. But wait till you see dat little place in Philly! Got a little "Rolls-Rough," too—gointer teach you to drive it, too.

EMMA. Ah been havin' a hard time, John, an' Ah lost you—oh, aint nothin' been right for me! Ah aint never been happy.

(*John takes both of her hands in his.*)

JOHN. You gointer be happy now, Emma. Cause Ah'm gointer make you. Gee Whiz! Ah aint but forty-two and you aint forty yet—we got plenty time. (*There is a groan from the bed.*) Gee, what's that?

EMMA (*ill at ease*). Thass mah chile. She's sick. Reckon Ah bettah see 'bout her.

91

JOHN. You got a chile? Gee, that great! Ah always wanted one, but didn't have no luck. Now we kin start off with a family. Girl or boy?

EMMA *(slowly)*. A girl. Comin' tuh see me agin soon, John?

JOHN. Comin' agin? Ah aint gone yet! We aint talked, you aint kissed me an' nothin', and you aint showed me our girl. *(Another groan, more prolonged.)* She must be pretty sick— let's see. *(He turns in his chair and Emma rushes over to the bed and covers the girl securely, tucking her long hair under the covers, too—before he arises. He goes over to the bed and looks down into her face. She is mulatto. Turns to Emma teasingly.)* Talkin' 'bout *me* liking high-yallers—*yo* husband musta been pretty near *white.*

EMMA *(slowly)*. Ah, never wuz married, John.

JOHN. It's alright, Emma. *(Kisses her warmly.)* Everything is going to be O.K. *(Turning back to the bed.)* Our child looks pretty sick, but she's pretty. *(Feels her forehead and cheek.)* Think she oughter have a doctor.

EMMA. Ah done had one. Course Ah cain't git no specialist an' nothin' lak dat. *(She looks about the room and his gaze follows hers.)* Ah aint got a whole lot lake you. Nobody don't git rich in no white-folks' kitchen, nor in de washtub. You know Ah aint no school-teacher an' nothin' lak dat.

(John puts his arm about her.)

JOHN. It's all right, Emma. But our daughter is bad off—run out an' git a doctor—she needs one. Ah'd go if Ah knowed where to find one—you kin git one the quickest—hurry, Emma.

EMMA *(looks from John to her daughter and back again.)* She'll be all right, Ah reckon, for a while. John, you love me—you really want me sho' nuff?

JOHN. Sure Ah do—think Ah'd come all de way down here for nothin'? Ah wants to marry agin.

EMMA. Soon, John?

JOHN. Real soon.

EMMA. Ah wuz jus' thinkin', mah folks is away now on a little trip—be home day after tomorrow—we could git married tomorrow.

JOHN. All right. Now run on after the doctor—we must look after our girl. Gee, she's got a full suit of hair! Glad you didn't let her chop it off. *(Looks away from bed and sees Emma standing still.)*

JOHN. Emma, run on after the doctor, honey. *(She goes to the bed and again tucks the long braids of hair in, which are again pouring over the side of the bed by the feverish tossing of the girl.)* What's our daughter's name?

EMMA. Lou Lillian. *(She returns to the rocker uneasily and sits rocking jerkily. He returns to his seat and turns up the light.)*

JOHN. Gee, we're going to be happy—we gointer make up for all them twenty years *(another groan)*. Emma, git up an' gwan git dat doctor. You done forgot Ah'm de boss uh dis family now—gwan, while Ah'm here to watch her whilst you're gone. Ah got to git back to mah stoppin'place after a while.

EMMA. You go git one, John.

JOHN. Whilst Ah'm blunderin' round tryin' to find one, she'll be gettin' worse. She sounds pretty bed—*(takes out his wallet and hands her a bill)*—get a taxi if necessary. Hurry!

EMMA *(does not take the money, but tucks her arms and hair in again, and gives the girl a drink)*. Reckon Ah better go git a doctor. Don't want nothin' to happen to *her*. After you left, Ah useter have such a hurtin' in heah *(touches bosom)* till she come an' eased it some.

JOHN. Here, take some money and get a good doctor. There must be some good colored ones around here now.

EMMA *(scornfully)*. I wouldn't let one of 'em tend my cat if I had one! But let's we don't start a fuss.

(John caresses her again. When he raises his head he notices the picture on the wall and crosses over to it with her—his arm still about her.)

JOHN. Why, that's you and me!

EMMA. Yes, I never could part with that. You coming tomorrow morning, John, and we're gointer get married, aint we? Then we can talk over everything.

JOHN. Sure, but I aint gone yet. I don't see how come we can't make all our arrangements now. *(Groans from bed and feeble movement.)* Good lord, Emma, go get that doctor!

(Emma stares at the girl and the bed and seizes a hat from a nail on the wall. She prepares to go but looks from John to bed and back again. She fumbles about the table and lowers the lamp. Goes to door and opens it. John offers the wallet. She refuses it.)

EMMA. Doctor right around the corner. Guess I'll leave the door open so she can get some air. She won't need nothing while I'm gone, John. *(She crosses and tucks the girl in securely and rushes out, looking backward and pushing the door wide open as she exits. John sits in the chair beside the table. Looks about him—shakes his head. The girl on the bed groans, "water," "so hot." John looks about him excitedly. Gives her a drink. Feels her forehead. Takes a clean handkerchief from his pocket and wets it and places it upon her forehead. She raises her hand to the cool object. Enter Emma running. When she sees John at the bed she is full of fury. She rushes over and jerks his shoulder around. They face each other.)*

EMMA. I knowed it! *(She strikes him.)* A half white skin. *(She rushes at him again. John staggers back and catches her hands.)*

JOHN. Emma!

EMMA *(struggles to free her hands)*. Let me go so I can kill you. Come sneaking in here like a pole cat!

JOHN *(slowly, after a long pause)*. So this is the woman I've been wearing over my heart like a rose for twenty years! She so despises her own skin that she can't believe any one else could love it!

(Emma writhes to free herself.)

JOHN. Twenty years! Twenty years of adoration, of hunger, of worship! *(On the verge of tears he crosses to door and exits quietly, closing the door after him.)*

(Emma remains standing, looking dully about as if she is half asleep. There comes a knocking at the door. She rushes to open it. It is the doctor. White. She does not step aside so that he can enter.)

DOCTOR. Well, shall I come in?

EMMA *(stepping aside and laughing a little)*. That's right, doctor, come in.

(Doctor crosses to bed with professional air. Looks at the girl, feels the pulse and draws up the sheet over the face. He turns to her.)

DOCTOR. Why didn't you come sooner. I told you to let me know of the least change in her condition.

EMMA *(flatly)*. I did come—I went for the doctor.

DOCTOR. Yes, but you waited. An hour more or less is mighty important sometimes. Why didn't you come?

EMMA *(passes hand over face)*. Couldn't see.

(Doctor looks at her curiously, then sympathetically takes out a small box of pills, and hands them to her.) Here, you're worn

out. Take one of these every hour and try to get some sleep. *(He departs.)*

(She puts the pill-box on the table, takes up the low rocking chair and places it by the head of the bed. She seats herself and rocks monotonously and stares out of the door. A dry sob now and then. The wind from the open door blows out the lamp and she is seen by the little light from the window rocking in an even, monotonous gait, and sobbing.)

THE FIRST ONE

A PLAY IN ONE ACT

BY ZORA NEALE HURSTON

Time: *Three Years After the Flood*
Place: *Valley of Ararat*
Persons: *Noah*
His wife
Their sons: Shem, Japheth, Ham
Eve, Ham's wife
The sons' wives and children (6 or 7)

SETTING

Morning in the Valley of Ararat. The Mountain is in the near distance. Its lower slopes grassy with grazing herds. The very blue sky beyond that. These together form the back-ground. On the left downstage is a brown tent. A few shrubs are scattered here and there over the stage indicating the temporary camp. A rude altar is built center stage. A Shepherd's crook, a goat skin water bottle, a staff and other evidences of nomadic life lie about the entrance to the tent. To the right stretches a plain clad with bright flowers. Several sheep or goat skins are spread about on the ground upon which the people kneel or sit whenever necessary.

ACTION

Curtain rises on an empty stage. It is dawn. A great stillness, but immediately Noah enters from the tent and ties back the flap. He is clad in loose fitting dingy robe tied about the waist with a strip of goat hide. Stooped shoulders, flowing beard. He gazes about him. His gaze takes in the entire stage.

NOAH *(fervently)*: Thou hast restored the Earth, Jehovah, it is good. *(Turns to the tent).* My sons! Come, deck the altar for the sacrifices to Jehovah. It is the third year of our coming to this valley to give thanks offering to Jehovah that he spared us.

(Enter Japheth bearing a haunch of meat and Shem with another. The wife of Noah and those of Shem and Japheth follow laying on sheaves of grain and fruit (dates and figs). They are all middleaged and clad in dingy garments.

NOAH: And where is Ham—son of my old age? Why does he not come with his wife and son to the sacrifice?

MRS. NOAH: He arose before the light and went. *(She shades her eyes with one hand and points toward the plain with the other.)* His wife, as ever, went with him.

SHEM *(impatiently)*: This is the third year that we have come here to this Valley to commemorate our delivery from the flood. Ham knows the sacrifice is made always at sunrise. See! *(He points to rising sun.)* He should be here.

NOAH *(lifts his hand in a gesture of reproval)*: We shall wait. The sweet singer, the child of my loins after old age had come upon me is warm to my heart—let us wait.

(There is off-stage, right, the twanging of a rude stringed instrument and laughter. Ham, his wife and son come dancing on down-stage right. He is in his early twenties. He is dressed in a very white goat-skin with a wreath of shiny green leaves about his head. He has the rude instrument in his hands and strikes it. His wife is clad in a short blue garment with a girdle of shells. She has a wreath of scarlet flowers about her head. She has black hair, is small, young and lithe. She wears anklets and wristlets of the same red flowers. Their son about three years old wears nothing but a broad band of leaves and flowers about his middle. They caper and prance to the altar. Ham's wife and son bear flowers. A bird is perched on Ham's shoulder.)

NOAH *(extends his arms in greeting)*: My son, thou art late. But the sunlight comes with thee. *(Ham gives bird to Mrs. Noah, then embraces Noah.)*

HAM *(rests his head for a moment on Noah's shoulder)*: We arose early and went out on the plain to make ready for the burnt offering before Jehovah.

MRS. SHEM *(tersely)*: But you bring nothing.

HAM: See thou! We bring flowers and music to offer up. I shall dance before Jehovah and sing joyfully upon the harp that I made of the thews of rams. *(He proudly displays the instrument and strums once or twice.)*

MRS. SHEM *(clapping her hands to her ears)*: Oh, Peace! Have we not enough of thy bawling and prancing all during the year? Shem and Japheth work always in the fields and vineyards, while you do naught but tend the flock and sing!

MRS. JAPHETH *(looks contemptuously at both Ham and Noah)*: Still, thou art beloved of thy father . . . he gives thee all his vineyards for thy singing, but Japheth must work hard for his fields.

MRS. SHEM: And Shem—

NOAH *(angrily)*: Peace! Peace! Are lust and strife *again* loose upon the Earth? Jehovah might have destroyed us all. Am I not Lord of the world? May I not bestow where I will? Besides, the world is great. Did I not give food, and plenty to the thousands upon thousands that the waters licked up? Surely there is abundance for us and our seed forever. Peace! Let us to the sacrifice. *(Noah goes to the heaped up altar. Ham exits to the tent hurriedly and returns with a torch and hands it to Noah who applies it to the altar. He kneels at the altar and the others kneel in a semi-circle behind him at a little distance. Noah makes certain ritualistic gestures and chants)*: "O Mighty Jehovah, who created the Heaven and the firmaments thereof, the Sun and Moon, the stars, the Earth and all else besides—

OTHERS: I am here

I am here, O, Jehovah

I am here

This is thy Kingdom, and I am here.

(A deep silence falls for a moment.)

NOAH: Jehovah, who saw evil in the hearts of men, who opened upon them the windows of Heaven and loosed the rain upon them—And the fountains of the great deep were broken up—

OTHERS *(repeat chant)*

NOAH: Jehovah who dried up the floods and drove the waters of the sea again to the deeps—who met Noah in the Vale of Ararat and made covenant with Noah, His servant, that no more would he smite the Earth—And Seed time and Harvest, Cold and Heat, Summer and Winter, day and night shall not cease forever, and set His rainbow as a sign.

NOAH AND OTHERS: We are here O Jehovah

We are here

We are here

This is Thy Kingdom

And we are here.

(Noah arises, makes obeisance to the smoking altar, then turns and blesses the others.)

NOAH: Noah alone, whom the Lord found worthy; Noah whom He made lord of the Earth, blesses you and your seed forever.

(At a gesture from him all arise. The women take the meat from the altar and carry it into the tent.) Eat, drink and make a joyful noise before Him. For He destroyed the Earth, but spared us. *(Women reenter with bits of roast meat—all take some and eat. All are seated on the skins.)*

MRS. NOAH *(feelingly)*: Yes, three years ago, all was water, *water,* WATER! The deeps howled as one beast to another. *(She shudders.)* In my sleep, even now, I am in that Ark again being borne here, there on the great bosom.

MRS. HAM *(wide-eyed)*: And the dead! Floating, floating all about us—We were one little speck of life in a world of death! *(The bone slips from her hand.)* And there, close beside the Ark, close with her face upturned as if begging for shelter—my *mother! (She weeps, Ham comforts her.)*

MRS. SHEM *(eating vigorously)*: She would not repent. Thou art as thy mother was—a seeker after beauty of raiment and laughter. God is just. She would not repent.

MRS. HAM: But the unrepentant are no less loved. And why must Jehovah hate beauty?

NOAH: Speak no more of the waters. Oh, the strength of the waters! The voices and the death of it! Let us have the juice of the grape to make us forget. Where once was death in this Valley there is now life abundant of beast and herbs. *(He waves towards the scenery.)* Jehovah meets us here. Dance! Be glad! Bring wine! Ham smite thy harp of ram's thews and sing!

(Mrs. Noah gathers all the children and exits to the tent. Shem, Japheth, their wives and children eat vigorously. Mrs. Ham exits, left. Ham plays on his harp and capers about singing. Mrs. Ham reenters with goatskin of wine and a bone cup. She crosses to where Noah reclines on a large skin. She kneels and offers it to him. He takes the cup—she pours for him. Ham sings—)

HAM:

"I am as a young ram in the Spring

Or a young male goat.

The hills are beneath my feet

And the young grass.

Love rises in me like the flood

And ewes gather round me for food."

His wife joins in the dancing. Noah cries "Pour" and Mrs. Ham hurries to fill his cup again. Ham joins others on the skins. The others have horns suspended from their girdles. Mrs. Ham fills them all. Noah cries "pour" again and she returns to him. She turns to fill the others' cups.

NOAH *(rising drunkenly)*: Pour again, Eve, and Ham sing on and dance and drink—drown out the waters of the flood if you can. (His tongue grows thick. Eve fills his cup again. He reels drunkenly toward the tent door, slopping the liquor out of the cup as he walks.) Drink wine, forget water—it means death, *death!* And bodies floating, face up! *(He stares horrified about himself and creeps stealthily into the tent, but sprawls just inside the door so that his feet are visible. There is silence for a moment, the others are still eating. They snatch tidbits from each other.)*

JAPHETH *(shoves his wife)*: Fruit and herbs, woman! *(He thrusts her impatiently forward with his foot. She exits left.)*

SHEM *(to his wife)*: More wine!

MRS. SHEM *(irritated)*: See you not that there is plenty still in the bottle? *(He seizes it and pours. Ham snatches it away and pours. Shem tries to get it back but Ham prevents him. Reenter Mrs. Japheth with figs and apples. Everybody grabs. Ham and Shem grab for the same one, Ham gets it).*

MRS. SHEM *(significantly)*: Thus he seizes all else that he desires. Noah would make him lord of the Earth because he sings and capers. *(Ham is laughing drunkenly and pelting Mrs. Shem with fruit skins and withered flowers that litter the ground. This infuriates her.)*

NOAH *(calls from inside the tent)*: Eve, wine, quickly! I'm sinking down in the WATER! Come drown the WATER with wine.

(Eve exits to him with the bottle. Ham arises drunkenly and starts toward the tent door.)

HAM *(thickly)*: I go to pull our father out of the water, or to drown with him in it. *(Ham is trying to sing and dance.)* "I am as a young goat in the sp-sp-sp-. *(He exits to the tent laughing. Shem and Japheth sprawl out in the skins. The wives are showing signs of surfeit. Ham is heard laughing raucously inside the tent. He re-enters still laughing.)*

HAM *(in the tent door)*: Our Father has stripped himself, showing all his wrinkles. Ha! Ha! He's as no young goat in the spring. Ha! Ha! *(Still laughing, he reels over to the altar and sinks down behind it still laughing.)* The old Ram, Ha! Ha! Ha! He has had no spring for years! Ha! Ha! *(He subsides into slumber. Mrs. Shem looks about her exultantly.)*

MRS. SHEM: Ha! The young goat has fallen into a pit! *(She shakes her husband.)* Shem! Shem! Rise up and become owner of Noah's vineyards as well as his flocks! *(Shem kicks weakly at her.)* Shem! Fool! Arise! Thou art thy father's first born. *(She pulls him protesting to his feet.)* Do stand up and regain thy birthright from *(she points to the altar)* that dancer who plays on his harp of ram thews, and decks his brow with bay leaves. Come!

SHEM *(brightens)*: How?

HIS WIFE: Did he not go into the tent and come away laughing at thy father's nakedness? Oh *(she beats her breast)* that I should live to see a father so mocked and shamed by his son to whom he has given all his vineyards! *(She seizes a large skin from the ground.)* Take this and cover him and tell him of the wickedness of thy brother.

MRS. JAPHETH *(arising takes hold of the skin also)*: No, my husband shall also help to cover Noah, our father. Did I not also hear? Think your Shem and his seed shall possess both flocks and vineyard while Japheth and his seed have only the fields? *(She arouses Japheth, he stands.)*

SHEM: He shall share—

MRS. SHEM *(impatiently)*: Then go in *(the women release the skin to the men)* quickly, lest he wake sober, then will he not believe one word against Ham who needs only to smile to please him. *(The men lay the skin across their shoulders and back over to the tent and cover Noah. They motion to leave him.)*

MRS. SHEM: Go back, fools, and wake him. You have done but half.

(They turn and enter the tent and both shake Noah. He sits up and rubs his eyes. Mrs. Shem and Mrs. Japheth commence to weep ostentatiously).

NOAH *(peevishly)*: Why do you disturb me, and why do the women weep? I thought all sorrow and all cause for weeping was washed away by the flood. *(He is about to lie down again but the men hold him up.)*

SHEM: Hear, father, thy age has been scoffed, and thy nakedness made a thing of shame here in the midst of the feasting where

101

all might know—thou the Lord of all under Heaven, hast been mocked.

MRS. SHEM: And we weep in shame, that thou our father should have thy nakedness uncovered before us.

NOAH *(struggling drunkenly to his feet)*: Who, *who* has done this thing?

MRS. SHEM *(timidly crosses and kneels before Noah)*: We fear to tell thee, lord, lest thy love for the doer of this iniquity should be so much greater than the shame, that thou should slay us for telling thee.

NOAH *(swaying drunkenly)*: Say it, woman, shall the lord of the Earth be mocked? Shall his nakedness be uncovered and he be shamed before his family?

SHEM: Shall the one who has done this thing hold part of thy goods after thee? How wilt thou deal with them? Thou hast been wickedly shamed.

NOAH: No, he shall have no part in my goods—his goods shall be parcelled out among the others.

MRS. SHEM: Thou art wise, father, thou art just!

NOAH: He shall be accursed. His skin shall be black! Black as the nights, when the waters brooded over the Earth!

(Enter Mrs. Noah from tent, pauses by Noah.)

MRS. NOAH *(catches him by the arm)*: Cease! Whom dost thou curse?

NOAH *(shaking his arm free. The others also look awed and terrified and also move to stop him. All rush to him. Mrs. Noah attempts to stop his mouth with her hand. He shakes his head to free his lips and goes in a drunken fury)*: Black! He and his seed forever. He shall serve his brothers and they shall rule over him—Ah—Ah—. (He sinks again to the ground. There is a loud burst of drunken laughter from behind the altar.)*

HAM: Ha! Ha! I am as a young ram—Ha! Ha!

MRS. NOAH *(to Mrs. Shem)*: Whom cursed Noah?

MRS. SHEM: Ham—Ham mocked his age. Ham uncovered his nakedness, and Noah grew wrathful and cursed him. Black! He could not mean *black*. It is enough that he should lose his vineyards. *(There is absolute silence for a while. Then realization comes to all. Mrs. Noah rushes in the tent to her husband, shaking him violently.)*

MRS. NOAH *(voice from out of the tent)*: Noah! Arise! Thou art no lord of the Earth, but a drunkard. Thou hast cursed my son. Oh

102

water, Shem! Japheth! Cold water to drive out the wine. Noah! *(She sobs.)* Thou must awake and unsay thy curse. Thou must! *(She is sobbing and rousing him. Shem and Japheth seize a skin bottle from the ground by the skin door and dash off right. Mrs. Noah wails and the other women join in. They beat their breasts. Enter Eve through the tent. She looks puzzled.)*

MRS. HAM: Why do you wail? Are all not happy today?

MRS. NOAH *(pityingly)*: Come, Eve. Thou art but a child, a heavy load awaits thee. *(Eve turns and squats beside her mother-in-law.)*

EVE *(caressing Mrs. Noah)*: Perhaps the wine is too new. Why do you shake our father?

MRS. NOAH: Not the wine of grapes, but the wine of sorrow bestirs me thus. Turn thy comely face to the wall, Eve. Noah has cursed thy husband and his seed forever to be black, and to serve his brothers and they shall rule over him.

(Reenter the men with the water bottle running. Mrs. Noah seizes it and pours it in his face. He stirs.) See, I must awaken him that he may unspeak the curse before it be too late.

EVE: But Noah is drunk—surely Jehovah hears not a drunken curse. Noah would not curse Ham if he knew. Jehovah knows Noah loves Ham more than all. *(She rushes upon Noah and shakes him violently.)* Oh, awake thou *(she shrieks)* and uncurse thy curse. *(All are trying to rouse Noah. He sits, opens his eyes wide and looks about him. Mrs. Noah caresses him.)*

MRS. NOAH: Awake, my lord, and unsay thy curse.

NOAH: I am awake, but I know of no curse. Whom did I curse?

MRS. NOAH AND EVE: Ham, lord of the Earth. *(He rises quickly to his feet and looks bewildered about.)*

JAPHETH *(falls at his feet)*: Our father, and lord of all under Heaven, you cursed away his vineyards, but we do not desire them. You cursed him to be black—he and his seed forever, and that his seed shall be our servants forever, but we desire not their service. Unsay it all.

NOAH *(rushes down stage to the footlights, center. He beats his breast and bows his head to the ground.)* Oh, that I had come alive out of my mother's loins! Why did not the waters of the flood bear me back to the deeps! Oh Ham, my son!

EVE *(rushing down to him)*: Unspeak the Curse! Unspeak the Curse!

NOAH *(in prayerful attitude)*: Jehovah, by our covenant in this Valley, record not my curses on my beloved Ham. Show me once again the sign of covenant—the rainbow over the Vale of Ararat.

SHEM *(strikes his wife)*: It was thou, covetous woman, that has brought this upon us.

MRS. SHEM *(weeping)*: Yes, I wanted the vineyards for thee, Shem, because at night as thou slept on my breast I heard thee sob for them. I heard thee murmur "Vineyards" in thy dreams.

NOAH: Shem's wife is but a woman.

MRS. NOAH: How rash thou art, to curse unknowing in thy cups the son of thy loins.

NOAH: Did not Jehovah repent after he had destroyed the world? Did He not make all flesh? Their evils as well as their good? Why did He not with His flood of waters wash out the evil from men's hearts, and spare the creatures He had made, or else destroy us all, *all?* For in sparing one, He has preserved all the wickedness that He creates abundantly, but punishes terribly. No, He destroyed them because vile as they were it was His handiwork, and it shamed and reproached Him night and day. He could not bear to look upon the thing He had done, so He destroyed them.

MRS. NOAH: Thou canst not question.

NOAH *(weeping)*: Where is my son?

SHEM *(pointing)*: Asleep behind the altar.

NOAH: If Jehovah keeps not the covenant this time, if He spare not my weakness, then I pray that Ham's heart remains asleep forever.

MRS. SHEM *(beseeching)*: O Lord of the Earth, let his punishment be mine. We coveted his vineyards, but the curse is too awful for him. He is drunk like you—save him, Father Noah.

NOAH *(exultantly)*: Ah, the rainbow! The promise! Jehovah will meet me! He will set His sign in the Heavens! Shem hold thou my right hand and Japheth bear up my left arm.

(Noah approaches the altar and kneels. The two men raise his hands aloft.)

Our Jehovah who carried us into the ark—

SONS: Victory, O Jehovah! The Sign.

OTHERS *(beating their breasts)*: This is Thy Kingdom and we are here.

NOAH: Who saved us from the Man of the Waters.

SONS: Victory, O Jehovah! The Sign.

OTHERS: We belong to Thee, Jehovah, we belong to Thee.

(There is a sudden, loud raucous laugh from behind the altar. Ham sings brokenly, "I am a young ram in the Spring.")

NOAH *(hopefully)*: Look! Look! To the mountain—do ye see colors appear?

MRS. NOAH: None but what our hearts paint for us—ah, false hope.

NOAH: Does the sign appear, I seem to see a faint color just above the mountain. *(Another laugh from Ham.)*

EVE: None, none yet. *(Beats her breast violently, speaks rapidly.)* Jehovah, we belong to *Thee*, we belong to *Thee*.

MRS. NOAH AND EVE: Great Jehovah! Hear us. We are here in Thy Valley. We who belong to Thee!

(Ham slowly rises. He stands and walks around the altar to join the others, and they see that he is black. They shrink back terrified. He is laughing happily. Eve approaches him timidly as he advances around the end of the altar. She touches his hand, then his face. She begins kissing him.)

HAM: Why do you all pray and weep?

EVE: Look at thy hands, thy feet. Thou art cursed black by thy Father. *(She exits weeping left.)*

HAM *(gazing horrified at his hands)*: Black! *(He appears stupified. All shrink away from him as if they feared his touch. He approaches each in turn. He is amazed. He lays his hand upon Shem.)*

SHEM *(shrinking)*: Away! Touch me not!

HAM *(approaches his mother. She does not repel him, but averts her face.)* Why does my mother turn away?

MRS. NOAH: So that my baby may not see the flood that hath broken the windows of my soul and loosed the fountains of my heart.

(There is a great clamor off stage and Eve reenters left with her boy in her arms weeping and all the other children in pursuit jeering and pelting him with things. The child is also black. Ham looks at his child and falls at Noah's feet.

HAM *(beseeching in agony)*: Why Noah, my father and lord of the Earth, why?

NOAH *(sternly)*: Arise, Ham. Thou art black. Arise and go out from among us that we may see thy face no more, lest by lingering the curse of thy blackness come upon all my seed forever.

HAM *(grasps his father's knees. Noah repels him sternly, pointing away right. Eve steps up to Ham and raises him with her hand. She displays both anger and scorn.)*

EVE: Ham, my husband, Noah is right. Let us go before you awake and learn to despise your father and your God. Come away Ham, beloved, come with me, where thou canst never see these faces again, where never thy soft eyes can harden by looking too oft upon the fruit of their error, where never thy happy voice can learn to weep. Come with me to where the sun shines forever, to the end of the Earth, beloved the sunlight of all my years. *(She kisses his mouth and forehead. She crosses to door of tent and picks up a water bottle. Ham looks dazedly about him. His eyes light on the harp and he smilingly picks it up and takes his place beside Eve.*

HAM *(lightly cynical to all)*: Oh, remain with your flocks and fields and vineyards, to covet, to sweat, to die and know no peace. I go to the sun. *(He exits right across the plain with his wife and child trudging beside him. After he is off-stage comes the strumming of the harp and Ham's voice happily singing: "I am as a young ram in the Spring." It grows fainter and fainter until it is heard no more. The sun is low in the west. Noah sits looking tragically stern. All are ghastly calm. Mrs. Noah kneels upon the altar facing the mountain and she sobs continually.)*

We belong to Thee, O Jehovah

We belong to Thee.

(She keeps repeating this to a slow curtain).

CURTAIN

THE POT MAKER

MARITA BONNER

CHARACTERS

ELIAS JACKSON: *The Son, "called of God"*
MOTHER: *Nettie Jackson, Elias' mother*
LUCINDA JACKSON: *Elias' wife*
FATHER: *Luke Jackson, Elias' father*
LEW FOX: *Lucinda's lover*

SETTING

See first the room. A low ceiling; smoked walls; far more length than breadth. There are two windows and a door at the back of the stage. The door is between the windows. At left and right there are two doors leading to inner rooms. They are lighter than the door at back stage. That leads into the garden and is quite heavy.

You know there is a garden because if you listen carefully you can hear a tapping of bushes against the window and a gentle rustling of leaves and grass. The wind comes up against the house so much awash—like waves against the side of a boat— that you know, too, that there must be a large garden, a large space around the house.

But to come back into the room. It is a very neat room. There are white sash curtains at the window and a red plaid cloth on the table. Geraniums in red flower pots are in each window and even on the table beside the kerosene lamp which is lit there. An old-fashioned wooden clock sits on a shelf in the corner behind the stove at the right. Chairs of various types and degrees of ease are scattered around the table at center.

As the curtain is drawn, see first MOTHER; *a plump colored woman of indeterminable age and an indeterminate shade of brown, seated at the table. The* FATHER, *Luke, whose brown face is curled into a million pleasant wrinkles, sits opposite her at left.* LEW *stands at the stove facing the two at the table. He* must be an over-fat, over-facetious, over-fair, over-bearing, over-pleasant, over-confident creature. If he does not make you long to slap him back into a place approaching normal humility, he is the wrong character for the part. You must think as you look at him: "A woman would have to be a base fool to love such a man!"

Then you must relax in your chair as the door at right opens and LUCINDA walks in. "Exactly the woman," you will decide. For at once you can see she is a woman who must have sat down in the mud. It has crept into her eyes. They are dirty. It has filtered through-filtered through her. Her speech is smudged. Every inch of her body, from the twitch of her eyebrow to the twitch of muscles lower down in her body, is soiled. She is of a lighter brown than MOTHER and wears her coarse hair closely ironed to her head. She picks up each foot as if she were loath to leave the spot it rests on. Thus she crosses the room to the side of ELIAS who is seated at the window, facing the center of the room.

It is hard to describe ELIAS. He is ruggedly ugly, but he is not repulsive. Indeed, you want to stretch out first one hand and then the other to him. Give both hands to him. You want to give both hands to him and he is ruggedly ugly. That is enough.

ARGUMENT

When you see ELIAS, he is about to rehearse his first sermon. He has recently been called from the cornfields by God. Called to go immediately and preach and not to dally in any theological school. God summoned him on Monday. This is Wednesday. He is going to preach at the meeting-house on Sunday.

SCENE 1

As the curtain draws back, expectation rests heavily on everyone. MOTHER is poised stiffly on the edge of her chair. Her face and her body say, "Do me proud! You're my son! Do me proud!" FATHER on his side rests easily on his chair; "Make all the mistakes you want. Come off top notch. Come off under the pile. You're my son! My son." That sums them up in general, too. Can you see them? Do you know them?

ELIAS: (rising and walking toward the table) You all set back kind er in a row like. (He draws chairs to the far end of the room right.) There, there, Ma here! Pa there! Lew—(He hesitates and LEW goes to LUCINDA's side and sits down at once. This leaves ELIAS a little uncertain but he goes on.) Now—(He withdraws a little from them.) Brothers and sisters.

108

MOTHER: M-m-m-m, Lias, can't you think of nothin' new to say first? I been hearin' that one since God knows when. Seems like there's somethin' new.

ELIAS: Well, what'll I say then?

MOTHER: Oh—"ladies and gent'mun"; somethin' refined like. (*At this point,* LEW *and* LUCINDA *seemed to get involved in an amused crossing of glances.*) But go on then, anything'll be all right. (*The* MOTHER *stops here and glares at* LUCINDA *to pay her for forcing her into back water.* LUCINDA *sees* LEW.)

ELIAS: (*continuing*) Well, Brothers and Sisters! There is a tale I'd like for to tell you all this evening, brothers and sisters; somethin' to cheer your sorrowing hearts in this vale of tears.

LUCINDA: What if their hearts ain't happen to be sorrowing?

FATHER: (*cutting in*) Boun' to be some, chile! Boun' to be! (*The* SON *flashes thanks to* FATHER. *He appears to have forgotten the jibe and to be ignorant of the look of approval too. He is a delightful mutual peacemaker.*)

ELIAS: A tale to cheer your sorrowing hearts through this vale of tears.—This here talk is about a pot maker who made pots.

LUCINDA: (*laughing to herself—to* LEW) Huh, huh; Lord, ha' mercy.

MOTHER: (*giving* LUCINDA *a venomous glance and rising in defense*) Look here, Lias, is that tale in the Bible? You is called of God and He aint asked you to set nothin' down He aint writ Himself.

ELIAS: This is one of them tales like Jesus used to tell the Pharisees when he was goin' round through Galilee with them.

MOTHER: Jesus ain't never tol' no tales to Pharisees nor run with them either! Onliest thing He ever done was to argue with them when He met them. He gave 'em a good example like.

ELIAS: Well this'n is somethin' like—wait you all please! Once there was a man who made pots. He lived in a little house with two rooms and all that was in those rooms was pots. Just pots. Pots all made of earthenware. Earthenware. Each one of them had a bottom and a handle just alike. All of them jes' alike. One day the man was talking to them pots—.

LUCINDA: (*just loud enough to be disagreeable*) What kinder fool was talking to pots?

ELIAS: (*ignoring her*) An he says, "Listen you all. You is all alike. Each one of you is got a bottom to set on and a handle. You all is alike now, but you don' have to stay that a way. Do jes' as I tells you and you can turn to be anything you want. Tin pots, iron pots, brass pots, silver pots. Even gold." Then them pots says—

MOTHER: Lias, who in the name of God ever heard tell of a minister saying pots talked. Them folks aint goin' to let you do it.

ELIAS: Ma! Then the pots said, "What we got to do?" And the man, he told them he was goin' to pour something in them. "Don't you all tip over or spill none of the things I put in you. These here rooms is goin' to get dark Mighty dark. You all is goin' to set here. Each got to set up by hisself. On his own bottom and hold up his handle. You all is goin' to hear rearin' and tearin'. Just set and don't spill on the ground." "Master I got a crack in me," says one of them pots, "I got a crack in me so's I can't hol' nuthin." Then the man took a little dirt and he spit on it and put in on the crack and he patter it—just as gentle like! He never stopped and asked "How'd you get that crack" and he patted it—just as gentle like! He didn't do like some folks would have done. He stooped right down and fixed the crack 'cause 'twas in his pot. His own pot. Then he goes out. Them rooms got so dark that a million fireflies couldn't have showed a light in there. "What's in the corner?" says one of the pots. Then they gets scared and rolls over on the ground and spilled.

LUCINDA: Uhm. (*She sees only* LEW *again.*)

ELIAS: (*still ignoring her*) It kept getting darker. Bye 'n bye noises commenced. Sounded like a drove of bees had travelled up long a elephant's trunk and was setting out to sting their way out thoo the thickest part. "Wah, we's afraid," said some more pots and they spilled right over. For a long time them rooms stayed right dark and the time they was dark they was full of noise and pitchin' and tarin'—but pres'n'y the dark began leaving. The gray day come creepin' in under the door. The pot maker he come in; "Mornin' ya'll, how is you?" he asks. Some of the pots said right cheery, "We's still settin' like you tol' us to set!" Then they looked at their selves and they was all gol'. Some of them kinder had hung their heads but was still settin' up. The pot maker he says, "Never min', you all, you all can be silver. You ain't spilled over." Then some of the pots on the groun' snuk up and tried to stand up and hol' up their heads. "Since you all is so bol' as to try to be what you aint, you all kin be brass!" An' then he looked at them pots what was laying on the groun' and they all turned to tin. Now sisters and brothers, them pots is people. Is you all. If you'll keep settin' on the truth what God gave you, you'll go be gol'. If you lay down on Him, He is goin' to turn you to tin. There won't be nothin' to you at all. You be as empty as a tin can . . .

FATHER: Amen, amen.

ELIAS: Taint but just so long that you got to be on this earth in the dark—anyhow. Set up. Set up and hold your head up. Don' lay down on God! Don' lay down on Him! Don' spill on the groun'. No matter how hard the folks wear and tear and worry you. Set up and don' spill the things He give you to keep for Him. They tore Him—but He come into the world Jesus and He went out of it still Jesus. He set hisself up as Jesus and He aint never laid down. (*Here,* LUCINDA *yawns loudly and gives a prolonged "Ah-h-h-h!"*) Set up to be gol' you all and if you ever feels weak tell God, He won't ask how you got cracked. "Master, I got a crack in me." He'll stoop down and take and heal you. He'll heal you; the pot maker done it and he warn't God. The pot maker he didn't blame the pots for bustin'. He knows that pots can bust and God knows that it wouldn't take but so much anyway to knock any gol' pot over and crack it an' make it tin. . . . That's the reason He's sorry for us and heals us. Ask Him. And set. Set you all. Don't spill on the groun'. Amen. (*There is a silence. The father looks along the floor steadily.* ELIAS *looks at him.* LUCINDA *sees* LEW. *The mother sees her son. Finally* ELIAS *notes* LUCINDA *has her hand in* LEW's *and that they are whispering together. But* LEW *releases her hand and smiles at* ELIAS, *rising to his feet at the same time.*)

LEW: (*in a tone too nice, too round, too rich to be satisfactory*) Well, well folks! I'll have to go on now. I am congratulating you, sister Nettie, on such a son! He is surely a leadin' light. Leadin' us all straight into Heaven. (*He stops and mouths a laugh.*) I'll be seein' you all at the meetin'—good night. (*He bobs up and down as if he were really a toy fool on a string.*) Ah— Lucinda—ah—may—I—ask—you—for—a drink of water if— ah—it do not bother you? (*The tone is hollow. There will be no water drunk though they may run the water.* LUCINDA *smiles and leaves behind him giving a defiant flaunt as she passes* ELIAS. *This leaves the other three grouped beside the table.*)

FATHER: That is a right smart sermon, 'pears to me. Got some good sense in it.

MOTHER: But them folks aint goin' to sit there and hear him go on to tell them pots kin talk. I know that. (*A door bangs within the room in which* LUCINDA *and* LEW *have disappeared.* LUCINDA *comes out, crosses the stage, goes into the room at right. A faint rustling is heard within.*)

MOTHER: (*calling*) 'Cinda, what you doin' in that trunk? Taint nuthin' you need in there tonight. (*The rustling ceases abruptly—you can almost see* LUCINDA's *rage pouring in a flood at the door.*)

LUCINDA: (*from within*) I ain't doin' nothing'—(*She appears at the doorway fastening a string of red beads around her throat.*)

MOTHER: Well, if you aint doin' nothin', what you doin' with them beads on?

LUCINDA: (*flaring*) None of your business.

MOTHER: Oh, it aint! Well you jes' walk back in there and rest my best shoes under the side of the bed please, ma'am.

FATHER: Now Nettie, you women all likes to look—

MOTHER: Don't name me with that one there!

ELIAS: Ma, don't carry on with 'Cinda so.

MOTHER: You aint nothin' but a turntable! You aint got sense enough to see that she would jam you down the devil's throat if she got a chance.

LUCINDA: I'm goin' long out of here where folks got some sense. (*She starts off without removing the shoes.*)

MOTHER: Taint whilst to go. I'm goin' callin' myself. Give me my shoes. (LUCINDA *halts at the door. There are no words that can tell you how she looks at her mother-in-law. Words cannot do but so much.*)

LUCINDA: (*slinging the shoes*) There. (ELIAS *picks them up easily and carries them to his* MOTHER. *She slips them on, and, catching up a shawl, goes off at back followed by her husband.* LUCINDA *stamps around the room and digs a pair of old shoes up from somewhere. She slams everything aside that she passes. Finally, she tips one of the geraniums over.*)

ELIAS: (*mildly*) Taint whilst to carry on so, Lucinda.

LUCINDA: Oh, for God's sake, shut up! You and your "taint whilst to's" make me sick. (ELIAS *says nothing. He merely looks at her.*)

LUCINDA: That's right! That's right! Stand there and stare at me like some pop-eyed owl. You aint got sense enough to do anything else. (ELIAS *starts to speak.* LUCINDA *is warmed up to her subject. What can he say? Even more rapidly*) No you aint got sense enough to do anything else! Aint even got sense enough to keep a job! Get a job paying good money! Keep it two weeks and jes' when I'm hoping you'll get a little money ahead so's I could live decent like other women—in my house—You had to go and get called of God to quit and preach!

ELIAS: (*evenly*) God chose me.

LUCINDA: Yas God chose you. He aint chose you for no preachin'. He chose you for some kinder fool! That's what you are—some kinder fool! Fools can't preach.

ELIAS: Some do.

LUCINDA: Then you must be one of them that does! If you was any kind of man you'd get a decent job and hold it and hold your mouth shut and move me into my own house. Aint no woman so in love with her man's mother she wants to live five years under the same roof with her like I done. (ELIAS *may have thought of a dozen replies. He makes none. LUCINDA stares at him. Then she laughs aloud. It is a bitter laugh that makes you think of rocks and mud and dirt and edgy weather. It is jagged.*) Yes you are some kinder fool. Standing there like a pop-eyed owl—(*there follows the inevitable*). The Lord knows what I ever saw in you!

ELIAS: (*still evenly*) The Lord does know Lucinda. (*At that LUCINDA falls back into her chair and curses aloud in a singsong manner as if she were chanting a prayer. Then she sits still and stares at him.*)

LUCINDA: Elias—ain't you never wanted to hit nobody in your life? (*Before he can answer, a shrill whistle is heard outside the window at left. LUCINDA starts nervously and looks at the window. When she sees ELIAS has heard the sound, she tries to act unconcerned.*) What kinder bird is that whistlin' at the window? (*She starts toward it. ELIAS puts out a hand and stops her.*)

ELIAS: Taint whilst to open the window to look out. Can't see nothin' in the dark.

LUCINDA: That aint the side that old well is on, is it? That aint the window, is it?

ELIAS: You ought to know! Long as you been livin' here! Five years you just said. (*There is a crackle of bushes outside the window close to the house. A crash. Then a sound of muttering that becomes louder and louder. A subdued splashing. LUCINDA starts to the window but ELIAS gets there first. He puts his back to the wall.*)

LUCINDA: Somebody's fallin' into that well! Look out there!

ELIAS: Taint whilst to.

LUCINDA: Taint whilst to! Of God—here um calling! Go out there! Taint whilst to! (*She tries to dart around* ELIAS. *They struggle. He seizes her wrist, drags her back. She screams and talks all the time they struggle.*) Call yourself a Christian! The devil! That's what you is! The devil! Lettin' folks drown! Might be your own mother!

ELIAS: Taint my mother—You know who it is!

LUCINDA: How I know? Oh, go out there and save him for God's sake. (*The struggles and splashings are ceasing. A long drawn out "Oh my God" that sounds as if it's coming from every portion of the room, sifts over the stage.* LUCINDA *cries aloud. It is a tearing, shrieking, mad scream. It is as if someone had torn her soul apart from her body.* ELIAS *wrenches the door open.*) Now Cindy, you was goin' to Lew. Go 'long to him. Go 'long to him. (*He repeats.*)

LUCINDA: (*trying to fawn at him*) Oh! No! Elias, Oh Master! Ain you no ways a man? I aint know that was Lew! I aint know that was Lew—Oh, yes I did. Lew, Lew. (*She darts past* ELIAS *as if she has forgotten him. You hear her outside calling*) Lew, Lew. (*Full of mad agony, the screams search the night. But there is no answer. You hear only the sound of the wind. The sound of the wind in the leaves.* ELIAS *stands listening. All at once there is the same crackling sound outside and a crash and a splash. Once more* LUCINDA *raises her voice—frightened and choked. He hears the sound of the water. He starts toward the door.*)

ELIAS: Go 'long to Lew. (*He shouts and then sits down.*) You both is tin. (*But he raises himself at once and runs back to the door*). God, God, I got a crack in me too! (*He cries and goes out into the darkness. You hear splashing and panting. You hear cries.*) Cindy, give me your hand! There now! You is 'most out.

(*But then you hear another crash. A heavier splashing. Something has given away. One hears the sound of wood splitting. One hears something heavy splashing in the water. One hears only the wind in the leaves. Only the wind in the leaves and the door swings vacant. You stare through the door. Waiting. Expecting to see* ELIAS *stagger in with* LUCINDA *in his arms perhaps. But the door swings vacant. You stare—but there is only wind in the leaves. That's all there will be. A crack has been healed. A pot has spilled over on the ground. Some wisps have twisted out.*)

CURTAIN

THE PURPLE FLOWER

A PRIZE PLAY

BY MARITA O. BONNER

Time: *The Middle-of-Things-as-They-are. (Which means the End-of-Things for some of the characters and the Beginning-of-Things for others.)*

Place: *Might be here, there or anywhere—or even nowhere.*

Characters: *Sundry White Devils. (They must be artful little things with soft wide eyes such as you would expect to find in an angel. Soft hair that flops around their horns. Their horns glow red all the time—now with blood—now with eternal fire—now with deceit—now with unholy desire. They have bones tied carefully across their tails to make them seem less like tails and more like mere decorations. They are artful little things full of artful movements and artful tricks. They are artful dancers too. You are amazed at their adroitness. Their steps are intricate. You almost lose your head following them. Sometimes they dance as if they were men—with dignity—erect. Sometimes they dance as if they were snakes. They are artful dancers on the Thin-Skin-of-Civilization.*

The Us's: *They can be as white as the White Devils, as brown as the earth, as black as the center of a poppy. They may look as if they were something or nothing.*

Setting: *The stage is divided horizontally into two sections, upper and lower, by a thin board. The main action takes place on the upper stage. The light is never quite clear on the lower stage; but it is bright enough for you to perceive that sometimes the action that takes place on the upper stage is duplicated on the lower. Sometimes the actors on the upper stage get too vocifer-*

ous—too violent—and they crack through the boards and they lie twisted and curled in mounds. There are any number of mounds there, all twisted and broken. You look at them and you are not quite sure whether you see something or nothing; but you see by a curve that there might lie a human body. There is thrust out a white hand—a yellow one—one brown—a black. The Skin-of-Civilization must be very thin. A thought can drop you through it.

Scene: *An open plain. It is bounded distantly on one side by Nowhere and faced by a high hill—Somewhere.*

Argument: *The White Devils live on the side of the hill, Somewhere. On top of the hill grows the purple Flower-of-Life-At-Its-Fullest. This flower is as tall as a pine and stands alone on top of the hill. The Us's live in the valley that lies between Nowhere and Somewhere and spend their time trying to devise means of getting up the hill. The White Devils live all over the sides of the hill and try every trick, known and unknown, to keep the Us's from getting to the hill. For if the Us's get up the hill, the Flower-of-Life-at-Its-Fullest will shed some of its perfume and then and there they will be Somewhere with the White Devils. The Us's started out by merely asking permission to go up. They tilled the valley, they cultivated it and made it as beautiful as it is. They built roads and houses even for the White Devils. They let them build the houses and then they were knocked back down into the valley.*

SCENE

When the curtain rises, the evening sun is shining bravely on the valley and hillside alike.

    The Us's are having a siesta beside a brook that runs down the Middle of the valley. As usual they rest with their backs toward Nowhere and their faces toward Somewhere. The White Devils are seen in the distance on the hillside. As you see them, a song is borne faintly to your ears from the hillside.
    The White Devils are saying:

        "You stay where you are!

        We don't want you up here!

        If you come you'll be on par

        With all we hold dear.

        So stay—stay—stay—

        Yes stay where you are!"

116

The song rolls full across the valley.

A LITTLE RUNTY US: "Hear that, don't you?"

ANOTHER US *(lolling over on his back and chewing a piece of grass):* "I ain't studying 'bout them devils. When I get ready to go up that hill—I'm going! *(He rolls over on his side and exposes a slender brown body to the sun.)* "Right now, I'm going to sleep." *(And he forthwith snores.)*

An old dark brown lady who has been lying down rises suddenly to her knees in the foreground. She gazes toward the hillside and speaks: "I'll never live to see the face of that flower! God knows I worked hard to get Somewhere though. I've washed the shirt off of every one of them White Devils' back!"

A YOUNG US: "And got a slap in the face for doing it."

OLD LADY: "But that's what the Leader told us to do. 'Work,' he said. 'Show them you know how.' As if two hundred years of slavery had not showed them!"

ANOTHER YOUNG US: "Work doesn't do it. The Us who work for the White Devils get pushed in the face—down off of Somewhere every night. They don't even sleep up there."

OLD LADY: "Something's got to be done though! The Us ain't got no business to sleep while the sun is shining. They'd ought to be up and working before the White Devils get to some other tricks.

YOUNG US: "You just said work did not do you any good! What's the need of working if it doesn't get you anywhere? What's the use of boring around in the same hole like a worm? Making the hole bigger to stay in?"

(There comes up the road a clatter of feet and four figures, a middle-aged well-browned man, a lighter-browned middle-aged woman, a medium light brown girl, beautiful as a browned peach and a slender, tall, bronzy brown youth who walks with his head high. He touches the ground with his feet as if it were a velvet rug and not sun-baked, jagged rocks.)

OLD LADY *(addressing the Older Man):* "Evenin', Average. I was just saying we ain't never going to make that hill."

AVERAGE: "The Us will if they get the right leaders."

THE MIDDLE-AGED WOMAN—CORNERSTONE *(speaks):* "Leaders! Leaders! They've had good ones looks like to me."

AVERAGE: "But they ain't led us anywhere!"

CORNERSTONE: "But that is not their fault! If one of them gets up and says, 'Do this', one of the Us will sneak up behind him and

117

knock him down and stand up and holler, 'Do that', and then he himself gets knocked down and we still sit in the valley and knock down and drag out!"

A YOUNG US: "Yeah! Drag Us out, but not White Devils." *(aside).*

OLD LADY: "It's the truth Cornerstone. They say they going to meet this evening to talk about what we ought to do."

AVERAGE: "What is the need of so much talking?"

CORNERSTONE: "Better than not talking! Somebody might say something after while."

(The Young Girl—Sweet—who just came up, speaks): "I want to talk too!"

AVERAGE: "What can you talk about?"

SWEET: "Things! Something, father!"

(The Young Man—Finest Blood—who is with them speaks): "I'll speak too."

AVERAGE: "Oh you all make me tired! Talk—talk—talk—talk! And the flower is still up on the hillside!"

OLD LADY: "Yes and the White Devils are still talking about keeping the Us away from it, too."

(A drum begins to beat in the distance. All the Us stand up and shake off their sleep. The drummer, a short black, determined looking Us, appears around the bushes beating the drum with strong, vigorous jabs that make the whole valley echo and re-echo with rhythm. Some of the Us begin to dance in time to the music.)

AVERAGE: "Look at that! Dancing!! The Us will never learn to be sensible!"

CORNERSTONE: "They dance well! Well!!"

(The Us all congregate at the centre front. Almost naturally, the Young Us range on one side, the Old Us on the other. Cornerstone sits her plump brown self comfortably in the centre of the stage.)

(An Old Us tottering with age and blind comes toward her): "What's it this time, chillun? Is it day yet? Can you see the road to that flower?

AVERAGE: "Oh you know we ain't going to get up there! No use worrying!"

CORNERSTONE *(to Old Man):* "No it's not day! It is still dark. It is night." (For the sun has gone and purple blackness has lain across the Valley. Somehow, though, you can see the shape of the flower on top of Somewhere. Lights twinkle on the hill.)

OLD MAN *(speaking as if to himself):* "I'm blind from working—building for the White Devils in the heat of the noon-day sun and I'm weary!"

CORNERSTONE: "Lean against me so they won't crowd you."

(An old man rises in the back of the ranks; his beard reaches down to his knees but he springs upright. He speaks): "I want to tell you all something! The Us can't get up the road unless we work! We want to hew and dig and toil!"

A YOUNG US: "You had better sit down before someone knocks you down! They told us that when your beard was sprouting."

CORNERSTONE *(to Youth):* "Do not be so stupid! Speak as if you had respect for that beard!"

ANOTHER YOUNG US: "We have! But we get tired of hearing 'you must work' when we know the Old Us built practically every inch of that hill and are yet Nowhere."

FIRST YOUNG US: "Yes, all they got was a rush down the hill—not a chance to take a step up!"

CORNERSTONE: "It was not time then."

(An Old Man on the back row): "Here comes a Young Us who has been reading in the books! Here comes a Young Us who has been reading in the books! He'll tell us what the books say about getting Somewhere."

(A Young Man pushes through the crowd. As soon as he reaches the centre front, he throws a bundle of books and cries): "I'm through! I do not need these things! They're no good!"

(The Old Man pushes up from the back and stands beside him): "You're through! Ain't you been reading in the books how to get Somewhere? Why don't you tell us how to get there?"

THE YOUNG MAN: "I'm through I tell you! There isn't anything in one of these books that tells Black Us how to get around White Devils."

OLD MAN *(softly—sadly):* "I thought the books would tell us how!"

YOUNG MAN: "No! The White Devils wrote the books themselves. You know they aren't going to put anything like that in there!"

YET ANOTHER OLD MAN *(throwing back his head and calling into the air):* "Lord! Why don't you come by here and tell us how to get Somewhere?"

A YOUNG MAN *(who had been idly chewing grass speaks):* "Aw, you ought to know by now that isn't the way to talk to God!"

OLD MAN: "It ain't! It ain't! It ain't! It ain't! Ain't I been talking to God just like that for seventy years? Three score and ten years—Amen!"

THE GRASS CHEWER: "Yes! Three score and ten years you been telling God to tell you what to do. Telling Him! And three score and ten years you been wearing your spine double sitting on the rocks in the valley too."

OLD US: "He is all powerful! He will move in his own time!"

YOUNG US: "Well, if he is all powerful, God does not need you to tell Him what to do."

OLD US: "Well what's the need of me talkin' to Him then?"

YOUNG US: "Don't talk so much to Him! Give Him a chance! He might want to talk to you but you do so much yelling in His ears that He can't tell you anything."

(There is a commotion in the back stage. Sweet comes running to Cornerstone crying.)

SWEET: "Oh—oo—!"

CORNERSTONE: "What is it, Sweet?"

SWEET: "There's a White Devil sitting in the bushes in the dark over there! There's a White Devil sitting in the bushes over in the dark! And when I walked by—he pinched me!"

FINEST BLOOD *(catching a rock):* "Where is he, sister?" (He starts toward the bushes.)

CORNERSTONE *(screaming):* "Don't go after him son! They will kill you if you hurt him!"

FINEST BLOOD: "I don't care if they do. Let them. I'd be out of this hole then!"

AVERAGE: "Listen to that young fool! Better stay safe and sound where he is! At least he got somewhere to eat and somewhere to lay his head."

FINEST BLOOD: "Yes I can lay my head on the rocks of Nowhere."

(Up the center of the stage toils a new figure of a square set middle-aged Us. He walks heavily for in each hand he carries a heavy bag. As soon as he reaches the center front he throws the bags down groaning as he does so.)

AN OLD MAN: "'Smatter with you? Ain't them bags full of gold."

THE NEW COMER: "Yes, they are full of gold!"

OLD MAN: "Well why ain't you smiling then? Them White Devils can't have anything no better!"

THE NEW COMER: "Yes they have! They have Somewhere! I tried to do what they said. I brought them money, but when I brought it to them they would not sell me even a spoonful of dirt from Somewhere! I'm through!"

CORNERSTONE: "Don't be through. The gold counts for something. It must!"

(An Old Woman cries aloud in a quavering voice from the back): "Last night I had a dream."

A YOUNG US: "Dreams? Excuse me! I know I'm going now! Dreams!!"

OLD LADY: "I dreamed that I saw a White Devil cut in six pieces—head here, *(pointing),* body here—one leg here—one there—an arm here—an arm there."

AN OLD MAN: "Thank God! It's time then!"

AVERAGE: "Time for what? Time to eat? Sure ain't time to get Somewhere!"

OLD MAN WALKING FORWARD: "It's time! It's time! Bring me an iron pot!"

YOUNG US: "Aw don't try any conjuring!

OLD MAN *(louder):* "Bring me a a pot of iron. Get the pot from the fire in the valley."

(Someone brings it up immediately).

OLD MAN *(walking toward pot slowly):* "Old Us! Do you hear me. Old Us that are here do you hear me?"

(All the Old Us cry in chorus): "Yes, Lord! We hear you! We hear you!"

OLD MAN *(crying louder and louder):* "Old Us! Old Us!! Old Us that are gone, Old Us that are dust do you hear me?"

(His voice sounds strangely through the valley. Somewhere you think you hear—as if mouthed by ten million mouths through rocks and dust—"Yes!—Lord!—We hear you! We hear you!")

OLD MAN: "And you hear me—give me a handful of dust! Give me a handful of dust! Dig down to the depths of the things you have made! The things you formed with your hands and give me a handful of dust!"

(An Old Woman tottering with the weakness of old age crosses the stage and going to the pot, throws a handful of dust in. Just before she sits down again she throws back her head and shakes her cane in the air and laughs so that the entire valley echoes.)

A YOUNG US: "What's the trouble? Choking on the dust?"

OLD WOMAN: "No child! Rejoicing!"

YOUNG US: "Rejoicing over a handful of dust?"

OLD WOMAN: "Yes. A handful of dust! Thanking God I could do something if it was nothing but make a handful of dust!"

YOUNG US: "Well dust isn't much!"

OLD MAN AT THE POT: "Yes, it isn't much! You are dust yourself; but so is she. Like everything else, though, dust can be little or much, according to where it is."

(The Young Us who spoke subsides. He subsides so completely that he crashes through the Thin-Skin-of-Civilization. Several of his group go too. They were thinking.)

OLD MAN AT THE POT: "Bring me books! Bring me books!"

YOUNG US *(who threw books down):* "Here! Take all these! I'll light the fire with them."

OLD MAN: "No, put them in the pot."

(Youth does so.)

OLD MAN: "Bring me gold!"

(The Man who brought the Bags of Gold): "Here take this! It is just as well. Stew it up and make teething rings!!" (He pours it into the pot.)

OLD MAN: "Now bring me blood! Blood from the eyes, the ears, the whole body! Drain it off and bring

(No one speaks or moves.)

OLD MAN: "Now bring me blood! Blood from the eyes, the ears, the whole body! Drain it off! Bring me blood!!"

(No one speaks or moves.)

OLD MAN: "Ah hah, hah! I knew it! Not one of you willing to pour his blood in the pot!"

YOUNG US *(facetiously):* "How you going to pour your own blood in there? You got to be pretty far gone to let your blood run in there. Somebody else would have to do the pouring."

OLD MAN: "I mean red blood. Not yellow blood, thank you."

FINEST BLOOD *(suddenly):* "Take my blood!" *(He walks toward the pot.)*

CORNERSTONE: "O no! Not my boy! Take me instead!"

OLD MAN: "Cornerstone we cannot stand without you!"

AN OLD WOMAN: "What you need blood for? What you doing any-how? You ain't told us nothing yet. What's going on in that pot?"

OLD MAN: "I'm doing as I was told to do."

A YOUNG US: "Who told you to do anything?"

OLD MAN: "God. I'm His servant."

YOUNG US *(who spoke before):* "God? I haven't heard God tell you anything."

OLD MAN: "You couldn't hear. He told it to me alone."

OLD WOMAN: "I believe you. Don't pay any attention to that simple-ton! What God told you to do?"

OLD MAN: "He told me take a handful of dust—dust from which all things came and put it in a hard iron pot. Put it in a hard iron pot. Things shape best in hard moulds!! Put in books that Men learn by. Gold that Men live by. Blood that lets Men live."

YOUNG US: "What you suppose to be shaping? A man?"

OLD US: "I'm the servant. I can do nothing. If I do this, God will shape a new man Himself."

YOUNG MAN: "What's the things in the pot for?"

OLD MAN: "To show I can do what I'm told."

OLD WOMAN: "Why does He want blood?"

OLD MAN: "You got to give blood! Blood has to be let for births, to give life."

OLD WOMAN: "So the dust wasn't just nothing? Thank God!"

YOUTH: "Then the books were not just paper leaves? Thank God!"

THE MAN OF THE GOLD BAGS: "Can the gold mean something?"

OLD MAN: "Now I need the blood."

FINEST BLOOD: "I told you you could take mine."

OLD MAN: "Yours!"

FINEST BLOOD: "Where else could you get it? The New Man must be born. The night is already dark. We cannot stay here forever. Where else could blood come from?"

OLD MAN: "Think child. When God asked a faithful servant once to do sacrifice, even his only child, where did God put the real meat for sacrifice when the servant had the knife upon the son's throat?"

OLD US *(in a chorus):*

> In the bushes, Lord!
> In the bushes, Lord!
> Jehovah put the ram
> In the bushes!

CORNERSTONE: "I understand!"

FINEST BLOOD: "What do you mean?"

CORNERSTONE: "Where were you going a little while ago? Where were you going when your sister cried out?"

FINEST BLOOD: "To the bushes! You want me to get the White Devil? *(He seizes the piece of rock and stands to his feet.)*

OLD MAN: "No! No! Not that way. The White Devils are full of tricks. You must go differently. Bring him gifts and offer them to him."

FINEST BLOOD: "What have I to give for a gift?"

OLD MAN: "There are the pipes of Pan that every Us is born with. Play on that. Soothe him—lure him—make him yearn for the pipe. Even a White Devil will soften at music. He'll come out, and he only comes to try to get the pipe from you."

FINEST BLOOD: "And when he comes out, I'm to kill him in the dark before he sees me? That's a White Devil trick!"

OLD MAN: "An Old Us will never tell you to play White Devil's games! No! Do not kill him in the dark. Get him out of the bushes and say to him: 'White Devil, God is using me for His instrument. You think that it is I who play on this pipe! You think that is I who play upon this pipe so that you cannot stay in your bushes. So that you must come out of your bushes. But it is not I who play. It is not I, it is God who plays through me—to you. Will you hear what He says? Will you hear? He says it is almost day, White Devil. The night is far gone. A New Man must be born for the New Day. Blood is needed for birth. Blood is needed for the birth. Come out, White Devil. It may be your blood—it may be mine—but blood must be taken during the night to be given at the birth. It may be my blood—it may be your blood—but everything has been given. The Us toiled to give dust for the body, books to guide the body, gold to clothe the body. Now they need blood for birth so the New Man can live. You have taken blood. You must give blood. Come out! Give it.' And then fight him!"

FINEST BLOOD: "I'll go! And if I kill him?"

OLD MAN: "Blood will be given!"

FINEST BLOOD: "And if he kills me?"

OLD MAN: "Blood will be given!"

FINEST BLOOD: "Can there be no other way—cannot this cup pass?"

OLD MAN: "No other way. It cannot pass. They always take blood. They built up half their land on our bones. They ripened crops of cotton, watering them with our blood. Finest Blood, this is God's decree: "You take blood—you give blood. Full measure—flooding full—over—over!"

FINEST BLOOD: "I'll go." *(He goes quickly into the shadow).*

(Far off soon you can hear him—his voice lifted, young, sweet, brave and strong): "White Devil! God speaks to you through me!—Hear Him!—Him! You have taken blood; there can be no other way. You will have to give blood! Blood!"

(All the Us listen. All the valley listens. Nowhere listens. All the White Devils listen. Somewhere listens.

Let the curtain close leaving all the Us, the White Devils, Nowhere, Somewhere, listening, listening. Is it time?)

EXIT, AN ILLUSION

A ONE-ACT PLAY

BY MARITA O. BONNER

FOREWORD

(Which presents the setting, the characters, and the argument)

The room you are in is mixed. It is mixed.

There are ragged chairs with sorry sagging ragged bottoms.—
There are lace curtains with sorry ragged holes—but all over the
chairs are scattered clothes, mostly lingerie of the creamiest, laci-
est, richest, pastel-crepe variety.

Everything is mixed.

Dishes are pushed back on the table. They may be yesterday's
dishes or they may be today's. But dishes are pushed back and the
table cloth is rumpled back. A pair of red kid pumps are on the
edge of the table. Your eyes skip from the scarlet omen of their
owner's hasty death—omen, if the bottom still holds in supersti-
tion—

Shoes mixed with dishes on the table.

Newspapers, pillows, shoes and stockings are scattered across
the floor, making a path straight to an exquisite dressing-table of
the variety type. This stands at the extreme right of the stage.

There is a window at right back—nearly at the centre—through
which you see snow falling. Directly beside the window there is a
door which must lead into an inner hall. It is not stout enough to
be an outer door. It is the brownish sort of non-de-script door that
shuts a cheap flat off from the rest of the world.

On the left side of the room is an open couch-bed. The sheets
and blankets depend almost to the floor in uneven jags. Easily,
then, you can see the figure of a woman lying there. Her hair

126

which is a light brown—lies with a thick waving around her head. Her face—thin—is almost as pale as the sheets. She is sleeping with an arm hung over the side of the bed. Even though she keeps tossing and twitching as if she would come awake, she holds her arm over the side.

Down on the floor on the same side, lying so that her arm falls across him—there is a man. A part of his face shows against the bed-clothes and you can see he is blackly brown with the thin high-poised features that mark a "keen black man."

You can see at a glance that his slender body is caste for high things. High things. High things of the soul if the soul is fully living—high things of the flesh if the soul is fully dead.

He is Buddy.

The girl is Dot.

You are in their flat.

They are most assuredly not brother and sister.

Neither are they man and wife.

The room is mixed.

—Dot suddenly leans over the side toward Buddy. You wonder how she awakens so easily.

DOT—"Well Buddy I got a date. I got to get gone. Buddy! Buddy! (*She leans over further and shakes him.*)

BUDDY—"Hunh—hunh? What say, Dot?" (*He wakes up*). "What say Dot?" (*He yawns*). "Uh-uh! Guess I was sleep. What say?"

DOT—"I say I got a date, Buddy."

BUDDY (*fully awake at once*)—"Date? Where you think you're going keeping a date sick as a dog and with the snow on the ground! (*He looks toward the window.*) Snowing now! Where you think you're going?"

DOT—"I got a date I tell you!"

BUDDY—"An' I tell you you ain't go-going to keep it!"

DOT—"Aw cut that stuff! How long since you thought you could tell me when to go and when to come! Store that stuff!"

BUDDY—"I ain't storing nothing! You ain't going, I say."

DOT—"Aw Buddy I been knowing the guy all my life! Played with him when I's a kid! Been on parties with him since I been going around!"

BUDDY—"Aw don't try that old friend stuff! What's his name?"

DOT—"Exit."

BUDDY—"Exit? Exit! Where'd he get that! off the inside of a theayter door? Exit! Exit! What's his other name or is that the onliest one he got?"

DOT—"Mann. Exit Mann. That's his name. Yeah—" (*She hesitates and seems to be uncertain.*)

BUDDY—"Well it sure is a rotten name! Must be hiding from the cops behind it!"

(*Dot takes this opportunity to rise from her couch. The filmy night garments cling to her almost as closely as her flesh. You see she is not curved. You see she is flat where she should curve, sunken where she should be flat. You wish she would lie down again but she gets up—almost falls back—takes hold of the back of the chair and passes across the room to the dressing table.*)

BUDDY—"Look at you! 'Bout to fall down! You better lay down again." (*Dot has begun to brush her hair before the dressing table. She brushes rapidly with strokes that grow vigorous as if each one made some new strength start up in her.*)

DOT—"Aw let me alone! I'm going out!"

(*Buddy sits on the floor and watches her. She rouges her cheeks and paints her lips and begins to powder heavily with white powder.*)

BUDDY—"You ain't fixin' to go out passing are you?"

DOT—"Aw don't ask so many fool questions!"

BUDDY (*growing angry*)—"Don't get too smart! Guess there's something after all in what the fellers been saying 'bout you anyhow."

DOT—"What your nigger friends been saying now?"

BUDDY—"Nigger friends? You're a nigger yourself for all your white hide!"

DOT (*shrugging*)—"I may not be—You'd never know!"

BUDDY—"Aw shut up! You'd like to think ya was white! You'd have never lived with niggers if you'd a been all white and had a crack at a white man!"

(*Dot starts to speak—changes her mind—and paints her lips again.*)

BUDDY (*after a second's silence*)—"Take some of that stuff off!"

DOT—"I can't! Mann likes a woman like me to paint up so I'll flash out above the crowd."

BUDDY—"Mann! what's Mann got to do with the way you look! Look here you! You been running 'round with this fellow Mann? (*He plunges to his feet and lunges toward her.*) Is he the white feller they been seeing you out with for the past three months?"

DOT—"They? What they? Some more of your—!"

BUDDY—"Don't call them niggers again you half-white—"

(*Dot catches him by the shoulder and pushes him away.—She selects a piece of clothes out of a drawer.*)

DOT—"I told you in the beginning I been knowing this guy all my life! Been out with him!"

BUDDY—"Is he white?"

DOT—"I don't know!"

BUDDY—"You don't know! Where'd you meet him?"

DOT—"Aw for God sake shut up and let me alone! I never met him! This is the last time I'm going to tell you I been knowing him all my life!"

BUDDY—"Naw I ain't lettin' you alone! Naw I ain't letting you alone! This is the guy the fellers been telling me about! This is the guy! Ol' lop-sided lanky white thing! Been hanging around you at all the cafes and dances and on the streets all the time I'm out of the city! I'm out of the city—working to keep you—you hanging around with some no 'count white trash! So no count he got to come in nigger places, to nigger parties and then when he gets there—can't even speak to none of them. Ain't said a word to nobody the fellers say! Ain't said a word! Just settin' 'round—settin' 'round—looking at you—hanging around you—dancin' with you! He better not show hisself 'round here while I'm here!"

DOT—"He can't never come when you're here."

BUDDY—"You right he can't come here. Can't never come! He better be afraid of me."

DOT—"He ain't afraid of you. He's afraid of your love for me."

BUDDY—(*laughing shortly*). "Aw for crap sake! My love! He ain't afraid of my love! He's afraid of my fist!"

(*Dot does not seem to hear him now. She talks to herself—"It's almost time!" It's almost time!"*)

Buddy hears her the second she speaks—"Almost time for what?"

DOT—"Him to come!"

BUDDY—"Who?"

DOT—"Exit!"

BUDDY—(*cursing*). "He ain't coming here! He ain't coming here! I'll knock his head clean off his shoulders if he comes here!"

DOT—"He's coming!"

BUDDY—"I'll kill you 'fore he gets here and then kill him when he comes!"

DOT—"Aw Buddy—don't take on so! If you love me he can't come in between your love and come to me!"

(Buddy curses until his veins are swollen—packed full of the poison of the curses.)

BUDDY—"Damn you! Damn you!! Trying to throw this 'your love' stuff out to cam'flage and hide behind. I tol' you when we were fussing before you went to sleep that I didn't believe you when you said everybody was lying on you! You said everybody was lying and you was tellin' the truth! Say you ain't never been with other men! Naw I don't love you!"

(He breaks off and rushes to a drawer and snatches out a mean, ugly, blue-black, short, pistol.)

DOT—(*screaming and overturning her chair*) "Aw Buddy—Buddy don't! You love me!"

BUDDY—"Shut up!!" (*He lifts the gun as if he were going to bring it down—raking her with fire the length of her body. He stops—*) "Naw I don't love you! Half-white rat!"

DOT—(*crawling to her knees away from him*) "Then he's got to come! I got to go with him!"

BUDDY—"Yas he's got to come! And when he comes I'll fix you both! Get up!" (*He prods her with his foot.*) Get up! Get up and dress to go out before your Exit is here! Exit! Exit! I'll Exit him when I get through with you!"

(Dot completes her powdering then she suddenly reaches her hat down from a hook above the table. It is a smart black turban. It is black crepe and is wound and wound around. She snatches up a sealskin coat that has been lying on another chair and begins to put it on.)

BUDDY—"You must be foolish! What you putting the coat on over the night-clothes for?"

DOT—"I ain't got time to put no more on."

BUDDY—"Aw yes you got time, sister! Put on all you want! I ain't going to run you off before he gets here! You ain't going 'till your Exit comes!"

DOT—"This is all I need—all I need! I'm ready."

BUDDY—"You're ready—where's your friend? Can't go without him!"

DOT—"He's here!" (*she points.*) "There he is." (*And close behind Buddy you see a man standing. He is half in the shadow. All you can see is a dark over-coat, a dark felt hat. You cannot see his face for his back is turned. You wonder how he came there. You wonder if perhaps he has not been there all the while.*)

BUDDY—(*starting back as he sees the man.*) "You're a regular sneak, ain't you! Ain't enough to sneak in and take a man's girl while he's out workin! Got to sneak in his house! Sneak in on him when he's minding his business!"

(*The man does not move or answer. Dot's color is bright. Her eyes glow in the semi-shadow. The lights in the room seem dimmer somehow. Dot is breathing so that the fur mounts and slides— mounts and slides on her bosom. She keeps wetting her lips as if they were drying out. She starts across the floor toward him but pauses and draws back almost at once.*)

BUDDY—(*still talking to the man.*) "Turn around and say something! Turn around and say something! They say all you do is hang around niggers' places and keep a still tongue!" (*To Dot*) "Go on over! Go on up to your Exit. Go on so you can go off the way I am sending you off. Go off like you lived! Lying in some man's arms—then lying to me* (*as if to himself*)—*That's the way to die anyhow: jus' like you lived!"

DOT—(*rubbing a hand across her face.*) "Buddy!" (*gasping*) "Buddy! Say you love me! I don't want to go! I don't want to go with him!"

(*Buddy's answer is an inarticulate wild roar:—"Get on to him! Get on over to him!"*)

(*With a scream and a quick run Dot crosses the little space and as quickly the man opens his arms and draws her to him without turning around.*)

DOT—(*crying smothered against the coat as if she were far away*) "Buddy—Buddy—Buddy! Do you love me? Say you love me before I go!"

(*As she cries out the man begins to walk toward the back door. Buddy curses and fires at the same time. A stray shot strikes the light. It goes out. Buddy scratches a match and you see the man standing in the doorway—about to cross the threshold. His back is still turned but as you look he slowly begins to turn around.*)

BUDDY—"Mann? Mann!! Dot! Dot!

(*At that the man turns fully and you see Dot laid limp—hung limp—silent. Above her, showing in the match light between the*

131

overcoat and the felt hat are the hollow eyes and fleshless cheeks of Death.

But almost at once the light flares back. You see the room as it was at first. Dot on her couch with her arms hanging over the side—Buddy lying beside the couch. The red shoes on the table.)

DOT—(*struggling awake*)—"Buddy! (*You can hear a rattling in her throat. A loud rattling. The rattling of breath soon to cease).* "Buddy!!! Buddy!! Aw God, he can't hear me!—Buddy, do you love me? Say you love me 'fore I go! Ah—ah—ah—!" (*The rattling is loud—loud. It stops on a high note. She stretches rigid and is still.*)

(The room is quiet an instant. You think you hear the rattling, though.)

BUDDY—(*striving in his sleep*) "Exit!! Mann!! Exit! (*He pauses— then cries aloud*) You lied! Naw I don't love you! (*He cries so loudly that he comes fully awake and sits up swiftly*)—"Say Dot—I had a—! Dot! Dot!! Oh my God (*he touches her*) My Dot! (*and he leans over her and begins to cry like a small boy*). Oh Dot!—! I love you! I love you!"

CURTAIN

THE HUNCH

BY EULALIE SPENCE

PERSONS IN THE PLAY

MAVIS

MRS. REED

MITCHELL

BERT

STEVE

LUCINDA

SCENE: *Harlem. (The living room in Mrs. Reed's apartment. Mavis rents this room for considerably more than she can afford. There is a day bed, a gate-leg table, a wing chair with its summer cover, two small chairs and an old book-case. The floor is covered with a gaily-colored fibre rug. At the left there are two windows with attractive ruffled curtains of cream voile. At the back a door opens upon the hall. Another door at the right leads into a bedroom. The door of a closet at the back is wide open, revealing several dresses on hangers. Pretty undergarments are lying about on chairs. Two pairs of new shoes are on the table. Several light summer wraps and sweaters are lying across the foot of the bed. Occupying a prominent place in the foreground is a wardrobe trunk partly packed.)*

TIME: *Evening in summer.*

AT RISE: *(Mavis Cunningham is seen packing her trunk. She sings softly as she goes leisurely about her work.*

>Everybody loves mah baby, but mah baby
>
>Doan love nobody but me—

Her graceful figure is enveloped in a lemon-colored smock with a loose black tie at the bosom. Her black hair is drawn smoothly back from her forehead. There is a soft prettiness about her, a joyousness in her step, a smile hovering about her lips.)

MAVIS. [*Going up to the mirror which hangs between the windows and holding an evening dress up against her body. She nods approval at her reflection.*] Not so bad, Honey. Not so bad. [*There is a knock on the door at the right. Mavis calls, "Come in!" Mrs. Reed waddles in. Her short, stout figure is encased in a pink crepe dress very much shorter than she can afford to wear it, and sleeveless. She flops into the wing chair as soon as Mavis has rescued two pretty hats.*]

MRS. REED. Well! Yuh pretty near packed, ain't yuh?

MAVIS. Almost! Did yuh go to the movies?

MRS. REED. Yeah. Seen "The Volga Boatman." The place was jes' jammed.

MAVIS. Like it?

MRS. REED. Yeah, pretty good. Say, them poor Russians warn't treated no better'n niggers, was they?

MAVIS. Not a bit.

MRS. REED. When'd yuh see de picture?

MAVIS. Couple uh weeks ago at the Strand. Bert took me.

MRS. REED. [*Enviously.*] Bert Jackson's a reg'lar daddy, ain't he?

MAVIS. [*With a smile.*] Say, you don't have to tell *me*.

MRS. REED. Reckon yuh knows it well 'nuff, seein' yuh's gwine tuh marry him ter-morrow. Say! Yuh doan seem de leas' bit excited.

MAVIS. Mebbe outside, I ain't Mis' Reed. But inside everything's jes' singin' an' jumpin'. I can't hardly keep still.

MRS. REED. Ah sure doan blame yuh none. Ah knows jes' how yuh feels.

MAVIS. I feel a little scared like, too. 'Tain't that I'm lonesome. I ain't lonesome, really, only every once in a while I get tuh thinkin' 'bout Mom an' my sister, Helen, back home in Raleigh. I didn't write 'em 'bout my gettin' married 'till yesterday. Yuh know, Mis' Reed, there's a plenty things can happen tuh break up a weddin', 'specially in Harlem.

MRS. REED. Yuh ain't tellin' me!

MAVIS. An' so I waited 'till the very last minute when I was sure.

MRS. REED. Yuh done jes' right. Yuh can't be sure uh no man dese days, 'till yuh's got the weddin' ring on yuh finger. Reckon thar ain't nuthin' slow 'bout Bert Jackson, neither. Bet thar's a plenty women chasin' him, right now.

MAVIS. Well, he's mine. They're not goin' tuh get him.

MRS. REED. Yuh ain't knowed him long, has yuh?

MAVIS. Only four weeks.

MRS. REED. Well, that's pretty quick, sure 'nuff, but Ah's heard tell uh quicker. It doan do no good tuh keep 'em hangin' too long. Whut's become uh dat feller uster follow yuh round? De one yuh was allus duckin'?

MAVIS. Steve? Oh, Steve's alright, only he ain't the kind of feller I could ever love. He knows I'm to marry Bert. I told him yesterday. Say! That reminds me! You know that long distance call I got last night from Philly—well, 'twas Steve! He call me up tuh ask me tuh put a number in fer him. Can yuh beat it? I didn't even know he was outer town. The money that boy wastes on numbers sure is a sin.

MRS. REED. Did yuh play it fer him?

MAVIS. Oh, sure, this morning. Guess! He asked me to put it in at two different places—fifty cents each. Steve's bin playin' that number more'n a month, dollar a day, sometimes two. He hopped over to Philly yesterday an' forgot tuh put it in. Said he couldn't trust nobody else tuh do it, only me. Yuh know, Mis' Reed, if yuh don't hand these agents the money, 'forehand yuh ain't got no kick comin' when they don't pay yuh.

MRS. REED. Well, yuh might uh tole me de number. 'Sposin' it had er come?

MAVIS. Steve's numbers don't never come. He ain't got no luck. He's a fool wastin' all that money.

MRS. REED. Ef he keeps it up, Honey, it's bound tuh come some time. It's when yuh drops 'em that dey comes right out. Whut number's Steve playin'?

MAVIS. 271.

MRS. REED. [*With a shriek.*] What? 271? My Gawd! Woman yuh's crazy! Crazy in love! Nutty!

MAVIS. Why, what's the matter?

MRS. REED. [*Angrily.*] You stan' thar an' tell me yuh doan know 271 hit ter-day?

MAVIS. [*In a dazed fashion.*] 271? But—Yuh's sure, Mis' Reed?

MRS. REED. [*Exasperated.*] Sure! Ef you ain't crazy Ah'd lak ter know! Ain't half uh Harlem seen it written on de sidewalks? Ain't yuh seen it in front uh Joe's?

MAVIS. [*Humbly.*] I forgot to look.

MRS. REED. How much yuh had on it fer yuhself?

MAVIS. [*Shaking her head.*] Nothin'. I doan play 'em no more. Bert's an agent, but I doan never play. I ain't got no luck. I played fifty cents with Bert fer Steve.

MRS. REED. Well! Ef you ain't a fool. Livin' right here in de house wid me an' never sayin' a word tuh me. We coulda cleaned up!

MAVIS. Yuh was sleepin' when I went out this mornin'. Gee! What a shame!

MRS. REED. [*Dropping her voice to a confidential tone.*] Say! Ah hope yuh ain't fool 'nuff tuh han' over all dat money ter Steve.

MAVIS. [*Quite taken back by the other's suggestion.*] But—but— Why, yes, Miss Reed. What yuh mean? It ain't my money. It belongs tuh Steve.

MRS. REED. [*Angrily.*] Like hell, it does—not! He didn't put dat money right in yuh han', did he? No! Well, he ain't got nuthin' tuh back up his case with. How he's gwine prove yuh put dat number in? Yuh'd be a darned fool not tuh put dat money in yuh pocket. Didn't yuh tell me t'other night yuh ain't got a cent? Thar ain't nobuddy knows 'bout dis but me, an' fer fifty bucks mah mouf'd stay shut de rest uh mah days. Whut yuh say?

MAVIS. [*Shaking her head firmly.*] Nothin' doin'! I ain't never played no skin game, yet! It's crooked, that's what!

MRS. REED. [*With withering scorn.*] Crooked! Say, who yuh think plays dis game on de level, anyhow? Dis ain't no square game. Everybuddy knows dat!

MAVIS. 'Tain't no use talkin', Mis' Reed. That money belong tuh Steve. He'll be lucky enough if he can collect off them fly bankers. That's all I'm worryin' 'bout.

MRS. REED. [*Incredulously.*] Yuh'd pass up five hundred—an' you gwine ter git married an' ain't got no money?

MAVIS. [*Stubbornly.*] I couldn't be happy knowin' I'd done Steve outa that money. He's always treated me on the level, an' he said he couldn't trust nobody but me tuh put that number in. Well, that's that! I'm only hopin' them bankers pay off. [*The door bell rings.*]

MRS. REED. Downstairs! Door's open. Well, Ah's gotta see dat money in Steve Collins' own han' 'fore Ah believes yuh could be such a fool. [*In answer to a loud knock, Mavis opens the door. A very dark man enters, carrying a brief-case. He is short and somewhat stout. His clothes are flashy, his manner breezy. He nods in the direction of Mrs. Reed and then turns towards Mavis.*]

MAVIS. [*Performing a necessary introduction.*] Mrs. Reed, meet Mr. Mitchell. Mr. Mitchell, my landlady.

MITCHELL. Delighted!

MRS. REED. Pleased, Ah'm sure!

MITCHELL. [*To Mavis.*] Well! Ah thought yuh'd be phonin' me long 'fore now. What's the matter? You doan look the least bit excited. Five cents ain't so bad, but fifty—Whew! Some haul, Ah'll tell the world! Only had a nickel on it mahself! Well, Mavis, yuh can't say Ah ain't treated yuh right. [*He opens the brief case and puts a package of money on the table. There are several small bills, but the greater part of the money is in small coins. Mrs. Reed's eyes almost pop out of her head.*]

MAVIS. It's awful good of you tuh bring it up so soon, Mitchell.

MITCHELL. Well, Ah doan grudge that boy nuthin'. He's bin plungin' fer more'n two months. Steve's game! Yuh shoulda put somethin' on it yuhself, Mavis. That's what Ah always do. Only a little, yuh know, but it helps.

MRS. REED. Did many people hit?

MITCHELL. Naw. Hardly anybody hit. That number weren't no favorite. It sure s'prise me Steve stuck tuh it so long. Well, yuh can't never tell.

MRS. REED. All de bankers payin' off on 271?

MITCHELL. Sure! Why?

MRS. REED. Oh, nuthin'.

MITCHELL. [*To Mavis.*] So yuh's goin' tuh get hitched ter-morrow?

MAVIS. Yes. Wish me luck, Mitch.

MITCHELL. All the luck in the world, kid! Bert's a lucky guy!

MRS. REED. [*With a sigh.*] Ah had a dream last night. Wish Ah knowed how tuh play it.

MITCHELL. Why'nt yuh see Aunt Sally? If she can't tell yuh straight, nobuddy kin.

MRS. REED. She ain't bin tellin' me straight fer some time. Reckon Ah needs another dream book.

MITCHELL. There ain't none like Sally. What'd yuh dream?

MRS. REED. Ah dream Ed an' me—Ed's mah fus husband'—Ah dream Ed an' me was lyin' in bed—

MITCHELL. Is he dead?

MRS. REED. Bin dead five years.

MITCHELL. That's 9.

MRS. REED. The door opened an' in walks Joe, mah secon' husban'—Lookin' mad tuh kill.

MITCHELL. Is he dead, too?

MRS. REED. Yeah. Died las' year.

MITCHELL. That's 2. Your number's 295. Play the combination an' yuh can't lose.

MRS. REED. Well, mebbe Ah'd better. [*She opens her purse, counts out some change and hands it to Mitchell who writes out a slip, gives her the original and pockets the duplicate.*]

MITCHELL. Guess Ah'll be hoppin' along. Got plenty stops tuh make. Anything fer you, Mavis?

MAVIS. Not ter-night, Mitch.

MITCHELL. Well, s'long! [*He goes out giving the door a breezy slam.*]

MRS. REED. Reckon Ah' oughta played one above an' one below— 296 an' 294. Mis' Hawley tole me las' night dat's how she come tuh hit. Played one above an' one below. [*She sighs deeply.*] Well, mebbe it won't come, nohow. Mah luck sho is gone back on me. [*Going up to the table and staring enviously at the little pile of money.*] Gee! It doan seem right dat we ain't gettin' a cent outa all dat money! Yuh won't take mah advice, Mavis, but yuh'll be sorry. See ef yuh ain't. [*The door bell rings.*]

MAVIS. [*Joyously.*] Mebbe it's Bert! [*She runs to the mirror and gives her hair a few hasty pats. There is a knock on the door and Mrs. Reed opens it to admit Bert Jackson. He is a tall thick-set fellow, rather good-looking in a heavy sort of way. His straight black hair is slicked to his head and highly polished. He scowls slightly as he sees Mrs. Reed.*]

MRS. REED. Come right in, Mr. Jackson!

BERT. [*To Mrs. Reed.*] Hello! Hot enough for you? [*He strides past her, takes Mavis in his arms and kisses her twice.*]

MRS. REED. [*Admiringly.*] Yuh's some shiek, ain't yuh!

MAVIS. [*Laughing.*] What's the matter, Mis' Reed? Jealous?

MRS. REED. Who, me? [*Mavis nods.*] Don't yuh believe it, Honey! Dis baby gets all de lovin' she can stand and doan yuh ferget it!

BERT. [*To Mavis.*] I see you're almost through packing.

MAVIS. Almost!

BERT. [*As he catches sight of the money on the table.*] Hello! Look at the coin! Somebody's rich around here!

MRS. REED. [*Fervently.*] Ah wish tuh Gawd we was!

MAVIS. It's Steve's money. Mitchell was up an' paid off!

BERT. Say, Mavis! I've had the devil's own luck!

MAVIS. [*Very much concerned.*] Why Bert, what happened? Sit down an' tell me.

BERT. There's nothing hurts me more'n a hard luck story. You know that slip I wrote Steve's number on? Well would you believe it, when I got to Miller's this morning, I found I didn't have Steve's slip! Hunted everywhere! Called up home and my landlady couldn't find it neither. Well then I called you and the operator said the line was busy.

MAVIS. [*Slowly.*] An'—an'—you didn't remember it, Bert? Yuh mighta remembered, when I only told yuh one number!

BERT. Gimme a chance, will you Honey? That's just what I tried to do! Neah as I could remember, it was 217. I remember the figures, but I clean forgot how you had 'em fixed!

MAVIS. [*In dismay.*] An' yuh didn't play nuthin'? Yuh mighta played the combination, Bert!

BERT. That's just what I did do! I put a dime on each. Of course I never had an idea 271 would hit! Too bad! I might have had something on it, myself! [*He takes a small roll of bills from his pocket and hands it to Mavis.*] Here you are! Sixty-seven to the good!

MRS. REED. Ah know it's de truth! [*Bert gives her an icy look.*]

MAVIS. It's too bad 'bout that slip, Bert! I can't see how yuh come tuh lose it! Reckon Steve'll be sore.

BERT. [*Lighting a cigarette.*] Steve ain't got no kick comin'. He's done pretty well, I should say!

MRS. REED. 'Deed he has! Ah was jes' tellin' Mavis, she's a fool handin' over all dat money tuh Steve.

BERT. Say, Mavis, how much did Steve make, anyhow?

MAVIS. Oh, I don't know. I haven't counted.

MRS. REED. Mr. Mitchell paid off on fifty cents, an' you jes' paid off on a dime.

BERT. Steve ain't got no kick coming. I say, Mrs. Reed, I'd like to speak to Mavis alone.

MRS. REED. [*Pulling her huge body slowly out of the arm chair.*] Ah get yuh! Ah jes' drop in fer a minute, anyhow. Thought

Mavis might need some help with 'er packin'. See yuh in de mornin', Mavis.

BERT. Good-night! [*He turns away impatiently, and Mrs. Reed withdraws with a last lingering look at the money on the table.*]. Darned old busy-body! Wonder if she planned to stay here all night!

MAVIS. She doan mean no harm, Bert. Let's ferget 'bout her! [*She pulls him down on the couch beside her and kisses him.*] Tell me somethin', Bert. I'm dyin' tuh know!

BERT. [*Returning her kisses with interest.*] What?

MAVIS. Where we goin', Bert? Yuh ain't tole me no plans.

BERT. An' I ain't telling you none, neither. Didn't I say it was going to be a surprise?

MAVIS. But Bert—

BERT. We're going to a little place in Jersey. Now, don't ask me where, for I ain't telling you.

MAVIS. Plenty colored people?

BERT. Nothing different! Wouldn't go no place else.

MAVIS. It ain't Asbury Park? Atlantic City?

BERT. I said a little place, didn't I?

MAVIS. Anyway, I'm goin' tuh love it. How long we goin' tuh stay, Bert?

BERT. A week, maybe two weeks, if you like it.

MAVIS. I'll love it! But Bert, what about my trunk? I doan know where tuh send it.

BERT. I'll send a feller for it first thing in the morning. He'll have a label ready. Don't worry. This is my surprise, and I ain't goin' to have it spoiled. Are you through packing?

MAVIS. I doan need tuh do no more ter-night.

BERT. Come on, then. Let's beat it. I'm hungry.

MAVIS. Where we goin', Bert?

BERT. Any place you say. How's Bamboo Inn?

MAVIS. Suits me! [*She jumps up just as the door bell rings.*] I wonder if that's fer me?

BERT. Ain't you had enough callers for one evening?

MAVIS. Well, I ain't stayin' in fer nobuddy.

BERT. Maybe it's Steve coming to bank his money. Wonder what took him to Philadelphia? He didn't say, did he?

MAVIS. Important business, he said. [*In answer to a knock on the door, Mavis admits Steve Collins. Steve is a slender brown skinned fellow with an appealing smile and a happy-go-lucky manner. His smile undergoes a perceptible change as he looks from Mavis to Bert.*]

STEVE. Hello, Mavis! [*He nods coolly in Bert's direction.*] Thought I'd find *you* here, but I wasn't sure.

MAVIS. Well, I suppose yuh's heard the good news, Steve?

STEVE. Meanin' 271?

MAVIS. Yes.

STEVE. Gotta thank you fer that, kid. I met Mitchell on the way here an' he told me he'd bin up. . . . You know what, Mavis, when I left Philly this evenin' I was dead broke.

MAVIS. Poor old Steve.

STEVE. Poor, nothin'! I've got five hundred dollars to the good, kid—thanks to you! I ain't likely to ferget that in a long time.

MAVIS. [*Unhappily.*] Steve—I—I got somethin' tuh tell yuh.

STEVE. Wait a minute! I got tuh tell you somethin', too. Bet yuh doan know what took me down tuh Philly?

MAVIS. No!

STEVE. [*To Bert.*] Give a guess!

BERT. Can't imagine! What?

STEVE. I had a hunch, see? An' I followed it! I never yet passed up a hunch. No Sir! Well, I had a hunch 'bout somethin' an' it led me straight tuh Philly an' I come across somethin' that near knocked me silly! Wait a minute an' I'll show yuh! [*He opens the hall door, returning almost immediately with a rather plump light-skinned young woman. She flashes a curious look at Mavis and a mocking one at Bert. Without waiting for an invitation she sits rather heavily, at the same time depositing a small overnight bag on the floor.*]

LUCINDA. Excuse me. I couldn't stand another minute. Guess you better introduce me, Mr. Collins.

STEVE. Mavis, this is Mis' Bert Jackson.

LUCINDA. Pleased to meet you, I'm sure. [*Mavis opens her mouth to speak but no sound comes.*]

STEVE. Reckon yuh doan need no introduction tuh yuh own husband, Mis' Jackson.

LUCINDA. Well, Bert, you sure don't look overjoyed to see me.

MAVIS. [*Running up to Bert and clutching his arm.*] It ain't true! Why'nt yuh give her the lie, Bert? Say it ain't true! [*But Bert does not answer. Mavis' hand falls to her side. She sways slightly and grasps at a chair for support. Steve holds out his hand to her but she draws sharply away.*]

LUCINDA. Fer Gawd's sake let's be sensible an' cut out all the fancy acting! [*To Bert.*] You oughta be caged, no foolin'! This ain't the first time you've tried this stuff, but it's the last time I'm gonna bother savin' you. You oughta be jailed, no foolin'! Ain't they got women enough in Harlem, without you staging another one of these fake weddings? I oughta let them send you up fer bigamy, I sure oughta!

MAVIS. Bert, it ain't true! Say it ain't true! [*Her voice fails suddenly on a sob.*]

LUCINDA. Say, I'm sorry fer you, kid, but it's all in the game. You ain't got nothing to cry about, take it from me! Bert is a no-good skunk if ever there was one. Mr. Collins here would make a dozen Berts with plenty left over to spare. He paid me fifty dollars to come over here an' put you wise. Bert ain't all there, if you ask me. . . . Well, I'm going, Mr. Collins. Guess there ain't nothing else I can do around here.

STEVE. Don't you want tuh take along yuh daddy?

LUCINDA. Be your age! [*She looks kindly down at the weeping Mavis.*] Say, kid, have a good time, an' don't be rushing after no husband. Take it from me! I didn't pick no daisy, I'll tell the world! [*With a final look of contempt in Bert's direction, Lucinda goes out. Steve looks from Bert to Mavis and back again to Bert. The latter appears to have recovered his poise now that his better half has departed. He takes a menacing step toward Steve.*]

BERT. I'll get you for this, you dirty sneak! Get outa here, quick, 'fore I knock you clean through that window!

STEVE. [*Derisively.*] I doan believe yuh, but say it again.

BERT. Clear out, I tell you!

STEVE. Suppose we put it up tuh Mavis?

MAVIS. [*Springing to her feet.*] Get out, both of yuh!

BERT. Lemme stay, Mavis. You ain't gimme no chance to set things right. I gotta explain—

MAVIS. [*Hotly.*] Yuh had yuh chance tuh explain an' yuh didn't take it! Now beat it, both of yuh!

STEVE. I'll go, Mavis. I know yuh's sore at what I done, but I couldn't a' done no different. I knowed Bert weren't on the level.

MAVIS. How'd yuh know so much? Yuh never tole me nothin'!

STEVE. Swell chance I woulda had makin' you believe. Well, I had a hunch an' a feller give me a tip 'bout goin' tuh Philly.

BERT. [*Savagely.*] What feller—

STEVE. Roy Davis—a feller yuh done outa some number money. Well, he had it in fer you an' squealed, that's all.

BERT. Davis lied. I ain't never done nobody outa no money.

STEVE. Well, I ain't got no kick coming 'long as yuh comes across with my dough. [*He walks to the table.*] This my winnings, Mavis?

MAVIS. Yes. That's what was give me. Mitchell paid up on fifty cents, but Bert said he lost yuh slip an' couldn't remember the number. He only played the combination for ten cents.

STEVE. [*In a low voice.*] But yuh gave him the fifty cents? Yuh seen him write down the number?

MAVIS. Yes. I got my duplicate.

STEVE. Yuh doan believe he lost that slip, do yuh, Mavis. [*Mavis does not answer but walks to the window and looks out into the night. Bert walks up to her and tries to take her hand but she repulses him.*]

BERT. You know I ain't no thief, don't you, Mavis? [*A low laugh breaks from Steve who has backed up against the door and drawn a revolver. Bert whirls angrily about to find himself being covered by Steve's weapon.*]

STEVE. Put up yuh hands an' be damned quick about it! [*Bert hesitates, looking at Mavis.*] Up with 'em or by Gawd! I'll rip yuh pockets open with the first shot! [*Bert puts his hands up.*] Now, Mavis look through his pockets! [*Mavis hesitates.*] I got a hunch that money's layin right in his pocket. [*Still Mavis does not move.*] Hold this gun, Mavis, an' I'll do the lookin'. Yuh owes it to him, Mavis, to prove that I'm wrong. [*Very reluctantly, Mavis takes the gun from Steve and keeps it aimed at Bert, while Steve looks through the latter's pockets.*]

BERT. Drop that gun, Mavis. I'm being robbed! [*Suddenly Steve holds up a roll of bills.*]

STEVE. [*Triumphantly.*] I knew it!

BERT. That's mine! That's my money!

STEVE. [*Taking the gun from Mavis and handing her the money.*] Count it!

BERT. [*In a choked voice.*] I'll get you for this! I'll get you for this!

STEVE. [*Coldly.*] Next time yuh see me yuh'd better run! How much, Mavis?

MAVIS. A hundred an' eighty-three dollars.

STEVE. Put it on the table. [*She obeys.*] Now, you skip along, big boy, an' watch yuh step! Try any funny business an' yuh friends'll be playin' yuh hearse number 'fore the week's out. Keep outa my way, an' doan lemme see yuh hangin' round Mavis! [*Without another word, Bert slinks out of the room. Steve returns the revolver to his pocket. He goes up to the table, takes up several bills and thrusts them into his pocket. Mavis watches him in silence.*]

STEVE. [*Cheerfully.*] Fifty-fifty! I've got mine, Mavis, and here's yours. Better put it away.

MAVIS. [*Bitterly.*] Think I'd touch a cent of it?

STEVE. Well, why not? Half's yours. Say, who played this number for me, anyway.

MAVIS. I wouldn' touch a cent. I had enough trouble 'bout that money. Pick it up an' clear out.

STEVE. [*With a grin.*] Can't do either one. The money's yours an' I ain't gonna leave yuh here tuh cry yuh eyes out. Nothin' doin'!

MAVIS. [*Fiercely.*] *You* done it all! *You* spoiled everything! Yuh think I hate Bert, doan yuh? Well, I don't, see? I love him!

STEVE. [*Incredulously.*] You love him *now,* knowin' everything?

MAVIS. Yes, an' hate *you.*

STEVE. Alright. If yuh love him go ahead an' have him. His wife doan care none. I wasn't gonna see him put anything over on you, that's all. . . . Gawd, but you wimmen 'er queer!

[*Mavis slips out of her smock. She puts on her hat and takes her pocketbook. Steve watches her miserably.*]

STEVE. Where yuh goin', Mavis?

MAVIS. To hell, fer all I care!

STEVE. [*Instantly more cheerful.*] Come on. I'm with yuh.

MAVIS. I ain't gonna stand much more from you. Clear out, I tell yuh!

STEVE. Nix. You're up against it, kid, that's why yuh feel that way. How do I know? Say, my head ain't all wood! Ain't I bin up against it too, pretty near all my life? I like yuh, kid. Honest. First time I saw yuh I knew yuh was on the level. I wouldn't a' butted in if I hadn't knowed yuh was on the level.

MAVIS. Wish I'd never seen yuh! I shoulda lied 'bout puttin' in that number an' gyped all, jes' like Bert was gyping some.

STEVE. You couldn't do it kid. 'Sides yuh didn't need tuh. Half that money goes tuh you anyway.

MAVIS. I wouldn't touch a cent!

STEVE. Bet yuh ain't got a cent? Spent all gettin' clothes fer yuh weddin'.

MAVIS. Yuh mind yuh own business.

STEVE. Bet yuh ain't got nothin' tuh pay yuh room rent.

MAVIS. I wish tuh Gawd I'd never seen yuh!

STEVE. Well, yuh can't help it. Yuh did see me. [*Hopefully.*] Say, yuh wouldn't marry me instead 'er Bert, would yuh?

MAVIS. [*With withering scorn.*] You doan hate yuhself, do yuh?

STEVE. Well, alright. Now get this. Yuh's plannin' tuh stay in here an' cry yuh eyes out. Mrs. Reed'll know yuh's bin jilted an' ain't got no money.

MAVIS. It ain't none 'er yo' business!

STEVE. Or mebbe yuh's plannin' tuh go tuh Bert, anyhow, 'spite uh what he's done tuh yuh.

MAVIS. It ain't none uh yo' business, what I'm plannin' tuh do!

STEVE. [*Grimly.*] I'm makin' it my business! If yuh goes tuh Bert, I'm gonna empty that gun uh mine on him, so help me Gawd! [*Mavis looks up startled. A pleading note replaces the sternness in Steve's voice.*] Yuh's angry an' yuh's hurt. Sure! Doan I know it? Now I've got five hundred dollars an' half of it's yours fer bein' on the level an' puttin' in that number fer me. If it hadn't come, I'd a' bin broke, flat. Bert's wife got my last fifty. Well, I'm flush now, see? You take what's comin' tuh yuh, kid, an' buck up. Ferget 'bout Bert an' have a good time. Why'nt yuh go home an' see yuh folks fer a spell?

MAVIS. I wish tuh Gawd I could, but—[*She turns away with a hopeless gesture.*]

STEVE. Well, you start ter-morrow. We're goin' fifty-fifty on this. Say yuh didn't leave a boy friend down in Raleigh, did yuh?

MAVIS. I couldn't never pay you back.

STEVE. Yuh doan have to. Say, yuh know I'm dead gone on yuh, Mavis. Yuh wouldn't never let me spend nothin' on yuh when I took yuh out, an' I ain't never give yuh a present. Now you take that money an' go home. I'll look after little Bertie an' see he doan die of a broken heart.

MAVIS. You—you—why Steve, you's a fool. A fool! Yuh knows the chances are you won't never see me no more. I won't come back.

STEVE. Rot. The chances are yuh won't stay home a month. Why kid, yuh couldn't stay away from Harlem on a bet. Not Harlem! No sir! An' say if yuh ain't back in a month, doan be surprised tuh see little Stevie crossin' the Mason Dixon tuh see an old pal!

MAVIS. Steve, I can't go! I'm ashamed! I wrote tuh tell them I was gonna get married. I didn' write 'till yesterday, when I was sure. I can't go! I can't! [*She throws herself on the day bed and sobs—slow, body-racking sobs. Steve's right hand goes into his pocket with a sudden thrust. Without a word he moves toward the door. As he turns the knob, Mavis springs up, runs toward him and seizes him by the arm.*]

MAVIS. Come back, Steve. Yuh's crazy tuh think uh such a thing!

STEVE. I gotta! [*He shakes her off.*]

MAVIS. Steve! Gimme that gun!

STEVE. No!

MAVIS. I'll go home, Steve! Honest! I'll do anything yuh say, but fer Gawd's sake, doan do no killin'. Steve! Please! Steve!

STEVE. Alright.

MAVIS. Yuh mean it?

STEVE. I said alright, didn't I?

MAVIS. But—I wish yuh'd smile, Steve. Yuh face doan look natural, not smilin'.

STEVE. [*Smiling.*] Well, what next?

MAVIS. Gimme that gun, Steve.

STEVE. [*Hands her the revolver. Mavis takes out the cartridges and puts the revolver into a drawer of her trunk. Steve watches her and smiles again.*] Now you do something fer me.

MAVIS. What?

STEVE. Put some powder on yuh face an' come on.

MAVIS. [*Obeying.*] Where we goin', Steve?

STEVE. We're goin' tuh a cabaret an' we're gonna dance an' dance an' then dance some more. Darned if I ain't thirsty, too. An' I doan mean maybe. [*He picks up the money on the table and crams it into Mavis' purse. Suddenly he laughs happily—joyously. Mavis stares at him in astonishment.*]

MAVIS. What yuh laughin' at, Steve?

STEVE. I was jes' thinkin', if I ain't the lucky guy, hittin' that number like that an'—an' everything! But I had a hunch! Say, Mavis?

MAVIS. What? [*She closes her trunk and locks it.*]

STEVE. [*Opening the hall door and looking around at Mavis.*] I have a hunch we're gonna have a bang up time. No foolin'!

MAVIS. [*Looking around the room.*] Got everything?

STEVE. I'll tell the world, I have!

MAVIS. [*Switching off the lights.*] Alright. Let's go!

STEVE. [*Joyously.*] An' I doan mean maybe!

[*The hall door closes and the key is turned in the lock.*]

(CURTAIN)

THE STARTER

A COMEDY OF HARLEM LIFE

BY EULALIE SPENCE

CHARACTERS

T.J. KELLY
FIRST WOMAN
SECOND WOMAN
GEORGIA

Scene: *Present-day Harlem.*
Time: *A summer evening.*

THE STARTER

AT RISE: THOMAS JEFFERSON KELLY *is sprawled upon the bench, his straw hat on one side, his coat on the other. T. J. KELLY as he signs himself, is reading a copy of "The News." From time to time, he chuckles, mutters aloud, whistles or hums in a low baritone. T. J. KELLY's face is the most important thing that ever happened to him. For the rest, T. J. is tall, dapper and in love.*

T. J. KELLY. Holy gee! What d'ye know 'bout that! (*He stares a bit, then turns the page*) Um! Some looker! Hello! 'Woman gives Birth To Four Healthy Sons'! Gee! A male quartet! Four! . . . 'Father Overjoyed!' Like hell, he is! (T. J. *throws the paper on the ground in disgust*) Gee! Suppose something like that was to happen to me! (T. J. *grabs his coat and hat and prepares for flight. Suddenly he stops short, laughing sheepishly. He resumes his seat. He takes his hat off and places it on the bench*) Reckon them things only happen to furriners. Sure! (T. J. *whistles a few lines from "'Tain't Gonna Rain No Mo'." Two tired looking women trudge into view. They stop short and look at* T. J. *in exasperation.*)

148

FIRST WOMAN. (*Mopping her face with a handkerchief*) Any wonder we kain't find no place tuh set? Looka him sprawlin' on dat bench, will yuh? Gawd, it's hot!

SECOND WOMAN. (*Addresing* T.J. KELLY) Say, move up, will yuh? Yuh ain't go' no lease on dat bench. . . .

T. J. KELLY. (*With a provoking grin*) Reserved! (*He spreads both arms along the back of the bench.*)

FIRST WOMAN. (*With a snort*) Reserved! Kin yuh beat dat fer nerve, Mis' Clark?

SECOND WOMAN. Ah should say not! (*To* T. J. KELLY) Take yo' arms off dat bench, you loafin' nigger!

T. J. KELLY. (*Calmly*) Now, see here Angel face, and you too, Grape Nuts! Ah know you're both dying for a real live hug from an honest tuh goodness he-man. Well, come on an' get it. I won't charge you nothing.

FIRST WOMAN. (*Indignantly*) Kin yuh beat it?

SECOND WOMAN. (*Angrily*) Ah like yo' gall!

T. J. KELLY. (*Pleasantly*) They all do! You're not the only one!

FIRST WOMAN. A woman kain't walk tru dis park no mo', 'thout bein' insulted!

SECOND WOMAN. Aw, come on, Mrs. Henry! Ah would'n' set thar now ef he was tuh scrub de whole bench—

FIRST WOMAN. Me neither. (*They turn scornfully away and walk on.*)

T. J. KELLY. (*Hums audibly*)

> Honey! Say doan' yuh know
> Honey! Ah love yuh so—
> Yuh's cute, yuh's sweet
> Yuh's mighty fine—
> Sweeter dan de watermelon hangin' on de vine.

(*A pretty brown girl in a light dress comes along the path from the direction in which the women are walking. She merely glances at their angry faces and passes on. They stop and look back at her. As she approaches* T. J. KELLY, *he rises, makes an elaborate bow and sweeps his belongings to one side. Then* T.J. KELLY *kisses the girl, Valentino-fashion. The women stand and stare.*)

FIRST WOMAN. Brazen!

SECOND WOMAN. Hussy! (*They pass on.*)

GEORGIA. (*With her very first breath*) Say, T. J., did yuh see them ole hens stare?

T. J. KELLY. No. I couldn't see nothin' but you, then, Honey.

GEORGIA. Well, they sure did stare! Reckon they was jealous all right!

T. J. KELLY. Not a doubt of it!

GEORGIA. Say, yuh doan' hate yuhself, do you?

T. J. KELLY. Naw! 'Tain't no use hating the person you have to live with.

GEORGIA. Meanin' who?

T. J. KELLY. Meaning me—Thomas Jefferson Kelly—at your service.

GEORGIA. Oh! (*She moves away, the length of the bench.*)

T. J. KELLY. Say, what's the idea of moving down there?

GEORGIA. Yuh gets along pretty well by yuhself—doan' yuh?

T. J. KELLY. Sure, but I gets along better when you're around. (*He reaches out and draws her close to him.*)

GEORGIA. (*Leaning against his shoulder*) 'Twas a helluva day, T. J. (*She sighs.*)

T. J. KELLY. It sure was! Ninety in the shade! To see the way people shop in all this hot weather! I don't see how they do it! I have to stand there by that cage till I'm ready to drop! An' talk about dumb-bells! Why those birds can't read, some of them. They stand by an elevator marked "down" an' expects it to go up— and other way 'round! An' the fool questions they asks! Gee! To think of all my education being lost on those people!

GEORGIA. Poor T. J. Yuh's had too much schoolin'—that's whut's the matter with yuh—

T. J. KELLY. (*Fully launched upon his grievances*) Two terms in High School, and don't you forget it. . . . Funny—me standing there in a Palm Beach suit with brass buttons, an' a hat to match with more brass buttons! Sometimes a man gets to thinkin'—Here I am a starter—a starter—just one step better'n the man who runs the cage—Gee! *That's* a helluva job?

GEORGIA. It sure is! I'm glad yuh's a starter, T. J.

T. J. KELLY. (*Bitterly*) Yeh! But there's something about the name that don't just hit me right. Starter! Starter! It seems to get over into a man's life—somehow—starter!

GEORGIA. (*Sitting up wide-eyed*) Gee! That's funny!

T. J. KELLY. Is it? Well, I don't just see the point—that's all.

GEORGIA. Why T. J.—yuh knows Ah does sewin' doan yuh? (*T. J. nods*) Well, Ah ain't never tole yuh 'bout mah place 'cause it's so low-down. Eyetalians and Jews and colored—all in tergether. It's a dump. Well, I'm what they calls a Finisher. Finisher on dresses! See? That's whut Ah meant—You bein' a Starter and me a Finisher!

T. J. KELLY. (*Giving a loud laugh*) Holy gee! That's a good one! Say, Georgia, we'd make a good team—we would. (*He gives her a tight hug.*)

GEORGIA. (*Pleased*) Quit yuh kiddin'.

T. J. KELLY. No kiddin'. Y'know, kid, I bin thinkin'—Say, why don't we get married? Huh?

GEORGIA. Ah dunno, 'cept yuh never mentioned it befo'.

T. J. KELLY. Well, I'm mentioning it now. See? Think it over, kid. Well, what's the answer?

GEORGIA. (*Slowly*) Has yuh got any money, T. J.?

T. J. KELLY. (*With an injured air*) Money! Say! Have a heart! That's a fine question.

GEORGIA. (*Slyly*) Fer a starter!

T. J. KELLY. (*Suspiciously*) Say—are you making fun of me?

GEORGIA. Co'se not, T. J.!

T. J. KELLY. Well, you're taking your time 'bout answering—ain't yuh?

GEORGIA. How much yuh got saved, T. J.?

T. J. KELLY. (*Frowning*) Ain't that a little personal, Honey?

GEORGIA. Ah doan' think so—but co'se ef yuh doan' feel like sayin'—

T. J. KELLY. I have fifty-five dollars! That's not so bad for—

GEORGIA. Fer a *starter!* (*She draws away from him coldly*) Yuh mean yuh ain't got mo'n fifty-five dollars an' you wukin' steady?

T. J. KELLY. An' me dressing like a gentleman an' paying dues in a club an' two Societies an' a Lodge? An' taking you to the theatre twice a week—

GEORGIA. *Movies*—an' doan' yuh ferget it!

T. J. KELLY. (*Angrily*) So, that's how you feel about it—is it? Don't I take you to dances? Didn't we go to Coney last week and a

151

cabaret Monday night? How the devil you expect me to have money?

GEORGIA. (*Coldly*) Nobuddy asked yuh nothin' 'bout marryin'—you's the one mentioned it—

T. J. KELLY. Sure, but that don't give you no right to ask 'bout my bank account. Reckon you wouldn't say how much *you've* got in your bank.

GEORGIA. Well, sence yuh's dyin' tuh fine out—

T. J. KELLY. (*Angrily*) Who—me?

GEORGIA. Sence yuh's dyin' ter know—Ah's got two hundred dollars!

T. J. KELLY. Whew! (*Almost immediately he recovers his air of superiority*) Well, that ain't so much!

GEORGIA. Mo'n you's got!

T. J. KELLY. (*Reflectively*) Two hundred dollars! Say, you know what, Georgia? That's enough money to start on. We could get a nice room—Why I've got a peachuva room. An' we could get new fixings—pay down a deposit, you know. I could arrange all that at the store. They know me—Two hundred dollars ain't so bad! Say! Say—many a man's got married on less!

GEORGIA. Yuh ain't sayin' nuthin' 'bout yo' fifty-five—

T. J. KELLY. Fifty-five's all right—as a starter—but it ain't nothing for a man to talk about.

GEORGIA. An' whut 'bout a ring, T. J.?

T. J. KELLY. A ring! (*He looks the picture of dismay.*)

GEORGIA. (*Sarcastically*) Yuh ain't never heard 'bout that befo' has yuh?

T. J. KELLY. Sure—but—Well,—Oh, all right! I'll get you a ring—a beauty, too, get me?

GEORGIA. See here, boy friend! Ah'm a regular girl! An' Ah knows a Woolworth Special when Ah sees one!

T. J. KELLY. (*Indignantly*) Say, d'you think I'd put a Woolworth over on you? How d'you get that way?

GEORGIA. Reckon it's frum 'sociatin' wid them Jews an' Eyetalians. Say, those folks sure wears diamonds.

T. J. KELLY. (*Incredulously*) To work?

GEORGIA. Sure!

T. J. KELLY. Fake, that's all!

GEORGIA. Fake nuthin'!

T. J. KELLY. Well, kid, what d'you say?

GEORGIA. Ah dunno, T. J. (*She sighs once more*) Ah was reckonin' on that two hundred fer rainy weather—(T. J. *whistles a bar or two from "'Tain't Gonna Rain no Mo'"*) In mah business thar's plenty rainy weather. Las' year Ah was outa wuk altogether four months.

T. J. KELLY. (*Aghast*) What? How come?

GEORGIA. Laid off. Nuthin' doin'—It's a reg'lar thing in mah line— dull season—strikes—union dues—

T. J. KELLY. But you could always find something else, couldn't you?

GEORGIA. Naw. Wuk's slack every place. An' then's the time Ah needs mah savin's.

T. J. KELLY. How 'bout waitress in some nice—

GEORGIA. Nuthin' doin'. Ah ain't no hash slinger!

T. J. KELLY. You're mighty fussy ain't you?

GEORGIA. Ef we got married yuh would'n' mind mah stayin' home when things was slow, would yuh, T. J. (T. J. *swallows painfully*) Gee, it would be great tuh be able tuh stay in bed mornin's. Yuh know, T. J., the thought uh hittin' de chillies has driv' plenty into matrimony befo' now. Gee! Tuh lie in bed on a cole winter mornin' when de sleet an' rain er batterin' at de winders!

T. J. KELLY. (*Impatiently*) Fer Gawd's sake, woman—

GEORGIA. (*Startled out of her dreaming*) What the matter, T. J.?

T. J. KELLY. (*Irritably*) Say—all this talk 'bout cold and sleet—an' stayin' in bed—Gee! It's enough to give a man cold feet.

GEORGIA. Cole feet! Well, if yuh has cole feet, now's the time tuh say so! (*She rises.* T. J. KELLY *grasps her hand. He draws her down again.*)

T. J. KELLY. Say, it's a fine way to spoil a good night—talkin' 'bout winter mornings—(*He kisses her*) Looka there, Honey!

GEORGIA. (*Reluctantly*) Whar?

T. J. KELLY. (*Pointing*) Over there. Going to be a moon to-night.

GEORGIA. Sure 'nuff.

T. J. KELLY. Not so bad! An' looka there Honey!

GEORGIA. Whar?

T. J. KELLY. (*Pointing*) Down there! All those lights an' those people an' this park—We owns the whole show!

GEORGIA. Quit yuh kiddin'.

T. J. KELLY. Gawd, Harlem sure is great! Looka them lights!

GEORGIA. Say, T. J.? (*She sits upright as though she has just remembered something.*)

T. J. KELLY. What you thinkin', Honey?

GEORGIA. Is we engaged?

T. J. KELLY. (*Annoyed*) Lawd! Do we have to go all over that? (*In a kindlier tone*) Keep yuh eyes on them lights, Honey an'—an' forget it. (*The park is very much darker now.* GEORGIA'S *head snuggles up against* T. J.'s *shoulder. His arm slips about her waist. The Moon-man hangs his lantern in the heavens, and we do the only kindly thing we can think of. We draw the Curtain.*)

CURTAIN

HOT STUFF

EULALIE SPENCE

CHARACTERS

FANNY KING: *The "Red Hot" Mama*
MARY GREEN: *Fanny's Friend*
JOHN COLE: *A Numbers Addict*
JENNIE BARBOUR: *John's Girlfriend*
ISADORE GOLDSTEIN: *A Jew*
WALTER KING: *The "Red Hot" Mama's "Daddy" (Husband)*

SCENE

The living room in Fanny's flat. The furnishings are simple and in good taste. A full length mirror is at left, and a door opening upon the hallway. At right, two windows overlook the street. Heavy portieres at center back separate the living room from the bedroom.

TIME

The present. About eight o'clock on a winter's night.

AT RISE: FANNY is sitting at a table busily assorting slips of paper. Her friend, MARY GREEN, is sitting close by waiting patiently for FANNY to finish what she is doing. FANNY's beauty is a kind called "striking." Large, flashing black eyes, small mouth, regular features and slick bobbed head. Her skin is a golden brown; her figure sensuous to a fault. MARY GREEN is very good-looking, slender and very fair. Although she is rouged and painted every bit as much as FANNY, she lacks the warmth and vividness of the latter's personality.

FANNY: *(looking at a slip)* Reg'lar Dumb Dora—this one! Plays high everyday, never sticks to a number and raises a helluva noise when they come the day she drops 'em! *(She adds the slip*

155

to her little pile.) Say, there's easy money in this game, Mary. I'm thinkin' uh droppin' the other, pretty soon if my luck keeps up! An' talk 'bout suckers! Believe me, it's here you find them.

MARY: Guess nobuddy can put anything over on you, Fanny.

FANNY: I'd like to see 'em try—just once!

MARY: I ain't got no luck in this game. It gets me how some people make out so well!

FANNY: I don't lose nuthin'; you take it from me. *(She slaps the last slip on the pile.)* Well, that's that! Good day for little Fanny.

MARY: How much?

FANNY: Two hundred fifty!

MARY: My Gawd! Ain't you a lucky kid! Gee! It makes me sick hearing you rattle off hundreds like that! How d'ye do it?

FANNY: Secrets of the trade. You gotta be on the inside! Say . . . who was that six foot sheik you was with at Craig's last night?

MARY: Bill Hogan! Met him in Atlantic City . . . doctor's convention last summer.

FANNY: I know it's the truth! He ain't a doctor, is he?

MARY: He ain't nothing but! Dr. Bill Hogan!

FANNY: Well, what d'ye know! Some looker!

MARY: An' that ain't all!

FANNY: I know he don't hang out round here . . .

MARY: Naw. No such luck. He comes from out West. He's only here for a week on business.

FANNY: Well, I know you're steppin' fast while he's here. I tried to get to your table but I didn't have a ghost of a chance. Walter was along an' you know what that means. A wasted evening! Try an' have some fun with a husband like mine dangling at your elbow.

MARY: Where's Walter tonight?

FANNY: He's gone to Brooklyn to see a feller 'bout a deal. He won't be back till late.

MARY: Well, I got a date myself. Gimme twenty-five pair, Fanny. Ten flesh, five black an' ten nude.

FANNY: Right! Don't know if I got ten flesh, though. *(She opens the drawer of a cabinet in the room and takes out a quantity of silk stockings.)* No, I ain't got but five flesh. You better take five uh these parchment. They're the latest.

MARY: All right. *(She examines the stockings.)* Reg'lar two fifty or I'm a liar.

FANNY: Nothing but! One thing about you, Mary, you sure does know good stuff when you see it!

MARY: An' it don't stop at stockings. I'll tell the world. *(She hands FANNY some bills.)* Twenty-five!

FANNY: Right! *(She tucks the bills in her dress.)* How much you lettin' 'em go at, Mary? I get a dollar sixty-five for the one's I sell.

MARY: That ain't hot enough for my customers. I can't charge more'n a dollar fifty. If I do, they say the price is cold—an' won't buy. Too much competition in this line. *(She puts the stockings in a small black satchel.)*

FANNY: Well, I have a side line, so it's different for me! I don't sell a single dress less'n fifteen.

MARY: An' they're worth forty every one of 'em. Well, kid, I'm off. Dr. Bill ain't got but one more day.

FANNY: What you done with Jack this last week?

MARY: Jack's outa town. Back Sunday!

FANNY: I get you.

MARY: S'long!

FANNY: S'long kid! *(As the door closes on MARY, FANNY picks up the stockings and returns them to the cabinet. The telephone rings. FANNY sits beside the table, takes the phone from beneath the rose tafetta flounces of a tall white-haired doll.)* Hello? Yes, this is Mis' King. What number you say? 429? Yes. 429. Ten cents on the combination. That's sixty cents. All right, Mis' Harris! No, I won't forget! Goodbye! *(She writes the number on a pad and is about to turn away when the phone rings once more.)* Who is it? Oh, that you honey? Not tonight! I'm tired, kid! . . . Well . . . Where we goin'? Half past nine at the usual place! Gone to Brooklyn, won't be back till eleven. I'll leave a note. Oh, Walter won't mind! I'll tell him Mary and me have gone to the theater. Naw . . . Walter don't snoop! If he did I wouldn't live with him five minutes. S'long, kid! *(She hangs up the receiver. There is a knock at the door, and FANNY admits JOHN COLE. COLE is a rather short, dark fellow with a jerky, nervous way of speaking. FANNY freezes instantly at the sight of him and closes the door with a little slam.)* Well? You got my message, didn't you?

COLE: Yes, Mis' King, but I couldn't believe it.

FANNY: Well, it's true. Of course, I'm awful sorry. If I knew any way I could help you out I sure would.

COLE: But . . . *(He swallows convulsively.)* Mis' King, I don't want to make no trouble, but . . .

FANNY: You better not! The idea!

COLE: Two hundred an' fifty dollars! You can't mean it.

FANNY: See here, I'm sorry, darned sorry. If I'd a seen your slip, I'd a played it. Why wouldn't I? I ain't no thief, am I? I dropped that paper. I don't know how I coulda done it! It ain't never happened before. Of course, I'll give you back your fifty cents.

COLE: *(with a gesture of protest)* Fifty cents! Don't talk of fifty cents! I gotta have that money. Mis' King! I gotta have my winnings!

FANNY: *(harshly)* See here! I know you're excited an' all that, but I won't stand fer no funny talk! You gotta have your money! What money! You ain't got no money! You ain't got no winnings!

COLE: *(fiercely)* I believe you took 'em! You ain't honest! You're lyin'! They told me you was like that, but I didn't believe 'em.

FANNY: Now you get outa here! Get right out! The idea! The very idea! *(She opens the door.)* You get right out!

COLE: *(walking to the door)* I'll go, but I ain't done with this. *(He plucks desperately at the band of his hat.)* Nobuddy's gonna rob me an' get away with it. *(FANNY slams the door after him.)*

FANNY: Well, if he ain't got gall! Hm. His two hundred and fifty! Try'n collect, you nut! *(She goes into the adjoining room and returns with an evening gown. She places it over a chair. The doorbell rings. FANNY goes close to the door and calls.)* Who is it?

FEMALE VOICE FROM WITHOUT: Customer, Mis' King.

FANNY: *(opening the door)* Hello! I can't seem to remember you. *(She looks keenly at the newcomer.)*

JENNIE: I ain't bin here before! A friend uh mine told me you had some pretty dresses. Have you got any more left.

FANNY: Sure. Come in. I got some just your size. *(She closes the door and motions toward the bedroom.)* Step right in here, will you?

JENNIE: *(She is a small dark girl with a sharp decisive quality about her voice.)* Just a minute, Mis' King. You're a number agent, ain't you?

FANNY: Yes. You want to play a number?

JENNIE: *(coldly)* Listen, I didn't come here 'bout no dresses . . .

FANNY: *(slowly)* Oh! Well, what the devil did you come fer?

JENNIE: John Cole's a friend uh mine—

FANNY: *(with a slight sneer)* Oh! Very interesting! He sent you to collect for him, did he?

JENNIE: No. I told him I'd come and collect. An' what's more, I'm goin' to keep my promise.

FANNY: *(sharply)* I ain't got no time to waste on you.

JENNIE: You'se got time to hand over that money.

FANNY: Try an' get it! You make me laugh, you do! *(She takes a seat, crosses her legs in a leisurely fashion and surveys the other insolently.)*

JENNIE: Mebbe yuh won't laugh when yuh hears what I gotta say.

FANNY: Say, are you as looney as your boyfriend?

JENNIE: *(angrily)* Yuh can steal all the silk dresses an' stockings yuh wants—I don't care! But when it comes to stealin' cold cash what don't belong to yuh, that's where I take a hand!

FANNY: Well, of all th—

JENNIE: Listen to me! I work in the same building with Walter King. I know the name of the firm he works for. Want to know their name? See yuh don't. Well, yuh shipping clerk daddy ain't pinin' to go up the river, is he?

FANNY: *(springing to her feet)* How dare you! Get outa here, right now, you dirty little . . .

JENNIE: Cut that! I know two people who bought dresses from yuh. They're friends uh mine. Do yuh want 'em to go down to twenty-eighth street with me as witnesses?

FANNY: That kinda bluff won't go here. You got some nerve, I'll tell the world!

JENNIE: Not more'n you'se got.

FANNY: Get outa here! You don't know nothing! Think you're smart, don't you?

JENNIE: Saltzberg and Olinsky. Fifth floor—I work on the sixth. If you don't come across, I'll be there first thing in the mornin'.

FANNY: You can go to hell for all I care—

JENNIE: *(walking over to the door)* All right. I see it suits you if your daddy takes a long rest in the cooler. But lemme tell yuh somethin' kid: he won't go alone. You're his accomplice an' yuh'll get yours same ez him! *(She opens the door, but FANNY, after a moment's hesitation, runs up to her and lays a detaining hand on her arm.)*

FANNY: Close that door.

JENNIE: What fer?

FANNY: I want to tell you somethin'.

JENNIE: *(closing the door)* Well? There's only one thing I'm willin' to hear.

FANNY: I'll give you the money. I can't afford to have you squeal. How do I know you won't tell no how?

JENNIE: Yuh don't know. But you got my word that I won't. I ain't no liar.

FANNY: You might. Just to get even.

JENNIE: I ain't got no love fer Saltzberg and Olinsky, an' I ain't got none fer you. But just the same, I ain't one fer doin' my own people like some folks I know.

FANNY: *(opens the cabinet once more. She takes out a roll of money and hands it to JENNIE.)* Just like it come in.

JENNIE: All right! I'll give it to John. This is a losin' game anyhow, but it could be played on the level. *(She goes out.)*

FANNY: *(closes the cabinet with a slam. She taps impatiently with her neatly slippered foot.)* Dirty little shine! She'd a done it too! *(She snatches up the evening dress and moves toward the bedroom. There is a discreet knock at the door. FANNY throws the dress over the chair once more and opens the street door with an angry jerk. On the threshold stands ISADORE GOLDSTEIN, a Jewish peddlar of questionable reputation. He is good-looking, sleek, possessing an ingratiating smile and a familiar manner. In his hand he carries a briefcase.)*

FANNY: *(shortly)* Well?

GOLDSTEIN: I got something what you should see.

FANNY: Beat it. I don't want nuthin'. *(She makes a movement to slam the door.)*

GOLDSTEIN: *(staying the door with his hand)* Why you should be so mean to me? A good friend of yours, Miss Green, she tells me . . .

FANNY: I ain't got no money to buy nothing.

GOLDSTEIN: I ain't ask you should buy what you don't see.

FANNY: *(stepping aside)* Well, come in an' be quick about it. I gotta go out.

GOLDSTEIN: *(opening his suitcase)* I got something here what is such a bargain you never see. Now, wait! I know you know good stuff. Miss Green she tell me you good picker. Now . . . What you say? *(He shakes out a beautiful ermine wrap.)* I see already you like it. Well, try it on.

FANNY: Gee, it's a beauty! *(She strokes the fur lovingly.)*

GOLDSTEIN: Try it on. It don't cost you nuthin' to try it on. *(He places the wrap about FANNY's shoulders. She glides up to the mirror and preens herself, like a bird. GOLDSTEIN watches her with a gleam of admiration in his eye.)* You look like one queen. Ain't a man wouldn't fall dead fer you in such a coat. Turn round. So. You don't need I should tell you nuthin'. You got eyes in your head. Well, what you say?

FANNY: *(unable to tear her eyes away from her image in the mirror)* How much?

GOLDSTEIN: Cheap. Dirt cheap. If I would sell this coat you couldn't buy it. I give it away, that's all.

FANNY: How much?

GOLDSTEIN: You want to know how much you pay for this coat in Jaeckels? In any big house?

FANNY: I ain't buyin' it from Jaeckels', see?

GOLDSTEIN: I know that. Now that coat—I am givin' it away fer two hundred fifty. I gotta have cash tonight. If I would wait till tomorrow, I could get twice that easy. But I can't wait, see? I gotta get rid of it tonight. Two hundred fifty an' it's a present. What you say?

FANNY: *(derisively)* Know anymore good jokes?

GOLDSTEIN: You think I'm jokin'?

FANNY: I know you're jokin'. *(She takes off the wrap and hands it to GOLDSTEIN.)* Here. I ain't crazy if you is. Say, do I look like two hundred fifty spot cash?

GOLDSTEIN: You look like a million dollar kid to me. Say, would you pass up such a coat like this? It don't suit nobody but you.

FANNY: Then you better give it to me. Make it a present like you said.

GOLDSTEIN: That's just what I'm doin'.

FANNY: Come off!

GOLDSTEIN: Mebbe we can make it a good business. How much you got?

FANNY: A clean hundred an' not another cent.

GOLDSTEIN: *(shaking his head)* Think again, kid.

FANNY: Pack up yuh coat! Reckon we can't do no business.

GOLDSTEIN: *(coming close to her and stroking her arm)* Mebbe you got something what ain't money.

FANNY: What you mean?

GOLDSTEIN: You know what I mean. *(He places his arms about FANNY's waist.)*

FANNY: *(without drawing away)* Get out. I'm a respectable, married woman, an' don't you forget it.

GOLDSTEIN: Who said you ain't? If you wasn't respectable, I wouldn't make no bargain with you. Get me?

FANNY: I got a husband.

GOLDSTEIN: Well, why not? A fine looking girl what you is don't have no trouble getting husbands. Mebbe we make a bargain. What you say? How much you got over a hundred?

FANNY: Not a red cent.

GOLDSTEIN: *(hesitating)* If you could make fifty more. *(FANNY shakes her head.)* Twenty-five? *(FANNY shakes her head.)*

FANNY: You said yourself, I was a million dollar kid. *(She goes up close to him, puts her arms slowly about his neck and kisses him. GOLDSTEIN holds her close, returning her kisses hotly.)* Well?

GOLDSTEIN: *(thickly)* You win, you little brown devil. *(He takes the coat and wraps it around FANNY.)* Well, where's the money? When do I get paid?

FANNY: C.O.D. *(She goes into the bedroom. The portieres close behind her. GOLDSTEIN hesitates and then follows her.)*

THE VOICE OF GOLDSTEIN: You say you got a husband?

THE VOICE OF FANNY: Sure.

THE VOICE OF GOLDSTEIN: He wouldn't come in now an' go for getting excited, would he?

THE VOICE OF FANNY: Naw. He's in Brooklyn. *(The living room door opens slowly. A tall, dark fellow enters. He closes the door and replaces the key in his pocket. He notices the suitcase, frowns in a puzzled fashion and then passes in his same quick manner into the bedroom. There is a loud exclamation, another and another. The sound of a blow and fall. GOLDSTEIN dashes wildly out of the room, WALTER KING in full pursuit. GOLDSTEIN grabs his hat and suitcase, but fumbles at the door. KING yanks him away, opens the door and with a well aimed kick sends the Jew sprawling. The latter scrambles to his feet and plunges out of the room. KING picks up the suitcase and hurls it after the peddlar, slamming the door. Breathing rapidly and heavily, he re-enters the bedroom.)*

VOICE OF FANNY: Lemme alone! I didn't do nuthin'. *(She utters a loud scream. There is the sound of scuffling and other loud screams, sos and moans. There is never a word from KING.)* Yuh's killin' me! Gawd! Oh! Murder! Murder! *(Shriek after shriek rents the air. There is a loud knocking on the hall door. The shrieks cease. KING comes out. He walks up to the mirror and adjusts his tie and collar. He flicks a bit of thread from his coat and puts it on. He takes up his hat and puts that on. He listens for a moment to the loud sobs and moans in the adjoining room. Then he walks to the hall door, opens it and goes out, baning the door behind him. The moans become noticeably fainter. There is a silence. The portieres are parted and there stands FANNY in a most dishevelled condition. Dangling from one hand is the beloved ermine wrap. She places the wrap close to her face, stroking it with her cheek. She braces up suddenly. She slips the coat about her shoulders. She walks across the floor, painfully, and then as she reaches the mirror, a little sob breaks from her.)*

FANNY: The dirty brute! Glad he didn't scratch my face none. *(She smooths her hair. She turns around and around.)* Some bargain! *(She walks to the telephone.)* Bradhurst 2400. Hello! Jim? Jim, this is Fanny. Yes, I'm home. Can't make it tonight, kid. Of course, it's Walter. Tomorrow night, same time. OK. Say, honey, I just bought some coat. It's a peach! You'll see me strut tomorrow night, all right. I don't mean maybe. Goodbye, honey. Goodnight. *(She hangs up the receiver with a sigh.)*

CURTAIN

UNDERTOW

BY EULALIE SPENCE

PERSONS IN THE PLAY

DAN *the man*
HATTIE: *the man's wife*
CHARLEY: *their son*
CLEM: *the other woman*
MRS. WILKES: *a lodger*

SCENE: *Harlem. The dining room in Hattie's private house. It is a cheerful room, never sunny, but well furnished and spotless from shining floor to snowy linen. The supper dishes have been cleared away, but the table is still set for one who did not appear. Double doors opening upon the hall are at center back. At right there is a door leading to the kitchen. At the left there are two windows facing the street.*

TIME: *About eight o'clock one winter's night.*

AT RISE: *Hattie is sitting at the head of the table frowning heavily at the place of the one who did not appear. She drums impatiently with her fingers for a few seconds then pushing her chair back with more violence than grace, rises. Hattie's dark face is hard and cold. She has a disconcerting smile—a little contempt and a great deal of distrust. Her body is short and spreads freely in every direction. Her dark dress is covered by an apron which makes her look somewhat clumsy. Charley, dressed in an overcoat and hat of the latest mode bursts noisily into the room. He is a slender fellow; about the same complexion of his mother, but possessing none of her strength of character. His good-looking face is weak, with a suggestion of stubbornness about it. His manner is arrogant and somewhat insolent.*

164

CHARLEY: Ah'm off, Ma.

HATTIE: So Ah see.

CHARLEY: *(His glance falls on the table)* Say, Ma—Gee whiz! Ain't Dad bin home fer supper yet?

HATTIE: *(Shortly)* No.

CHARLEY: *(With a low whistle)* Dat's funny, he ain't never stayed out befo' has he?

HATTIE: Not sence Ah married him—'cept—

CHARLEY: *(Curiously)* 'Cept whut, Ma?

HATTIE: 'Cept wunce 'fo yuh was born.

CHARLEY: *(With an uproarous laugh)* An' the old man ain't tried it sence! Reckon yuh fixed him, didn't yuh, Ma! *(He sits down beside the table and laughs once more.)*

HATTIE: *(Sharply)* Ah ain't trained yuh half's as well's Ah's trained yo' Dad. *(She resumes her seat)* Ah shoulda made yuh stay in school fer one thing.

CHARLEY: Yuh had mo' sense Ma! If yuh'd a bossed me lak yuh's bossed Dad, Ah'd runned away long 'fo now.

HATTIE: Thar ain't no danger uh Dan runnin' off. He ain't got de nerve. Sides, nobuddy'd want him.

CHARLEY: Now doan' fool yuhself, Ma! An easy simp lak Dad'd be snapped up soon 'nuff ef he ever got it intuh his head dat he could do sech a thing.

HATTIE: Dan's a fool, but he knows which side his bread's buttered on.

CHARLEY: *(Giving his thigh a loud slap)* Holy smoke!

HATTIE: *(Irritably)* Whut's eatin' yuh?

CHARLEY: Nuthin'.

HATTIE: *(Impatiently)* Never mind lyin'! Whut's on yuh mind?

CHARLEY: Oh, nuthin'! Ah jes' thought er sumpth'n dat's all. Say, Ma—

HATTIE: Well?

CHARLEY: Ah gotta have five bucks ter-night,—Need 'em bad.

HATTIE: It doan do no harm tuh need 'em. Thar's a plenty things Ah's wanted dat Ah ain't never got.

CHARLEY: *(Roughly)* Where the devil do yuh think Ah kin git it, ef Ah doan ask yuh?

HATTIE: Yuh might wuk 'cassionally. Dan ain't bin home a day dese twenty-five years.

CHARLEY: *(With a sneer)* An' yuh's jes' done callin' him a fool, ain't yuh? The guys in mah crowd doan do no work see? We lives by our brains.

HATTIE: Not by exercisin' 'em, Lawd knows!

CHARLEY: How come yuh think we hits de Number ev'y week? Brain work!

HATTIE: Ef yuh hits so often whut yuh allus comin' ter me 'bout money fer?

CHARLEY: Ef dat ain't lak a woman! It takes money ter make money!

HATTIE: Charley, yuh's gotta cut out dis gamblin'. Ah ain't goin' give yuh no mo' money.

CHARLEY: *(Insolently)* Yuh think Ah'm Dad, doan' yuh? Well, Ah ain't! Ah wish ter Gawd Ah knew whut yuh's got over on him. No free man would er stood yuh naggin' all dese years.

HATTIE: *(Coldly)* Dem whut can't stan' fer mah ways knows whut dey kin do.

CHARLEY: Wouldn't 'sprise me none ef Dad has walked off—

HATTIE: *(Quickly)* Whut makes yuh think so?

CHARLEY: Reckon yu'd like tuh know, wouldn't yuh?

HATTIE: 'Tain't likely whut yuh could say's wurth five dollars tuh hear.

CHARLEY: Whut Ah seen wouldn't uh bin wuth nuthin' las' week, but sence Dad ain't showed up, fer supper, it's wuth a damn sight mo'. Yuh'd never guess whut Ah seen him doin' one night las' week up on Lenox Avenue.

HATTIE: Well, yuh might's well say it. Yuh kin have dat five, but lemme tell yuh dat yuh'll be de loser, later, if yuh's lied tuh me.

CHARLEY: Whut Ah's gotta lie fer? *(He stretches his hand across the table, palm upturned.)* Hand it over, Ma. *(Hattie takes a bill, from her stocking and puts it on the table, beside her. She places her closed fist upon the money. Charley frowns and back.)*

HATTIE: Ah ain't never refused tuh pay fer whut Ah gits.

CHARLEY: Oh, all right. Here goes. Me an' Nat Walker was strollin' up Lenox Avenue one night las' week 'bout half past six. Right ahead uh me Ah seen Dad. He was walkin' 'long, slow ez usual wid his head bent, not seein' nobuddy. All uv a sudden, a woman comin' down de Avenue, went up tuh him an' stops him. He looked up kinda dazed like an' stared at her lak he'd seen a ghost. She jes' shook him by de arm an' laughed. By dat

166

time, we come along side an' Ah got a good look at her. She warn't young an' she warn't old. But she looked—well—As jes' doan know how she did look—all laughin' an' happy an' tears in her eyes. Ah didn' look at her much fer starin' at Dad. He looked—all shaken up—an' scared like—Not scared like neither fer Ah seen him smile at her, after a minute. He ain't never smiled lak that befo'—not's Ah kin remember. Nat said— "Reckin yuh Dad's met an' ole gal 'er his"—But Ah only laughed—Struck me kinda funny—that! Dad meetin' an 'ole flame uh his—Ah meant tuh ask Dad 'bout her but it went clean outa mah hed. *(He reaches once more for the money. This time he takes it easily, enough. Hattie has forgotten it.)*

HATTIE: *(After a pause)* Was she tall?

CHARLEY: Kinda. Plenty taller'n you. *(He rises and takes his hat from the table.)*

HATTIE: *(After a pause)* Light?

CHARLEY: So—So,—lighter'n you. *(He moves toward the door.)*

HATTIE: Pretty?

CHARLEY: Mebbe. She warn't no chicken—but she was good tuh look at. Tain't no use mopin', Ma. Dad ain't de fus' husban' tuh take dinner wid his girl friend. Funny, though his never doin' it befo'. Well, s'long! *(He goes out and the door slams noisily. Hattie rouses up at that and starts clearing the table. She has just left the room with the last handful of dishes when the hall door is opened quietly and Dan enters. He is a dark man of medium height, slender of build. He looks a little stooped. There is a beaten look about his face—a tired, patient look. He takes off his overcoat and still stands there hesitating. Hattie re-enters, frowns darkly but does not speak. She places a scarf upon the table and a little silver-plated basket from the sideboard.)*

DAN: *(Dropping his coat and hat upon a chair)* Sorry, Ah'm late, Hattie. *(She does not answer)* Ah ain't had no supper. Reckon Ah'll get it an' eat in de kitchen.

HATTIE: *(Icily)* Reckon yuh'll hang dat coat an' hat in de hall whar dey belongs.

DAN: *(Apologetically)* Sure. Dunno how Ah come tuh ferget. *(He goes out with his clothes and returns almost immediately He looks timidly at Hattie, then passes on toward the kitchen door.)*

HATTIE: *(Fiercely)* Keep outa dat kitchen!

167

DAN: But Ah'm hungry, Hattie. Ah ain't had nuthin' tuh eat.

HATTIE: Whar yuh bin, dat yur ain't had nuthin 'tuh eat? *(Dan doesn't answer)* Yuh kain't say, kin yuh?

DAN: Ah went tuh see a friend uh mine.

HATTIE: Half past six ain't callin' hours! *(Dan looks unhappily at the floor)* Less'n yuh's asked ter dine!

DAN: It was important! Ah had tuh go.

HATTIE: Had tuh go whar? Yuh ain't said whar yuh's bin. *(Dan does not answer.)* An yuh ain't got no intention uh saying, has yuh? *(Dan does not answer. He moves once more toward the kitchen.)*

HATTIE: *(In a shrill voice)* Yuh keep outa thar! Keep outa mah kitchen! Ah kep yuh supper till eight o'clock. Yuh didn' come, an Ah's throwed it out!

DAN: Ah'll fix sumpth'n else. Ah doan want much.

HATTIE: Yuh ain't goin' messin' in mah kitchen! Yuh's hidin' sumpth'n, Dan Peters, and' Ah's gwine fine it out 'fo' long. Yuh ain't gonna trow no dust in mah eyes no second time—not ef Ah knows it!

DAN: All right. Ah doan' want no fuss, Hattie. Ah'll go out an' git sumpth'n.

HATTIE: Yuh kin fix de furnace 'fo' yuh go. Ah's got 'nuff tuh do runnin' a lodgin' house, 'thout fixin' fires day an' night.

DAN: Charley was home. Yuh coulda asked Charley tuh do it.

HATTIE: Charley doan' never fix no furnace. It's yo' job when yuh's home an' Ah ain't got no reason tuh wish it on Charley.

DAN: Ah'll fix it when Ah gits back. Ah'm hungry, now an' Ah's gwine tuh git sumpth'n tuh eat. *(He goes out. Hattie listens for the click of the iron gate, then hurries to the window and peers after him. The door is opened softly and a little brown woman sidles in. Her eyes rove constantly always seeking—seeking. Hattie turns around and glares fiercely at her.)*

HATTIE: What yuh want?

MRS. WILKES: *(Starting slightly at the grimness of the other's voice)* Ah declare, Mis' Peters, yuh sho' does look put out! Anything de matter?

HATTIE: *(Shortly)* Did yuh come down here tuh tell me dat?

MRS. WILKES: *(With an uneasy laugh)* C'ose not, Mis' Peters! . . . It's pretty cold upstairs. Ah s'pose de fire's goin' ez usual?

HATTIE: Yes.

MRS. WILKES: It's gettin' colder, Ah reckon. *(Hattie does not answer.)* It's warmer down here. As Ah always tells Mr. Wilkes, gimme a parlor floor an' basement any time. Ef thar's any heat goin' yuh's sure tuh git it—Co'se, Ah ain't complainin', Mis' Peters—

HATTIE: H'm!

MRS. WILKES: See Mr. Peters got home pretty late tuh-night, didn' he? *(Hattie answers only with a venomous glance.)* Thar's a man with reg'lar habits. Ah often tells Mr. Wilkes dat Ah wish tuh goodness he was a home lovin' man lak Mr. Peters. . . . Well, reckon Ah'll be gwine up again' seein' ez yuh's got comp'ny.

HATTIE: *(With a puzzled frown.)* Comp'ny?

MRS. WILKES: Thar's a lady tuh see yuh. She's upstairs settin' in de parlor.

HATTIE: Who let her in?

MRS. WILKES: Mr. Wilkes did. He seen her on de stoop. She was jes' gwine tuh ring de bell when Mr. Wilkes come up wid his key. She ask tuh see Mis' Peters an' he tole her tuh set in de parlor. Ef thar's ever a stupid man it sure is mah husban'. 'Stead uh goin' down an' tellin' yuh, 'er hollerin' tuh yuh, 'er sendin' her on down, he comes up-stairs an' tells *me* ter go down an' tell yuh. He'd oughta sent her down de basement do' fust place.

HATTIE: Send her down, will yuh? Some fine day, Ah 'spec we'll be cleaned out, ef yuh all's gwine let strangers in de house that 'a way.

MRS. WILKES: *(With a little cough.)* Thought yuh might want tuh see her in de parlor. Ah reckon she ain't no thief, not judgin' from her looks.

HATTIE: H'h! Whut she look lak?

MRS. WILKES: She's tall—but not too tall.

HATTIE: *(Forcing her stiffening lips to move)* Light?

MRS. WILKES: Lighter'n yuh an' me—

HATTIE: *(With a supreme effort)* Pretty?

MRS. WILKES: Well, yuh knows her all right! She ain't never bin here befo' ez Ah knows—but yuh knows her frum de way yuh's 'scribed her. Well, 'slong! Ah'll send her down. *(She opens the hall door)* B'r! *(She shivers)* Dis hall cert'nly is cold! *(The door closes after her. For a moment Hattie looks bewildered. But only for a moment. With a sudden harsh laugh she rips the apron from about her waist and pushes it quickly into the side-board drawer. She goes up to the mirror over the mantle, but one look at herself is all that she can bear. As she turns sharply away the door opens and Clem enters. In one glance Hattie's burning eyes take in the tall, well-dressed figure. The graying hair, the youthful face. If Clem's glance is less piercing, it is nevertheless, just as comprehensive.)*

CLEM: *(Softly)* It's bin a long time, Hattie. *(Hattie opens her lips to speak, but she doesn't. She sits, rather heavily, and continues to stare at Clem)* Ah doan' wonder yuh's 'sprised Hattie. *(She hesitates and then drawing up a chair facing Hattie, she too, sits.)* Ah know yuh's waitin' tuh hear whut brought me . . . It's a long story, Hattie. *(At that, Hattie moves impatiently)*

HATTIE: Yuh kin start—at de end—

CLEM: At de end?

HATTIE: At de end. Whut yuh come fer? Yuh's come ter git sumpth'n—Is it—Dan?

CLEM: *(Leaning back in her chair with a sigh)* De same ole Hattie! De years ain't changed yuh, none.

HATTIE: *(With a bitter laugh)* An' de years ain't changed *you*, none.

CLEM: Yes. Ah reckon they has, Hattie, Ah's suffered a-plenty.

HATTIE: *(With a curl of her lip)* An' yuh think dat yuh's de only one?

CLEM: Oh no! Ah kin see yuh's not bin over happy, Hattie, an' Ah knows dat Dan ain't bin happy.

HATTIE: Whut reason yuh got ter bring up all dis talk 'bout suff'rin'? Yuh bin seein' Dan agin', ain't yuh?

CLEM: Yes. Ah met him jes' by accident one night las' week.

HATTIE: An' yuh bin seein' him sence?

CLEM: Yes, ev'y night. Ah's bein' gwine down town ter meet him 'roun six o'clock an' Ah's ride home wid him in de "L".

HATTIE: An' tuh-night yuh had him out tuh dinner. *(Hattie's voice has a deadly calm.)*

CLEM: No. Tuh-night Ah couldn' go tuh meet him. Ah was called away on business. Ah ain't seen him tuh-night.

HATTIE: Did he know yuh was comin' here?

CLEM: No.

HATTIE: Why'nt yuh tell him, yuh was comin'.

170

CLEM: He wouldn' 'er let me come.

HATTIE: Well, say whut yuh's come fer, an' go. It ain't easy settin' here an' listenin' tuh yuh talkin' 'bout Dan.

CLEM: *(Abruptly)* Yuh's almost driv' him crazy. An' yuh said yuh loved him. *(Hattie's fingers clench slowly)*

HATTIE: Whar'd yuh go to? Whar you bin all dese years?

CLEM: South—Virginia, whar I come frum.

HATTIE: H'm!

CLEM: Ef Ah'd knowed yuh was gwine tuh be unkind tuh him, Ah'd never let him go! Dan ain't knowed a day's happiness sence Ah went away.

HATTIE: He—he tole yuh dat?

CLEM: Yes! Ah kin fergive yuh fer takin' him 'way frum me—an' de way yuh done it—but it ain't easy fergivin' yuh fer makin' him suffer.

HATTIE: An' dat's whut yuh's come here tuh tell me?

CLEM: *(Passionately)* Dan's dyin' here, right under yo' eyes, an' yo' doan see it. He's dyin' fer kindness—He's dyin' frum hard wuk. He's dyin' frum de want uv love. Ah could allus read him lak a book. He won't talk 'gainst yuh, Hattie, but Ah kin see it all in de way he looks—in de way he looks at me. *(Clem dabs at her eyes with her handkerchief)*

HATTIE: Go on. *(She marvels at her own quietness!)*

CLEM: *(Accusingly)* He's shabby—all uv him—hat an' shoes an coat. Ef he had one suit fer ev'y five dat yuh son has, he'd be pretty well dressed.

HATTIE: *(Slowly)* Yuh fergit, Charley is Dan's son ez well ez mine.

CLEM: An' yuh's set him 'gainst his dad. He sides with yuh ev'y time, doan' he?

HATTIE: *(With a faint sneer)* Did yuh read dat too, in de way Dan—looked—at yuh?

CLEM: Ef yuh had a brought Charley up diff'rent yuh mighta held on tuh Dan. 'Stead uh dat, yuh's brought him up tuh look down on him.

HATTIE: *(She is breathing heavily, her voice comes thick and choked.)* Is yuh tru? *(Rises)*

CLEM: Yuh doan' need Dan an yo' son doan' need him. Well, sence yuh ain't got no use fer him, Ah's gwine take him frum yuh,

Hattie. Now yuh knows why Ah's come. *(She rises also and looks down at Hattie, much to the latter's disadvantage.)*

HATTIE: *(Forcing the words out, as though each one pains her)* Funny—how—thoughtful yuh's got sence Ah's las' seen yuh. Yuh come inta mah house twenty years ago as a frien'—an' yuh took Dan when Ah hadn't bin married ter him a year. Yuh didn' give no 'nouncement den 'bout whut yuh was gwine ter do. Yuh jes' took him—an' me expectin' tuh be de mother uv his chile. Gawd! *(A deep shudder runs through her body)* But now—dat yuh's got mo' stylish—mo' lady-like in yuh ways yuh come tuh tell me ve'y politely, dat yuh's gwine tuh take him agin. Is it mah blessin' yuh's waitin' fer? Yuh doan' need no permission.

CLEM: Yuh, yuh doan' un'erstan'—Yuh never did un'erstan', Hattie.

HATTIE: Mebbe not. Some things is hard tuh un'erstan'.

CLEM: Co'se Dan an' me could go off tergether, 'thout yuh permission. Yuh knows dat well 'nuff. It's bein' done ev'y day. But we doan' want ter go lak dat.

HATTIE: Yuh mean Dan doan' want ter go that 'a-way!

CLEM: Yuh's wrong, Hattie. Dan ain't thinkin' 'er nuthin' 'er nobuddy but me. He's fer quittin' an' never sayin' a word tuh yuh but jes' goin' off, me an' him together. But Ah ain't gwine tuh go lak dat. Dis time it's gotta be diff'rent.

HATTIE: Diff'rent—how?

CLEM: Hattie, Ah wants yuh tuh free Dan. Yuh owes it tuh him. He ain't never bin free sence he's knowed yuh. Will yuh free him?

HATTIE: Free him—how?

CLEM: Give him a divo'ce.

HATTIE: A divo'ce—tuh marry you?

CLEM: *(Pleadingly)* Yes. 'Taint lak yuh loved him Hattie. Ef yuh loved him. Ah couldn' ask yuh. But yuh only holds onta him tru spite—Yuh hates him, mebbe—Yuh treats him lak yuh does.

HATTIE: Yuh knows Ah kain't keep him ef he wants tuh go. Reckon Ah knows it, too. Well, ef he wants tuh go he kin go.

CLEM: *(With an exclamation of relief)* Thank Gawd! Ah didn' think yuh'd do it, Hattie.

HATTIE: Yuh coulda spared yuh-self de trubble comin' here—an jes' gone off. It woulda bin more lak yuh.

CLEM: But—but—how? Yuh'd have ter know 'bout de devo'ce, Hattie.

172

HATTIE: Devo'ce? Ah ain't said nuthin' 'bout gettin' no devo'ce!

CLEM: But—but—yuh—Ah thought—Whut yuh mean, Hattie?

HATTIE: Yuh didn' need no devo'ce de fust time, did yuh?

CLEM: *(Biting her lips to keep back the tears)* Dat—Dat was diff'rent.

HATTIE: Ah doan' see it.

CLEM: Well, it was. It's gotta be a divo'ce dis time.

HATTIE: Ah see Dan's morals has improved some sence *you* went away.

CLEM: It ain't Dan whut's holdin' out fer devo'ce—It's—it's me.

HATTIE: *(Hattie's laugh has a bitter edge)* Den it's yo' morals dat's bin improvin'—Well, dey could stan' improvin' a-plenty. *(The fierce edge returns suddenly to her voice)* Yuh's wastin' yo' time an' mine an Dan's! 'Bout lettin' him go—He coulda gone all dese years—Ah warn't holdin' him back! He'd gone too, ef he'd knowed whar to find yuh. Ah knowed ef he ever found yuh, he'd leave me. Well, he didn' find yuh tell now. But long's Ah's got breaf tuh breathe, Ah ain't gwine say "Yes"! 'bout no divo'ce. Ef he kin git one 'thout me, let him git it! Yuh hear me? Now ef yuh's tru, yuh better get outa here. Ah ain't 'sponsibl' fer whut Ah says frum now on!

CLEM: Hattie, 'fore Gawd, yuh's hard!

HATTIE: Ah was soft 'nuff, when yuh fust stepped on me. Ef Ah's hard now, 'tis yo' fault!

CLEM: Hattie—Ah ain't tole yuh de real reason why Ah wants dat di'voce—*(A note of despair has crept into her voice)*

HATTIE: No? Well, Ah ain't in'trested none.

CLEM: Still Ah wants yuh tuh hear! It's sumpthin' dat Ah ain't tole Dan. *(The door is opened quietly and Dan enters. He starts— looks fearfully from Clem to Hattie and then back again to Clem)* Come in, Dan. Ah hope yuh doan' mind mah comin' tuh see Hattie. Ah jes' had tuh come.

DAN: *(Swallowing painfully)* It won' do no good. *(Hattie is gazing at him curiously)*

CLEM: Mebbe not, but Ah had tuh come.

DAN: Ah'm sorry, Hattie. We—we—*(He turns away as if ashamed)*

CLEM: Hattie knows ev'ything Dan. Ah's tole her. *(Dan turns toward her)*

DAN: Clem, whut was yuh sayin' when Ah come on in? Ah heard yuh—

CLEM: *(Embarrassed)* Ah didn' want tuh tell yuh—lak dis—

DAN: *(Gently)* We kain't go back now, Clem. Sence we's in de middle we's gotta git tru, somehow.

CLEM: *(Turning from him to Hattie)* Ah didn' mean tuh beg, 'less'n Ah had tuh—

HATTIE: *(Coldly)* Yuh doan' have tuh—

CLEM: Ef 'twas only me—but it ain't. It's fer mah Lucy,—Dan's chile *(There is a terrible silence)* Dan's chile—Ah didn' tell yuh, Hattie, an' Ah didn' tell Dan. Whut woulda bin de use? She's a woman now an' good—an' pretty. She thinks her dad died when she was a baby an' she thinks—she thinks—Ah'm a good woman. She's proud uh me. *(As if unconscious of Hattie's presence, Dan grips Clem's hands. They look at each other.)*

HATTIE: *(As if to herself. She seems to be trying to get it all quite clear)* She thinks yuh's a good woman! An' dat's why yuh expects me tuh give Dan a divo'ce.

CLEM: *(Eagerly)* Yes, Yes! Yuh see, doan' yuh?

HATTIE: Yes, Ah see. Gawd, ef dat ain't funny! She thinks yuh's a good woman. *(She laughs loudly,—hysterically)* Oh, my Gawd!

DAN: *(Sharply)* Hattie!

HATTIE: *(Ignoring him)* Tell me mo'—'bout dis—dis new relation uh Dan's.

CLEM: Ah's wuked hard tuh git her de chances Ah didn' have. She's bin tuh school—she's got an' eddication. An' now she's goin' tuh git married tuh a fine feller whut'll be able tuh take care uv her. Now yuh see dat Ah kain't jes' go off wid Dan. It's got tuh be proper—a divo'ce an' all. Yuh see, doan' yuh, Hattie?

HATTIE: *(Nodding)* Mother an' daughter—double weddin'

CLEM: *(Anxiously)* An yuh'll do it, Hattie? Gawd'll bless yuh, Hattie.

HATTIE: *(Derisively)* How come *you's* passin' on blessins? Yuh knows a lot, doan' yuh 'bout blessins? Wonder ef yuh knows ez much 'bout curses?

CLEM: Now, Hattie—

HATTIE: *(Darkly)* Yuh doan know nuthin' much 'bout curses, does yuh? Well, yuh's cursed, Clem Jackson! Cursed! Yuh's allus bin cursed sence de day yuh cast yuh eyes on Dan!

DAN: *(Harshly)* Hattie, yuh ain't got no call tuh go on lak dat.

HATTIE: *(Who does not seem to hear him)* Dan was cursed when he set eyes on yuh. An' Ah was cursed when Ah took yuh fer a frien'.

CLEM: *(Hurriedly)* Ah'm goin', Hattie! Ah see yuh ain't gwine give in.

HATTIE: Whut's yuh hurry? Yuh better hear whut Ah's gwine tuh say. . . . Curses. Yes, we's all bin cursed, Clem. Mah Charley's cursed an' yo' Lucy—too bad.

CLEM: *(Angrily)* Doan' yuh call mah Lucy's name 'long uv ours.

HATTIE: *(With a sneer)* Too bad. Wonder how she'll feel when she hears whut a good woman yuh is?

CLEM: *(Shrinking as if from a blow)* Whut? Yuh—yuh wouldn'—yuh wouldn'—

HATTIE: Wouldn'—wouldn'—*(She laughs again—crazily)* Sure, Ah'll fine her! Ef it takes de rest uh mah life, Ah'll fine her. It's too good—tuh keep. How she'll stare when she knows her ma was a prostitute an' her dad—

DAN: *(Hoarsely)* Damn yuh, Hattie! Doan yuh say no mo'.

HATTIE: Ah'll tell her all—all—leavin' out nuthin'.

CLEM: *(Pleading as if for life)* Yuh couldn', Hattie! Yuh couldn'! Hattie—Hattie—

HATTIE: How she play me false—when Ah trusted her—an' how she lie tuh me—How she ruin' mah life—an' come on back tuh take de leavin's once more—

DAN: Doan yuh say no mo, Hattie!

HATTIE: Yuh'd shut mah mouf' wouldn' yuh? How? How—

DAN: Let's go, Clem. Let's go—

HATTIE: *(Shrilly)* G'wan. Is Ah keepin' yuh? Take yuh street walker back whar she come frum. Yuh kin give Lucy mah regahds. Tell her dat a frien's gwine call on her—real soon—an' ole frien' uv her ma's.

DAN: *(With a cry of rage, grips Hattie by the shoulder and shakes her)* Yoh'll shut yo' mouf, Hattie. Promise, 'er fo' Gawd-A-Mighty.

HATTIE: *(Scornfully)* How yuh's thinkin' 'er shuttin' mah mouf, Dan Peters?

DAN: Yuh'll keep 'way frum Lucy. Yuh'll promise not tuh say nuthin' 'bout Clem. *(Dan shakes her again roughly)*

HATTIE: *(Her speech broken with little gasping cries)* Never! An' yuh kain't make me! Ah'll tell her 'bout dis good woman! Dis thief! Dis dirty minded whore! *(Without a word, Dan grips her by the throat and forces her back—back against the table. Her arms claw awkwardly and then drop to her sides. Clem utters a low cry and springs upon Dan, tearing wildly at his fingers.)*

CLEM: Dan! Leggo! Leggo, fer Gawd's sake! Dan! *(With a violent movement of disgust he thrusts Hattie from him. She falls heavily from the chair, her head striking the marble base of the mantle—an ugly sound. She lies very still. Dan looks at her stupidly. Clem throws her arms about his neck, sobbing hysterically)* Dan! Dan! Yuh come near killin' her!

DAN: *(Breathing heavily)* Ah'd a done it too, ef yuh hadn't bin thar.

CLEM: *(Stooping over Hattie)* She hit her head an awful crack!

DAN: Hattie's head's harder'n mos'. Come on, Clem. We kain't stay here, now. She'll be comin' to, 'fo' long! An raisin' de roof.

CLEM: *(Who is still peerin at Hattie)* Dan, thar's blood comin' out de corner uv her mouf.

DAN: She'll be waggin' it again' fo' yuh knows it.

CLEM: *(Going up to Dan and putting her hand on his shoulder)* Dan, Ah wish yuh hadn't done it! 'Twon' do no good!

DAN: Ah couldn' stan' it no longer. Ah clean los' mah head when she call yuh—whut she did.

CLEM: Yes, Ah know. Poor Danny boy! Ah doan see how yuh's stood it all dese years.

DAN: *(Putting his arms about her)* Ah was allus thinkin' uv yuh, Clem. Yuh shouldn' 'a lef' me behin'. Yuh'd oughta tole me whar tuh fine yuh. Yuh shoulda tole me 'bout Lucy.

CLEM: Yes, Ah see dat now. But yuh b'longed tuh Hattie 'n Ah thought—

DAN: Ah never b'longed tuh Hattie. *(He kisses her)* Let's go, Clem *(She draws away from him)* Why, whut's wrong?

CLEM: Ah's gotta think uh Lucy.

DAN: Lucy?

CLEM: Yes, Lucy. She's yo' chile Dan, an' she doan' know—'bout us.

DAN: An' me—Whut 'bout me, an you—Clem—Clem—

CLEM: Ah you musn'. Then thar's Hattie. Yuh's gotta think uv Hattie—*(They both turn and look at the figure huddled there on the floor)* Dan, we'd better try'n bring her to. Get some water, Dan.

DAN: Ah won' touch her!

CLEM: It ain't human leavin' her lak dat. Help me lif' her, Dan. She'll catch her death uh cold on dat flo'! *(Very unwillingly Dan assists. Together he and Clem get Hattie into a chair. Her head lolls persistently to one side. Clem rubs her hands)* Lak ice! Why, Dan, her fingers all stiff! An'—an' Dan! Feel her pulse! Dan! *(She draws back terrified. Hattie's body, unsupported, sags awkwardly against the table. Dan quickly seizes her hands, feeling her pulse. He tilts her head backward, looks into her face—feels her heart, then straightens up—his face distorted, his eyes blank.)*

CLEM: *(In a whisper)* Dan—she ain't—dead?

DAN: Dead. *(He looks down at his hands in horror)*

CLEM: *(Wildly)* Dan! Whut'll we do! Whut'll we do!

DAN: Yuh'll go back tuh Lucy. She needs yuh.

CLEM: You needs me mo', Dan!

DAN: Yuh kain't help none! Ah doan stan' no chance—reckon Ah owes it tuh Lucy tuh send yuh back tuh her. Ah ain't never had de chance tuh do nuthin' fer her—but dis.

CLEM: Ah kain't go, Dan! Doan' mek me. *(Her body is wracked with sobs.)*

DAN: *(Taking her in his arms and kissing her)* We's gotta think 'bout Lucy—We's brung each other bad luck, Clem. Hattie was right.

CLEM: But Ah loved yuh Dan, an' yuh loved me.

DAN: Ah ain't never loved nobuddy else.

CLEM: Whut'll dey do tuh yuh Dan? Dey won't kill yuh? *(She clings tightly to him.)* Will dey, Dan?

DAN: Co'se not, Honey! Reckon Ah'll git twenty—er fifteen years— mebbe ten—*(He buttons her coat and draws her firmly toward the door.)*

CLEM: Ten years! *(She wrings her hands with a low moaning cry.)*

DAN: Ah'll spend 'em all dreamin' 'bout yuh, Clem, an'—an' Lucy! Yuh musn' grieve, Honey. Go, now, fer Gawd's sake! Ah hears sombuddy comin' down! *(He pushes her out, forcibly. And then the door is shut. The outer door slams. Dan listens for the click of the gate. Finally he turns and looks down at Hattie.)* Ah'm sorry, Hattie! 'Fore Gawd, Ah didn' mean tuh do it!

CURTAIN

EPISODE

A DOMESTIC COMEDY

BY EULALIE SPENCE

PERSONS IN THE PLAY

JIM	MRS. JENNINGS
MAMIE	WALT
MRS. ROBINSON	HARRY

SCENE I. *The Jackson's apartment about eight o'clock one Saturday night.*

SCENE II. *Another Saturday night in the same apartment, six weeks later.*

(The curtain will be lowered after scene one, for perhaps ten seconds.)

SCENE I. *Let us spend half an hour with the* JACKSONS *on the second floor of "The Rutherford," an expensive apartment house in Harlem.* MAMIE JACKSON'S *living room is as like every other living room in "The Rutherford" as are the peas in the same pod.* MAMIE *had seen to that, and felt a glow of satisfaction and content in knowing that in furnishings, at least, all was as it should be. But there were other anxieties.*

When the curtain rises, we start to inspect the living room, but our attention is immediately attracted by the sound of voices beyond the rose-draped doorway at left.

MALE VOICE [*Exasperated*]: Lawd, there yuh go agin'!

FEMALE VOICE [*Tearful*]: Kain't yuh even tell the truth? Yuh oughta say there *you* go agin'. Seems ter me yuh bin out every night for more'n a month.

MALE VOICE [*Placatingly*]: Sorry, honey, but Ah's got a date ter-night with some uv the boys.

178

FEMALE VOICE [*Fiercely*]: Seems ter me Ah've heard that before! Well, lemme tell yuh somethin'. Ah's got a date on ter-night, myself, with one uv the boys! [*The rose portière is parted angrily and Mamie enters, throwing herself upon the lounge. Every fibre of her body expresses indignation. What though her skin is somewhat brown? Her sleek, shining head does not own one errant hair. The cut of her bob is flawless. Her eyes, which are snapping now, with little flames of wrath, can be soft and gentle, and a more charming figure than Mamie in her red dress does not dwell within the confines of "The Rutherford."*]

MALE VOICE: Aw, quit yuh kiddin', Mamie.

MAMIE: H'm. See yuh doan believe me.

MALE VOICE: Sure, Ah doan. Say, honey, why'nt yuh ask Mis' Jennings ter the movies ter-night? They's got a mighty fine picture at the Renaissance.

MAMIE: When'd yuh see it?

MALE VOICE [*Guardedly*]: Ah didn't say Ah seen it, did Ah?

MAMIE: Well, how'd yuh know it's so good? Bet yuh seen it with some other woman.

MALE VOICE [*In deep exasperation*]: Listen, sister. Let me tell yuh, once fer all—[*The Male, tie in hand, emerges angrily from behind the rose portiere.*]

MAMIE [*Scathingly*]: Ah ain't yuh sister, though Ah might jes' well be fer all the 'tenshin Ah gets. [*A pleading note creeping into her voice.*] Aw, Jim, kain't yuh take me ter the movies, yuhself? Ah'm lonesome, Jim. Seems like yuh out with the boys every night since we bin married. It ain't like what Ah thought marriage was goin' ter be. Ah pictured you an' me—jes' you an' me—settin' here on this couch, same's we useter—in Mom's parler; or mebbe you smokin' or readin' the paper, or mebbe talkin' ter me. Yuh ain' never got nuthin' ter say ter me no more.

JIM [*Uneasily*]: No, honey—

MAMIE [*Unheeding*]: Ah pictured yuh bringin' home yuh friends ter see me. That's what we got a home fer—so's we kin ask friends up an' have some fun. Ah pictured yuh takin' me out places like yuh useter—But now everything's different. Yuh doan love me no more Ah reckon.

JIM: Lawd, there yuh go agin'.

MAMIE: Bet Ah kin tell where *you* goin'.

JIM: 'Tain't no place fer *you*, honey.

MAMIE [*Scornfully*]: Low-down prize fights. That's what's takin' yuh out. Yuh'd rather hang around every night with a lot uv tough guys, than—

JIM: [*Soothingly*]: Now, honey, yuh listen ter me. Ah bin plannin' a s'prize fer yuh all week. Bin plannin' it all week.

MAMIE [*Doubtfully*]: Honest, Jim?

JIM: [*With fine gusto*]: Sure, honest! Ah declare ter hear yuh ask a man "honest" every time he opens his mouth, sure gits mah goat.

MAMIE: Ah doan mean nothin'—Jim, only sometimes yuh fergits promises.

JIM: Fergits? Well, any feller kin fergit, kain't he? That ain't sayin' yuh got ter hand him no "honest", every time he opens his mouth. Ah 'spec you wimmin fergits more'n we men, any ole time.

MAMIE: Mebbe so, Jim. But yuh knows Ah doan fergit nothin'.

JIM: H'm. Wouldn't be so bad ef yuh did fergit once'n a while. Well, keep yuh mind on this s'prize Ah's gettin' yuh. [*He slips hurriedly into his coat. Mamie jumps up suddenly, her face alight with an idea.*]

MAMIE [*Seizing Jim by his coat lapels as he darts toward the door*]: Jim, Ah got ter have somethin' ter keep thinkin' 'bout ter-night, so tell me what that s'prize is. Please, Jim.

JIM [*Annoyed*]: 'Twon't be no s'prize, then.

MAMIE: Please Jim. 'Sides yuh might fergit. If yuh tell me what it is Ah kin remind yuh.

JIM: So, that's it. Yuh can remind me. What's the matter with me remindin' mahself?

MAMIE: Aw, Jim, tell me. What you bin plannin' ter s'prize me with?

JIM: Ah bin plannin' ter take yuh ter—ter the Cap'tol ter-morrow night. Now, what do yuh say? Why, what's the matter? Ef yuh doan beat all—

MAMIE [*Drawing back with a bitter laugh*]: Oh, yuh bin thinkin' uv me ain't yuh? Yuh bin plannin' so hard yuh doan remember ter-morrow's Sunday and we got ter spend the evenin' with yer folks in Newark. Oh, yes, yuh bin thinkin' 'bout me hard.

JIM [*Very much annoyed*]: Ah knows what yuh thinkin', but Ah did fergit.

MAMIE [*Sneeringly*]: But yuh didn' fergit this was Saturday night, did yuh? Yuh never fergits yuh dates with yuh pals and yuh wimmen friends—only yuh dates with me. [*Her voice trembling on the verge of tears.*] Well, Ah'm goin' ter try mah hand at s'prize makin' mahself. Ef yuh thinks Ah needs ter be lonesome, one minute longer'n Ah wanters ter—

JIM [*Angrily*]: Aw, shut up an' go ter bed. Yuh naggin'd drive any man crazy! [*Goes out, slamming the door. Mamie throws herself on the couch once more and smothers her sobs in the pillows for a full minute. A discreet knock makes her start up. She dries her eyes hastily. Producing a powder puff from a convenient jar she dusts her face. Before the caller has knocked a third time, Mamie is presentable enough to open the door. She admits Mrs. Jennings, her neighbor on the same landing, and Mrs. Robinson, an acquaintance of Mamie's. Mrs. Robinson, plump, plain and homey, wears a coat and hat. Mrs. Jennings, tall, lean, and shrewd, wears an apron as a badge of her meticulous housekeeping. No sooner are the callers seated, than the tongues begin to fly.*]

MRS. JENNINGS: Ah see Jim's out agin'.

MRS. ROBINSON: We seen him rushin' out. He give the door an awful slam. Didn' seem ter see us.

MRS. JENNINGS: He sure looked mad. 'Spose yuh had words agin' 'bout him goin' out. Yuh sure has mah symp'thy. As Ah always tells mah friends, it doan do no harm ter marry a feller what runs on the road. He does his runnin' 'way from home an' stays in of a night when he *is* home. Joe ain' give me no trouble that way.

MAMIE: But yuh never out tergether. Joe's too tired ter take yuh out when he's home. Seems ter me, it's most as bad as Jim's never takin' me out.

MRS. JENNINGS [*Positively*]: It ain' the same at all. Ah has mah own friends, an' Joe—he has his. Ah never stays home, lessn' Ah wants ter. Ah sure got friends ter take me where Ah wants ter go.

MAMIE [*Curiously*]: But ain't Joe ever mad 'cause yuh go without him? Jim'd be awful mad.

MRS. JENNINGS: Doan yuh fool yuhself, honey. Jim ain' no diff'rent than Joe or any other man.

MAMIE: All men ain't the same, Mis' Jennings. Why, ef Ah had half's many men friends as some women has, Jim'd kill me.

MRS. JENNINGS [*Derisively*]: He would—not! It ain' bein' done this year. Lemme tell yuh somethin'. Yuh ain't bin married long an' Ah hates ter see yuh makin' a fool uv yuhself. 'Long's yuh Jim knows yuh hangin' roun' here yearnin', he'll let yuh yearn, an' have a wonderful time watchin' yuh doin' it. Yuh wants ter start the way yuh goin' ter keep up. Ain' that so, Mis' Robinson?

MRS. ROBINSON [*With a reminiscent smile*]: Sure, ef yuh kin. We doan all start right, an' that's the truth. Now, take me. Ah bin always fat, or almost fat. When Ah met Charlie, Ah was reducin'. Ah soon found out that he didn' care 'bout no fat girl, so Ah set ter work ter lose fifty pounds. Well, Ah lost thirty-five an' Ah married Charlie. Now Ah'm a home body, always was, an' always will be, Ah reckon. Charlie likes ter go—but Ah kain't stan' chasin' 'round. Pretty soon, Charlie was goin' without me. Nobody's fault but mine. Well, 'long 'bout the time Ah had put back them thirty-five pounds an' twenty-five more, Ah began ter see lessn' less uv Charlie. Now, guess what happen— Most two years ago, Charlie come one night with a man an' a big bundle. 'Twas a radio set. Well, would yuh believe it, honey, sence that night, Charlie bin settin' home, reg'lar. Yuh kain't git him out. Ah declare, he hates ter leave it uv a mornin' an' he kain't speak ter no one at night 'till he turns it on. So now we sets home, nights, an' Ah ain' bin so happy in the five years we bin married.

MRS. JENNINGS [*With a faint sniff*]: Ah kain't stand the things, mahself, more'n a few minutes. 'Course, ef Ah was dancin'—but jes' settin' still listenin'—not fer me, Ah kin tell yuh.

MRS. ROBINSON: Ah doan mind. Ah likes it. We has some right wonderful concerts sometimes. Ah reckon Ah likes it most as much as Charlie does.

MAMIE [*Thoughtfully*]: Ah think Ah'd like a radio set. Ah wonder—[*She stops, her face radiant with another Big Idea*] Oh, Ah wonder ef Jim'd like one, too. Mebbe—Oh, Mis' Robinson, do yuh think he'd stay home ef Ah got a radio?

MRS. JENNINGS [*In disgust*]: Well, Ah never!

MRS. ROBINSON: Well, yuh kain't be sure, but he might. Mis' Taylor was tellin' me last Sunday that her husband bin stayin' in nights sence they got their radio. An' Lawd knows Willie Taylor sure is some gad-about. Seems like ef Willie Taylor would stay in ter fool with a radio, an' mah Charlie—

MAMIE [*Trembling with the dawn of a new hope*]: Ah tole Jim Ah'd give him a big s'prize, an' Ah'm goin' ter! Ah'm goin' ter buy a radio out'n mah own money an' s'prize Jim. Won't he be s'prized though! [*Mamie laughs in sheer delight.*]

MRS. JENNINGS: Well, uv all the fool ideas, ef that doan beat all! What yuh want ter git a radio ter stay in fer? Though yuh wanted ter go *out?*

MAMIE: Oh, yuh doan understan' Mis' Jennings. Ah doan care ef Ah goes or stays, 'slong's Jim's with me. Ah loves him, an' Ah'm terrible lonesome without him.

MRS. ROBINSON: Ah reckon Ah knows jes' how yuh feels.

MAMIE [*Gratefully*]: Ah'm so glad yuh gave me that idea. Oh, but won't Jim be s'prized?

MRS. JENNINGS: Well, Ah doan think much uv the idea mahself, but then everybody knows his own business best.

MRS. ROBINSON [*Rising*]: Well, Ah'll be gettin' 'long. Ah wish yuh all the luck in the world, honey.

MRS. JENNINGS [*Also rising*]: Well, Ah 'spose we'll be hearin' plenty music 'cross the hall 'fore long.

MAMIE [*At the door*]: Yuh's cheered me up jes' wonderful. This time next week Jim'n Ah'll be listenin' ter some wonderful music.

MRS. JENNINGS [Skeptically]: Ah hope so, Ah'm sure.

MRS. ROBINSON: It's worth tryin' honey. Good-by.

MAMIE: Oh, good-night. Good-night. [*Mamie's friends go out. Happy Mamie! She rushes into the room beyond the rose portiere, returning immediately with a bankbook. She turns the pages eagerly.*] Four hundred dollars! [*Mamie attempts to express her emotion in the rapid whirl of the Black Bottom. Suddenly she stops short.*] Ah wonder what kind Mis' Robinson got. Ah fergot ter ask her. Mebbe she's still at Mis' Jennings! [*As Mamie opens the door she almost collides with Jim, standing on the threshold with a short, pudgy young man.*]

JIM: What's the matter, honey?

MAMIE: Jim! [*She glances in deep surprise from Jim to the stranger.*]

JIM: [*With a chuckle*]: Doan say Ah didn' give yuh some s'prize, then. This is Walt Gilbert, a chum Ah ain' seen fer years. Walt—mah wife.

WALT: Delighted ter meet yuh, Ah'm sure. [*Transferring a cornet case from his right hand to his left, he shakes hands solemnly. The party finds seats.*]

JIM: Ain't it a small world, though. Here Ah runs into Walt an' Ah ain' seen him in years. Me an' Walt uster be close pals 'fore he moved out Chicago way. An' say, honey, Ah runs into Walt at the club—Jes' accident, pure an' simple. Heard a feller playin' the cornet an' oh boy! Ah'll tell the world he kin play. An' when Ah takes a good look at the feller, ef it ain't Walt Gilbert! Walt kin sure make that cornet talk!

MAMIE [*Forcing herself to be polite, although she has taken an instinctive dislike to Walt*]: Do yuh play in an orchestra, Mr. Gilbert?

JIM [*Enthusiastically*]: Ah'll tell the world, he does. The Jim-Jam-Jem Orchestra. Mamie, that boy sure kin play the cornet!

MAMIE [*Opening her eyes in surprise*]: Ah didn' know yuh liked music so much, Jim. Ah'm awful glad, though.

JIM: Ah should say Ah was musical! Say, Mamie, yuh won't have ter fuss 'bout me stayin' home no more. Guess what?

MAMIE: Oh, Jim dear, tell me. Ah kain't guess.

JIM: Aw, guess! Ah jes' bought somethin' sence Ah left here.

MAMIE: Oh, Jim, what? Tell me, quick!

JIM: Well, Ah figgered Ah bin kinder mean, leavin' yuh home so much. So ter-night, when Ah left here, Ah thought Ah'd get mebbe a radio.

MAMIE [*Throwing her arms around him with a squeal of delight*]: Oh, Jim dear, Ah knew yuh was wonderful!

JIM [*Immensely pleased*]: Thought Ah didn' love yuh no more, didn' yuh? Well, Ah was on mah way ter the club ter ask one uv the boys 'bout a good radio, when Ah runs into Walt, here, an' heard him play the sweetest tune yuh ever want ter hear. Gee, but that feller kin play! [*Walt, in a wooden fashion, tries to look modest.*]

MAMIE: Oh, Jim dear, Ah'm so happy yuh goin' ter buy a radio. Yuh couldn't give me nothin' ter make me happier.

JIM: Oh, that was 'fore Ah met Walt. Walt talked me out'n the radio an'—

MAMIE [*Sharply*]: No—no!

JIM: Yuh bet he did, an' he talked me into buyin' a cornet. Jes' think, Mamie! The one he was playin' on ter-night. An' dirt cheap, too. Ain't it Walt?

WALT: Dirt cheap.

MAMIE [*Faintly*]: Not a cornet!

JIM [*Cheerfully*]: Yes, mam, a cornet. Yuh little Jimmie's goin' ter be the biggest cornet man in this burg 'lessn' a year, 'ceptin' Walt, here. How 'bout it, Walt?

WALT: Give yuh six months ter play real well.

JIM [*Delighted*]: Hear that, Mamie? He gimme six months. What's the matter, honey? Ain't yuh glad? Thought yuh was so keen on me stayin' home, evenin's. Now, Ah'll be here right by yuh side six nights out'n six.

MAMIE: Jim—Jim—Yuh doan mean it. Not the cornet. [*Shuddering violently.*] Ah hate 'em. Lawd, how Ah hate 'em! Once, Mom lived next door ter a man who was learnin' the cornet. He never did learn, Jim. Seems Ah kin hear the neighbors now, hollerin' fer him ter quit. [*Desperately*] Jim—Ah reckon yuh only teasin' me.

JIM: Teasin' yuh? Mah Lawd! Ef you wimmin ain' enuf ter drive a man crazy—

MAMIE [*Hoarsely*]: Jim—Yuh didn't buy *that* cornet?

JIM: Ah sure did.

MAMIE: An' yuh goin' ter learn ter play?

JIM: Ah sure am.

MAMIE [*Pleading as if for dear life*]: Jim yuh wouldn't git a radio instead ter please me? Ah'd buy it mahself, Jim. It wouldn't cost yuh a penny. Lemme buy it, Jim. Please!

JIM [*Loftily*]: Yuh ain't got no ambition, Mamie. That's what's the matter with yuh. Yuh wants ter listen ter other folks playin' but yuh doan' want yuh own husband ter learn. [*Turning coldly away.*] Open 'er up, Walt. [*Walt obeys. Relenting, Jim turns once more toward his wife, purposely ignoring the stricken look in her face.*] Now, honey, ef yuh wants ter see how the trick's done, keep yuh bright eyes on Walt Gilbert an' yuh old man. [*Jim raises the instrument to his lips and blows a frightful, gasping note. Mamie staggers weakly to a chair.*]

WALT: Fine. Now, try agin'. [*Jim obeys.*] Fine. Now try 'er agin'. [*Jim obeys in a sort of ecstasy.*] Fine. Now try 'er agin'. [*Jim obeys, and at the first choking, wheezing blast, Mamie begins to laugh, loudly, hysterically, painfully, the tears streaming down her face. The curtain descends while the two astonished men gaze in grave disapproval at the outrageous and unaccountable conduct of Mamie.*]

SCENE II. *Six weeks later.* MAMIE *is sitting dejectedly upon the couch in the living room, her elbows propped on her knees, her head clasped in her hands.* HARRY WILLIAMS, *one of* JIM's *pals, is standing, hat in hand, looking down at* MAMIE. *He seems anxious to go, yet unwilling to leave* MAMIE *without some ray of hope.*

HARRY: It sure is tough on yuh, Mamie. Gee! Seems like it kain't be true, Jim gone nuts on a cornet! [*Shaking his head sorrowfully*] Well—yuh got ter shake the blues, Mamie. Things got ter brighten up soon.

MAMIE [*Shaking her head slowly*]: 'Tain't no use, Harry. Ah useter hope it wouldn't last, but it's gettin' worse. [*Sitting up suddenly*] What'd yuh say, Harry, ef Ah tole yuh, he blows at that cornet in his sleep?

HARRY [*Horrified*]: Good Lawd, Mamie! 'Tain't bad as that?

MAMIE: He doan know Ah'm livin'. Ah 'spec he'll lose his job, soon. He doan think 'bout nothin' but that cornet.

HARRY: We got ter do somethin'. The boys' tired askin' him out. He's give up everythin'. Gawd, but it's funny—a thing like that happenin' ter Jimmie Jackson!

MAMIE: Yuh know, Harry, Ah kain't stand it much more. All the folks in the house stop speakin' ter me, 'causin' that cornet—

HARRY: Yuh poor kid!

MAMIE: Mis' Jennings slam the door in mah face last week. An' that ain't all. Harry. This mornin' Ah heard her talkin' over the dumbwaiter ter Mis' Simmons. She tole Mis' Simmons that all the tenants had got up a petition ter the landlord ter have us put out. Mis' Simmons said 'twas time we *was* kicked out.

HARRY: Lawd, but Jim oughter be shot!

MAMIE: Do yuh 'spose they kin get us put out, Harry?

HARRY: Sure not. Leastways, Ah doan think so.

MAMIE: 'Course Ah kain't blame them. Jim plays that cornet after twelve, some nights, never stoppin' ter say a word.

HARRY: Well, kid, yuh got ter chase them blues. Yuh lookin' bad, Mamie. Say, 'sposin' Ah takes yuh out ter-night. Aw, come on—

MAMIE: Jim ain't had his supper.

HARRY: Yuh waits on him too much. Quit hangin' 'round here an' mebbe 'fore yuh knows it, Jim'll be follerin' yuh ter see where yuh goin'.

MAMIE [*Shaking her head*]: Jim's awful jealous. He'd be sore ef Ah went out with yuh.

HARRY: See here, Mamie. Yuh makin' a big mistake. Now listen, kid. Ah'm goin' ter run along now. When Jim comes in, tell him that some uv the fellers looked him up an' ask him ter drop in ter the club ter-night. Ef he says he kain't go, get on yuh hat an' coat an' tell him yuh goin' out with one uv the boys. Yuh needn't mention mah name, 'lessn yuh has ter. That'll jolt him some. Make up a string er lies ef yuh has ter. Tell him yuh goin' ter a dance or a cabaret, or somethin' that'll fetch him. See? An' doan yuh wait ter see ef he's follerin'. Jes' put yuh things on an' go out, Jim'll be after yuh 'fore'n yuh kin say Jack Robinson.

MAMIE: Oh, Harry, do yuh think so?

HARRY: Ah sure do.

MAMIE: But where'll Ah meet yuh?

HARRY: Meet me at Hattie Smith's. But, Lawd, Mamie, Jim won't let yuh go—Ah knows Jim—

MAMIE: Ah ain' so sure Ah knows him, Harry. He's 'most a stranger ter me, now.

HARRY: Well, kid, buck up. Ef Ah doan see yuh by 'leven o'clock, Ah'll know everything's all right.

MAMIE [*Gratefully*]: Yuh awful good ter me, Harry.

HARRY: Aw, save yuh thanks. Ah ain't done nothin' but give yuh some good advice.

MAMIE: An' yuh doan mind takin' me out, 'casin' yuh has ter?

HARRY: Gee, Mamie, yuh cert'nly funny. Ah'll be right proud ter take yuh out. Yuh prettier'n most girls, Mamie, an' when it comes ter style—

MAMIE: Yuh awful good, Harry.

HARRY: Aw, fergit it. Well, 'slong, kid. 'Member, now, ter do like Ah tole yuh. [*Giving Mamie's hand a firm grip, Harry hurries out.*]

MAMIE [*The telephone rings and Mamie answers it*]: Hello! Yes— This Mis' Jackson. Mr. Cohen, the landlord? Yes—Ah wish yuh'd speak ter him yuhself, Mr. Cohen. Yes. Ah knows it disturbs the neighbors, but Yes—Yes—All right. Ah'll tell him. Yes. [*The door opens and Jim enters just as Mamie hangs up the receiver.*]

JIM: Hello, Mamie—[*Giving her a hurried kiss on her ear, and ducking into the room beyond the rose portières.*]

MAMIE: Hurry, Jim. Ah's kept yuh supper hot.

JIM [*Reappearing, cornet in hand*]: Doan need no supper, honey. Run into Walt an' we had a bite tergether. He was 'splain'n ter me—

MAMIE [*Abruptly*]: Jim. That was Mr. Cohen Ah was talkin' ter on the phone when yuh come in—

JIM: Cohen? Who's he. Ah doan know no Cohen.

MAMIE [*Bitterly*]: Yuh *uster* know him, before. Well, seems he knows *you;* all about *you.*

JIM: Yes? How come?

MAMIE: He's yuh landlord, Jim.

JIM: Oh! Well, what'd he want? Yuh paid the rent, didn' yuh?

MAMIE: 'Tain't no rent he wants ter see yuh 'bout. He says the neighbors bin complainin' 'bout yuh cornet an' yuh's got ter stop.

JIM: Ah's got ter stop, has Ah? Well, kin yuh beat that fer nerve?

MAMIE: Stop playin' or move.

JIM: Ah'd like ter see him or anybody else that kin make me stop playin'. Gawd! an' they calls this a free country!

MAMIE: The boys was up ter-night.

JIM [*Surprised*]: Here?

MAMIE: Yes. They wants yuh ter come ter the club ter-night? Somethin's on.

JIM: Nothin' doin'. Ah knows that bunch.

MAMIE [*Eagerly*]: Ah wish yuh'd go, Jim. Yuh ain't bin out fer more'n a month.

JIM: Not ter-night.

MAMIE: Jim, Ah wants ter go ter a dance ter-night. Won't yuh take me?

JIM: Sorry, kid, but yuh knows how Ah hates dances. 'Sides, Walt's comin' up later ter give me a lesson.

MAMIE [*Seats herself on the couch. Jim adjusts his music and begins a slow tortuous nerve-racking rendition of "Old Black Joe." Each note falls just a little short of the true pitch*]: Oh, Ah'm goin' out with one of the boys ter-night, Jim. [*An answering snort is her only answer.*] [*Bravely*] Goin' ter a cabaret after, too. [*Another staggering blast is her only answer.*]

MAMIE [*Desperately*]: Doan wait up fer me, Jim.

EPISODE

JIM [*Who has reached a stopping place*]: Have a good time, honey. [*The low wail starts once more.*]

MAMIE: Sure yuh doan mind mah goin', Jim?

JIM [*Irritably*]: See here, sister! If yuh goin', go on! Yuh keep on interrupting so An kain't git no decent practice.

MAMIE: Ah's goin' with Harry Williams. Harry's *some* feller!

JIM [*Patiently*]: Sure he is. Have a good time.

MAMIE: Ef Ah has a good time, Ah may not git home 'fore mornin', Jim.

JIM [*Just before he places the cornet to his lips*]: Take yuh key, Mamie.

MAMIE [*Who has slipped into her coat and hat*]: 'Sposin' Ah doan never come back, Jim? What then? [*A hoarse blare of sound is her only answer. Stifling a quick sob, Mamie wheels abruptly and rushes out. At the slam of the door, Jim looks up, relieved. He relaxes, sprawling upon the couch, adjusts the cornet at a more convenient angle and blows once more a thundering blast from his beloved instrument.*]

CURTAIN

MOTHER LIKED IT

BEING A PLAY IN TWO ACTS

BY ALVIRA HAZZARD

CHARACTERS

PRINCE ALI KAHN: *The Problem*
MEENA THOMAS: *Who is in love with the Prince*
ALTA FIELDS: *Whose practical jokes miss fire*
TESS: *Who takes life as she finds it*
JAY WINDSOR: *Who helps to solve the Problem*

ACT ONE

SCENE I.

The lobby of a local theatre. Alta is rather a spoiled, wilful girl of twenty. She is pretty, but impatient and self-centered. Throughout the play she pays much attention to her nose and hat. As the curtain rists, she is seated near Tess, a pleasant, plain girl of twenty-two. They are both dressed for the street, Tess very plainly, Alta smartly. They are seated Left.

ALTA (*rising and going to mirror to arrange her hat*). Are you sure you told her to meet us here?

TESS. Yes, in this lobby.

ALTA (*turning and looking at watch*). But we've waited twenty minutes! Meena is usually so very punctual.

TESS. Where are we going from here, to your home or to Crandall's?

190

ALTA. We can hardly make Crandall's if she doesn't hurry, and I must drive slowly today. I've paid two fines already this month.

TESS (*powdering nose*). Well, Alta, my conscience is clear. I gave the message as you left it. Meena said that she already had a seat for the performance, but would meet us here at 4 o'clock. You haven't mentioned the show. Did you like it?

ALTA. All except that stupid Indian Prince. His stunts were all chestnuts, his make-up atrocious, and his manner entirely too artificial. He was condescending. Doubtless, by this time, he thinks every girl in town is penning him love notes. (*Poses before mirror.*) Let's go and leave Meena.

TESS. I thought the juggling act was exceptionally good. They usually bore me to distraction. I'm getting hungry. Alta, did you ever eat at the La Ming? The food is wonderful.

ALTA (*visibly impatient, fixing hat*). Confound meeting an old maid! I suppose she's lengthening her newest gown, or hasn't come at all lest the Indian Prince shock her.

(*Meena is a charming girl of eighteen years. One should get the idea that up to now she has been very retiring, and reserved. She enters quietly with her hat in her hand. Alta has her back turned and does not see her enter. She tosses the hat on Tess' lap, and, tipping up behind Alta, covers her eyes. Tess rises.*)

ALTA (*embarrassed, turning as Meena releases her*). You, Meena? We're out of sorts waiting!

MEENA (*putting on hat before mirror*). So I judged by your last remark. (*Laughs, with show of anger.*) Cat!

ALTA. Oh, forgive me. I was a bit rude. But you yourself often admit that you are—

MEENA (*with a dramatic gesture*). Practical—I've stopped calling myself an old maid. I'm sorry to be late, but I stayed over to see Ali Kahn again. For one mellow glance from him I'd—Oh, pshaw! Practically speaking, he's just another individual, but he *is* wonderful. Don't you think so?

ALTA (*grimacing*). No, and we are late.

TESS (*who, leaning against the wall, shows interest in the conversation*). And we are famished. (*General primping and powdering as Tess starts toward right.*)

MEENA (*dramatically, as she lags behind*). That adorable Prince! Practically speaking he is—.

ALTA. Come to earth, Meena, let's move.

MOTHER LIKED IT

SCENE II.

The lobby of Crandall's fashionable Cafe. This scene is much the same as the first. Lounge chairs, and a mirror in the center of the back wall. There is a writing desk right. The girls enter right, Alta going immediately to the mirror, Tess sitting and powdering her nose. Meena perches on the arm of a chair.

ALTA (*without turning*). I know I'm a sight, and with this added excitement! Why I ever planned to come here is more than I can understand—now!

MEENA. Alta, I'm a bit worried. Don't you think we should have stopped? Did you notice how embarrassed that boy looked? I'm sure he has your number, and will report you to the Highway Commission.

ALTA (*coming down center, and peering left*). Now I am disgraced! There's Mary Tallman in a gorgeous new wrap. Is that Tommy Boyle with her? And he has shaved off his mustache! Why *did* I go to that beastly show? I feel all awry.

TESS (*happily—rising*). Do we care about Tommy Boyle and Mary Tallman? Queen Elizabeth's ghost could not stop me now. I crave nourishment (*gesturing toward dining hall*). Let us repair to the dining room and partake of the marvelous dishes that Monsieur Crandall has had prepared for us.

MEENA. I'll be satisfied to partake of the FOOD. Tess, dear, you missed your calling when you didn't follow the stage. But I'm with you and famished. (*Turns to Alta, who has slumped into a chair.*) We're off to the victuals Alta. (*They go into the dining hall.*)

ALTA (*rising reluctantly to follow them is attracted by something off right. She screams faintly, and drops back into the chair; rises again, goes quickly toward dining hall, then returns to center stage. She is very nervous, and her voice shakes*). The man, the very man I struck, and with Jay Windsor! Whatever shall I do? He'll surely recognize me! I—I—I'll—

(She turns from right to left several times, and finally faces away from them. Jay and the stranger enter right. The stranger is limping. He has no hat, and his tie is twisted. Jay is a plain, modern young man of twenty-five. The stranger is the better looking and five years younger. His muddy clothes have a collegiate cut. Alta is looking off left, but cannot, as they near her, resist looking at them.)

ALTA (*facing them*). Jay, Jay, is he hurt! What can I do? Is it serious?

MEENA (*sighing deeply*). Well, smarty, I've done it, and I'm not disgraced. He was so kind and polite—and gracious. Say something, Alta Fields! Are you quite satisfied?

ALTA (*fiercely*). That Jay Windsor to double-cross me!

TESS. Nothing to do but go in to dinner. Oh, Alta, you're a clever little fixer, you are. (*She laughs: Meena and Tess go into dining hall.*)

ALTA (*hanging back*). As if I could have depended on Jay! I could swear real damns!

(*She flounces after other girls. She is not quite off when Jay enters. He is ridiculously costumed: turban awry, trousers too large. He yoo-hoos to Alta, who turns one fierce glance on him and turns again into the dining hall. Jay slumps into a chair.*)

JAY. Late, and all this tomfoolery for nothing. (*The Prince enters. Jay does not see him. He studies Jay, and walking to him, speaks in perfect English.*)

PRINCE (*leaning over Jay*). What's this, old man, competition? You might have waited until I left town.

JAY (*starting*). It's Mr. Smith, the man of the accident, or I lose my guess. And are you really the guy who has drawn such crowds to the Empire?

PRINCE. Soft pedal! I have two days more, and the public doesn't need to know the bare facts. You see, I'm a student and this act as a summer job pays my tuition at the University of Chicago. I begin my last year next month. But why the impersonation?

JAY. It's a long story, but fate must intend us to be friends. Why, this is the second unforeseen meeting in a week. I must get out of here at once. I say, how would you enjoy going home with me, where we may have a pleasant smoke-chat?

PRINCE. I'd like it, my friend, but there (*waving toward dining hall*) in that hall is the girl of the golden smile, the liquid eyes. The very girl I had never dared hope to meet.

JAY (*with vim*). Well I'll be . . .

PRINCE. As I entered this lobby, she and two other young ladies were talking low and gesturing as if some conspiracy was afoot. As I came nearer, the girl of girls very timidly and reluctantly spoke to me. Never, never was I so distressed! This beastly make up! If I discard it she'll probably loathe me, but I *do* want to meet her as Jonas Smithly.

JAY (*making a face*). Ye gods, man, is that your real name?

PRINCE. It is.

JAY. Well, I suppose that can't be helped, but I know the young lady. She is Miss Taylor, and a charming young lady, indeed.

PRINCE (*in anticipation*). Can we dress and get back here by the time she comes out from dinner?

JAY. 'Fraid not. We've talked some time already. I can't be found here like this. (*He rises.*) I'll arrange a meeting for tomorrow.

PRINCE. "No time like the present." "He who hesitates is lost." And so on. May I use your name?

JAY (*moving toward exit*). Yes, use my name but make it snappy. I'll wait out there in that taxi.

(*Jay goes out. The Prince sits at table where paper is provided. He writes and tears up six sheets. Finally he writes a note to his satisfaction. This he encloses in an envelope, kisses it lightly, and takes it with him out after Jay. The girls come out, and the doorman enters immediately and says, "Note for Miss Taylor." She opens it hurriedly, then gives a little scream. Others, who have been primping, turn.*)

MEENA. Listen to this! (*She reads.*) "Dear Miss Taylor: I'm not an Indian Prince, but a husky college half-back and one-hundred-percent American. My act is only a summer diversion. Can you like me the tiniest bit, just the same? Mr. Windsor promises to see that we are properly introduced. Despite the fact that my real name is Jonas Smithly, I trust that soon, very soon, we will be better acquainted.

"Very sincerely yours,

"J. SMITHLY

"P. S.—If you can't stand the name, it *could* be changed, but mother liked it.

"J. S."

(*Meena smiles to herself and holds the letter to her breast. The other girls stand in utter surprise and bewilderment.*)

CURTAIN.

LITTLE HEADS

ONE-ACT PLAY OF NEGRO LIFE

BY ALVIRA HAZZARD

CHARACTERS

BEE
JOE } *Twelve-Year-Old Twins*

MRS. LEE: *Their mother*
FRANCES: *Their sister*
EDNA: *A friend*

The scene is a comfortable living room. There is a window, right, and an entrance from the front door and the rest of the house at the left. The arrangement of the furniture is optional. There should be a reading table in the room. Joe and Bee are discovered at opposite ends of the table, studying.

JOE *(looking up)*. What's the good of studying, Bee. Let's quit.

BEE *(looking around cautiously)*. You know what mother said.

JOE *(in whisper)*. She wouldn't know.

BEE. But you know what Miss Perry said about your conscience!

JOE. When?

BEE. Oh, you were there. She says that a little voice inside worries us most awful if we do something wrong, whether anyone knows it or not.

JOE. How does she know?

BEE. Don't be a big silly! She's smart, like Frances. Mother says that Francie'll be a teacher some day, just like Miss Perry.

JOE *(chin in hands)*. Miss Perry's white.

BEE. All the same, Francie's just as smart.

JOE. She's smarter, I think—except when she reminds me about behind my ears and all that nonsense. *(Pauses.)* Say, Bee, wouldn't you like to be white sometimes?

BEE. No.

JOE. Aw, be yourself! I saw you almost cry the other day in geography. *You* saw Allen Farnsworth look and grin when they were saying about the black race havin' kinky hair and all that junk.

BEE. Well, anyway, I wouldn't be white.

JOE *(pointing finger).* You're bein' stubborn!

BEE *(slapping finger).* Get your finger out o' my face.

JOE *(catching her hand and laughing).* Who'll make me?

BEE *(rising, he holds her tightly).* Stop, Joe,

JOE. Make me.

(They come forward. Joe is pleasant and teasing, but Bee is getting cross. She cannot get away.)

BEE *(kicking).* MOTHER! Joe's hurting me! *(Mrs. Lee enters.)*

MRS. LEE. Joe, what are you doing to your sister?

JOE *(letting go).* Nothin'.

BEE. He hurt my wrist. *(She rubs it.)*

JOE *(quickly).* She slapped me.

BEE. You started it.

JOE. I didn't.

MRS. LEE *(firmly).* Stop it! *(They eye her, and are silent.)* Back to your books, both of you.

BEE. But mother . . .

MRS. LEE. Not another word. Frances is coming tomorrow night, and you won't want to study then.

JOE. Bee said . . .

MRS. LEE. Don't make me speak to either of you again.

(Slowly, silently, they flop into chairs again. They cast sly glances at each other, trying to keep sober. Finally both grin sheepishly.)

BEE *(softly).* You didn't hurt me much.

JOE. Why'd you holler?

BEE. I wanted you to stop.

JOE. I'll squeeze you hard next time.

BEE *(hands behind her).* Dare you.

JOE. Say it again, and see what happens.

BEE. Double dare.

(Joe jumps at her so suddenly that in evading him she falls over chair. He trips also. They are in awkward positions on floor when Mrs. Lee appears.)

BOTH *(giggling)*. It was Bee—Joe.

MRS. LEE *(entering and re-arranging things)*. March right off to bed, the two of you. Do you hear me?

(They get up and face left. At sound of door bell Mrs. Lee goes out. Voices are heard outside: "Frances!" "Hello, mother," etc. Children rush out. They come back immediately with each a bag. Frances and mother follow. Frances is the center of attention. She takes off hat and coat and sits down. Mrs. Lee stands near table. The children stand at a distance from Frances, eyeing her.)

MRS. LEE. Well, this is a surprise, Frances. How did it happen?

JOE *(to Bee)*. I will!

BEE *(alarmed)*. You needn't.

JOE *(teasing)*. I will!

BEE. Don't, Joe, please . . .

JOE. Frances, she got a C in 'rithmetic.

BEE *(running out)*. You mean, hateful boy! I hate it, anyway.

FRANCES *(laughing)*. Come back, Bee, it can't be helped. I hate it, too. *(Bee comes back and hangs over Frances's chair. Joe sprawls near his mother. They cast glances at each other.)* Oh, yes, you were asking me why I am ahead of time. Well, you see, there is to be a most wonderful week-end party at Oak Manor given by one of the wealthiest girls on the campus. Mary says that my name is actually on the list. I had to get home and sort of get together. I cut a class to do it, but the party is worth it.

MRS. LEE. We'll miss having you here.

FRANCES. I know it, but this time I'm not able to be sensible and resist.

MRS. LEE. Of course you want to go. They are all white though, aren't they?

FRANCES. Yes, but they are all so nice to me that I shall be quite at home. Then, too, Palmer is going. We can be together, and I just know it will be great.

MRS. LEE. Does everyone in the school go?

FRANCES. Indeed not. That's the thrill of it. Only a dozen or fifteen couples are to be favored. No one but Mary could make me believe that I'm actually included.

MRS. LEE *(trying to hide worry)*. Won't it be expensive, Francie?

FRANCES. About a hundred dollars extra would do wonders. Isn't my endowment policy due about now? You know I'm twenty-one. *(She hugs her knees in anticipation.)*

MRS. LEE. We'll see about it. But run and rest a while now, and I'll get you a bite to eat.

FRANCES *(rising)*. Sounds good to me. I'm famished. But such oodles of news as I still have to tell you. Don't bother fixing anything special, for I could chew shingle nails. *(She goes out. Bee follows, making a face at Joe as she reaches the door. Joe bolts after her.)*

MRS. LEE. Right back here, young man. I'll have no more fussing in this house tonight.

(A voice is heard outside. A pleasant young girl of about Frances's age enters.)

EDNA. Hello, folks. I walked right in, since the door was open.

MRS. LEE. Fine. Come right in, Edna.

EDNA *(coming in and ruffling Joe's hair; he frowns)*. I saw Frances come in, and couldn't wait to greet her. Isn't she ahead of time?

MRS. LEE *(blankly)*. Yes, we were not looking for her until tomorrow. It was a real surprise. She is upstairs, and will be right down. Make yourself at home. *(Edna leans on the table and thumbs a book. Mrs. Lee rises.)* Edna, my dear—*(noticing Joe)*—Joe, mother wants to speak to Edna. *(He scuffs out.)* I suppose I shouldn't bother you with this, but, well, it's like this . . .

EDNA *(encouraging)*. What is it?

MRS. LEE *(in an attempt to get it over with)*. Frances had some money from an endowment policy. We spent it, and cannot replace it at once. I didn't think of Francie wanting it so soon. I had planned to give it to her in gold for her birthday. *(She sits down again and fingers her beads or scarf nervously.)*

EDNA. Do you think that Frances will really mind?

MRS. LEE. Oh, she won't mind, because I deposited it to Bob's account. He finishes Howard this year, you know, and he is always broke. Poor Bob's pitiful plea came with the check—the same mail. It was pampering him to send so much, but, as I told you, the money was handy, and I planned getting it in gold from the bank the first of the month. What worries me is that Francie has her mind set on a party for this very week-end. I'd rather do anything than spoil her fun.

EDNA. That is a shame. What can we do?

MRS. LEE *(leaning toward Edna)*. I don't know, but I thought you might help me think. I'm rather upset about it. She wants new clothes, I'm sure.

(Edna gets up and walks to the window. There is an awkward silence.)

EDNA *(turning)*. I'll tell you what, let's not tell her until the last moment—that is, let's wait a day and see if she decides to do without many new things. I'll try to talk her into making the trip as cheaply as possible.

MRS. LEE *(rising and going toward door)*. All right, Edna, you do that, and we'll both sleep on it before we tell her. You just make yourself comfortable while I fix her something to eat. She ought to be down any minute now. *(She goes out.)*

EDNA *(coming down center and sitting on chair arm)*. Just like a mother. A couple hundred—it must have been that much—to that spendthrift of a son. And to be paid back to a gem of a daughter from the interest of the family income. Well, Frances deserves it, there is no doubt about that. *(She goes back to the window and looks out. Frances comes in on tiptoe, and surprises Edna. They hug each other. Edna whispers something.)*

FRANCES. Not really! Is he keen?

EDNA. You'll see him. How about yourself—heartbreaker?

FRANCES. No news here, except that the adorable Palmer Brennon is to be invited to Dolores' party, and Mary says she saw my name on her list. I hope the invitation comes tonight.

EDNA *(sitting, while Frances lounges on the arm)*. Your mother told me. Isn't it thrilling!

FRANCES. Positively! They evidently are asking *both* of us, to make it pleasant all around. We must shop tomorrow. I have an insurance that is most handy at this particular time. I really think mother has it already, but wants to be mysterious.

EDNA. Yes?

MRS. LEE *(from outside)*. Come on, girls. I'm all ready.

(They go out with their heads together. Joe comes in and sits down in deep thought, his head in his hands. He snaps his fingers as if an idea had struck him.)

JOE *(calling)*. Bee, O Bee! *(She enters.)* Listen, silly, I've got news.

BEE. Foolin?

JOE. No, I'm not.

BEE *(going to window)*. Joe, the mailman is coming here. I can just see him.

JOE *(over her shoulder)*. Gee, Sis, I've a hunch it's that letter.

BEE. What letter?

JOE. You wouldn't understand, but wait. *(He runs out, coming back with a letter in his hand. Bee stays at the window.)* See, I was right. It's a special for Frances. Can you keep a secret?

BEE. Of course.

JOE. Well, this is that letter inviting Frances to the party, and her money is spent, so she can't go.

BEE. I've got five dollars in my bank.

JOE *(with disgust)*. What's five dollars? The check was for ever so much over a hundred. Sit down. *(She does.)* Now, listen. If Frances does not get this mother won't have to worry about sending her money to Bob. She'll think the rich girl forgot to invite her, after all.

BEE *(in alarm)*. Oh, Joe, we can't keep it.

JOE. Well, what shall we do?

BEE *(frowning)*. I can't think.

JOE *(fingering the letter)*. We might open it.

BEE *(covering her ears)*. Oh, Joe, never, never!

JOE *(with an air of importance and standing with feet apart, near her)*. Bee, remember you're a girl. I'm going to pry it open and read it to see if that helps.

BEE. How?

JOE. My jackknife. *(They bend eagerly over the table as Joe prys the letter open carefully. As it is done they both sigh heavily.)* Listen to this. "Dear Frances, I'm having a week-end party at the Oak Manor, and want you to come. Palmer, we hope, will come also. You are both so clever, we want you to help enter- tain. Haven't you some old things so that you can dress like— well, you know—sort of old-fashioned, and sing some of those delightful spirituals? Palmer will probably bring his sax. You will have some fun, besides serving your schoolmate, Dolores Page."

BEE. Then Frances won't need much money, after all.

JOE. Won't you ever grow up a little!

BEE. I'm as old as you are.

JOE *(strolling to window, and looking back at her in contempt).* In years.

BEE. You're not so awful smart, see.

JOE *(coming back to the table).* Well, we can't argue this time, and you can't ever tell, because you helped me. *(He tears the letter into bits and stuffs it into his pockets, while Bee looks on in wonder and amazement. She jumps up and runs to door to peep and see that no one has seen them.)*

BEE. Don't you feel most awfully wicked, Joe?

JOE *(with feeling).* No, I don't, but I just hate that Dolores Page. Let's go now. *(Voices are heard).* We'll feel—guilty—a little bit—when they come in. *(They tiptoe out hand in hand.)*

Two Gods

A MINARET

By Doris Price

CHARACTERS:

CORRINNE BARBER: *a widow.*
AMY GREY: *a neighbor.*
REVEREND SIMPSON.
VIRGINIA KELTON.
Place: A swamp region near the Sabine
River, dividing Alabama and Texas.
Time: About 1890.

SCENE:

*Kitchen of a Negro farmhouse. There is a table in the center piled
with kitchen utensils for pie making. There is no fireplace in the
room only a big, monstrous black stove in the center back. To the
left of the stove is a paneless window with wooden shutters and
to the right of it is an old fashioned kitchen cupboard, called a
'safe.' One of the wooden shutters is unfastened and flaps back
and forth with an irritating clatter throughout the play. Through
the partly opened window, and the open door to the left of the
window one can see the fields of corn in the distance. It is near-
ing dusk and the hue of the horizon changes from that of a daz-
zling setting sun to the quiet deep purple of an approaching summer evening.*

*As the curtain rises Corrinne, slender, brown and tall, her
head tied loosely with a green scarf is bending at the cupboard
trying to extract a tin pie pan. She finally obtains it and stands
up in relief from her former uncomfortable position. She moves
towards the table on which is spread flour, milk in a pitcher,
cloves, apples to be peeled and some partly peeled. It is easy to
see that she is following no systematic plan of work and that very*

probably her mind is on something entirely different from the process of pie making. As soon as she reaches the table she turns back with annoyance to the cupboard and dipping her fingers into a can hidden somewhere in its recesses she brings them out dripping with fat and spatters the tin carelessly but vigorously.

CORRINNE—Ah, shoot, now, where dat—? *(She finally secures some dried spice and returns to the table.)*

AMY—*(Fat, brown, comfortably middle-aged, sticks her uncovered head in the open doorway.)* Correen-n! *(Her voice drawls.)* Is yer busy, chile? *(She turns her head searchingly.)* Oh, dere yer be! *(She steps in.)*

CORRINNE—*(With a start of surprise.)* Come on in, Amy! Lor, yer sho give me a fright. I's thot may be dat preacher wuz trapsing over heah ergin.

AMY—*(Seating herself solidly in a wooden rocker near the doorway.)* Naw, jes me dis time. I guess yer kinner sorry taint der preacher do, aint yer?

CORRINNE—*(Angrily.)* I aint en what's mo, yer knows I aint!

AMY—*(Placidly.)* Well, tain no need to be putting yer back up ter me count er der preacher. Sho, is I git worried er plenty answering der dousands er questions he always askin 'bout yer.

CORRINNE—I aint wantin ter heah noffin 'bout 'im.

AMY—I ain sayin yer want ter heah 'bout him—what I's sayin es dat he mos worrin me ter deaf tryin ter heah 'bout you. Jes der odder night—

CORRINNE—En I aint wantin' ter heah dat nedder.

AMY—*(Stopping at the half-way of putting a "goober" into her mouth.)* Yer sho is a queer gal!

CORRINNE—Maybe I is, en maybe I aint!

AMY—Humph! *(Changing to a more diplomatic subject but not in the least disposed or intending to leave the matter as it now stands.)* Is yer makin apple pie?

CORRINNE—From der tree Albert planted when we furst came heah en he built dis house.

AMY—Dey fine lookin apples. *(She takes one putting the remaining "goobers" in her pocket.)*

CORRINNE—Aint dey! Albert sho wuz anxious ter see hit bloom. En der very year after he died—*(Her voice becomes more hard and bitter)* der ver' nex yeah after he died den hit blooms!

AMY—Dis is sho good furst fruit.

207

CORRINNE—Uh huh, der ver' furst. Dare been blooms on hit las yeah en yeah befo, but dis is der furst time dat we got real red apples.

AMY—Hits a fine tree en sweet.

CORRINNE—One der ver' bes in dese parts. Ole' Mars gave hit ter him when he heard we's don got marr'ed. (*She stops her work at the table as though lost in some refreshing memory then returns to it kneading the dough a little more viciously.*) 'Taint right, 'taint right!

AMY—Yer always quarreling wid der Lord 'bout der deaf of Albert. Odder folkses men don died en dey got over hit.

CORRINNE—Odder folks ain helpin me none!

AMY—(*Warningly*) You bettah watch out, gal. I's tellin yer what der Lord loves. He's mighty, en his ways is hard ter understand—lak Reverend Simpson said der odder—

CORRINNE—I ain wantin ter heah nuffin' 'bout Reven Simpson. I don tole yer onst.

AMY—Yer sho is agin dat po downtrodden soul. What's he don ter yer?

CORRINNE—He ain done nuffin an he ain gon do nuffin!

AMY—Well, hit beats me as ter why yer take on so, en eny one can see dat he es ez hard after yer ez a steer is after er—

CORRINNE—(*Angrily—her voice vibrating with anger*) I done tole yer I ain wantin ter heah nuffin 'bout 'im, aint I!

AMY—(*Beginning to grow uncomfortable*) Well, you talk den, if I cain say nuffin but you got ter git all riled up. A body'd think— (*She stops suggestively*).

CORRINNE—A body'd think what?

AMY—I ain sayin—ain yer don tole me ter shut up? Well, when folks don be wantin ter heah what I got ter say, Amy Grey ain nobody's fool! I shut up!

CORRINNE—I ain meant nuffin en yer knows it. Lor, hit sho is hot in dis kitchen! (*She gets a paper and fans excitedly*). Amy aint yer hot too? Yer better set more over in der doorway. Dere's mo breeze dere. When yer been ter town?

AMY—Not en mor'n er month. I got me some new shoes. We stopped en took Reveren—(*She stops—looking at Corrinne expectantly. Corrinne remains unshaken, fanning as tho she has not heard*).

CORRINNE—(*Putting down paper*) Guess I'd better finish up dis pie do I declare, hit's so hot in heah! (*She begins rolling out the dough with a wooden roller.*)

AMY—I'm gitting kinda thirsty! (*She goes into a corner and drinks looking out the window.*) I kin see yer husband's grave from heah.

CORRINNE—Uh huh, aint you knowed it? Dere's der tree right above hit.

AMY—Is yer still going up dere ter pray lak yer did when he furst died?

CORRINNE—Uh huh, ebber day, I goes by dere en I pray, but things is different now.

AMY—(*Still absorbed at the window*) Look lak somebody at der fence up dere.

CORRINNE—Who is hit? Jenny?

AMY—Uh, huh, I guess so. I cain jes tell. Is she still pesterin yer lak she used ter?

CORRINNE—Pesterin me? I ain nebber said she pested me. Where yer git sech ideas.

AMY—Dat wuz er long time ergo befor yer Alburt died. En yer said 'bout her always comin ter borrow sompun.

CORRINNE—Oh, naw, she ain pestin me none now.

AMY—(*Looking at her slyly*) Is yer still thinkin she's don got queer from so much livin alone?

CORRINNE—Is ah ebber said dat 'bout her?

AMY—Uh, huh, when yer en Alburt furst come. Yer used ter talk all der time 'bout how queer Jenny wuz en Alburt did too. Don yer remember?

CORRINNE—Yer mus be mistaken, Amy, I don' remember er thing 'bout all dat!

AMY—Humph, naw, I guess yer ain rermembin hit *now!*

CORRINNE—Now, what yer mean?

AMY—Nuffin but dat you is much alone ez she is.

CORRINNE—Huh, yer ain said nuffin. I is mor er alone den she is! Her folks ain died! Ebber one of mine—died—God took em! God took ebber one erway! Mah mudder, mah fadder, mah sisters en my budder—he took all, ebber last one ov dem en den on top er dat he took Alburt. En ain lef nuffin dat berlongs ter me. She's still got some kin folks, even if dey don lib wid her but God don dook all mine. Yes, suh, God done hit! En I wuz jes ez tru harted ez eny in der lan!

AMY—Is she been comin ter see yer offen?

CORRINNE—Offen? Naw, what she gon come ter see me offen fer?

AMY—Nuffin. I jes wondered dat's all.

CORRINNE—Naw!

AMY—Der sun is settin o'ber behin der marsh. Hit sho look pretty.

CORRINNE—I sho glad 'cause hit's too hot in heah fer eny good use.

AMY—Why don yer tak dat scarf from roun' yer head den, if yer so hot? Hit cool yer head off some.

CORRINNE—Naw, I don wanna, besides, I jes washed hit.

AMY—Oh, I's wonderin what yer had hit tied up fer. Yer ain been had hit tied up when yer washed hit befo.

CORRINNE—Naw. (*Very emphatically*) I ain but I tied hit up dis time!

AMY—Lor, if yer ain jes ez touchy. Yer ought ter git out more en talk ter folks. Lor, if yer ain jes ez touchy. A body is mos scared ter open his mouf. I guess I better be goin myself if I cain say nuffin.

CORRINNE—(*Half heartedly*) Naw, tain no nede fer yer ter go. Sit down. (*She looks at her sideways with a little frown of irritation.*)

AMY—(*Seating herself complacently*) Well, I guess I stay till yer git der pie baked, anyway.

CORRINNE—Uh huh, stay en have er piece—'twon take long. I putting one in der oben right now. (*She does so.*)

AMY—Yer sho look queer wid dat scarf aroun yer head.

CORRINNE—Hit's er pretty scarf; Alburt gibe hit ter me.

AMY—He did! En yer ain nebber showed hit ter me. Yer sho is a secrertive creature.

CORRINNE—How's Maddy?

AMY—Well, she wasn't so well so I heard. She ain been ter prayer meeting fer two weeks now, but I 'pose sh'll be dere termerrer. She's right down religious. Yer ain gon cach cher backslidin' lak some folks does. We haben barbecue termerrer night. You ought to come out, Renny. Revern sho would 'joy smackin his lips on one dose pies!

CORRINNE—I ain comin.

210

AMY—Well, seen ez yer ain been ter church, er prayer meetin, er baptizin, er nuffin, folks is sayin yer's a backslider!

CORRINNE—I ain carin what folks say. Dey ain feedin me is dey? I got my own farm. I do all my work en Alburt's too, en I ain askin not er single one of dem for a potato er a grain er wheat! Dey kin jes min dere own business!

AMY—Gal, when folks is gittin er way from der Lord it's der Lord's business en we dat's tryin ter bring folks inter der fold is rersponsible. God hold's us rersponsible when we don lif er han ter save drownin backsliders.

CORRINNE—Der Lord ain got nuffin ter do wit it. He thru wid me now dere ain nobody else fer him ter kill!

AMY—Don be gittin sacrerligious before me! I declare, if yer ain aiming ter be struck down dead wid lightin' der way yer carrin on!

CORRINNE—I'd be glad of it! I'd be glad of it!

AMY—Maybe dat's why he ain takin yer den. Dere's things worse en deaf—in dat's livin in a world er sin en diserpation. Reveren' sho needs ter come en talk ter yer. Yer headed straight fer Hell, 'corrdin' ter my notions. (*Pause*) But I guess I had better go enyway—how is der pie?

CORRINNE—*I look at it. (She takes it out viciously)* Yeah, hit's done. (*She gets a knife cuts and places a piece in a saucer and gives it to Amy.*)

AMY—Is yer heard about dose folks over at der marsh?

CORRINNE—What folks?

AMY—I ain knowin. Dey call dem debbil worshipers en dey got a strange temple built of green pine en oak and dey doin all kinda queer things! Aint yer been hearin of dem?

CORRINNE—Naw, I ain heard nuffin.

AMY—Dey say ez dey got a red altar built in dis green shed.

CORRINNE—Red en green dey Christmas an Christian colors aint dey?

AMY—Yes, but dis red means hell, en der green—

CORRINNE—What der green stand fer?

AMY—I ain heard what der green's fer. Dey say dat's a secret punisherible by deaf. Won none of dem tell yer a thing about hit.

CORRINNE—*Is* yer asked dem?

AMY—Dem? I don talk wid none of dem debbil worshippers. Dat Jenny's one.

CORRINNE—How yer know?

AMY—Henry saw her strappin her saddle on en round her left ankle wuz a silver band! Dey don boun demselves ter der debbil en fersaken God entirely!

CORRINNE—Well, what's God gon do fer 'em? Dat's what I'd lak ter kno!

AMY—(*Rising in horror*) Dat's blasphemy—Dat's blasphemy!

CORRINNE—(*Calmly but firmly*) I ain carin what hit is. I's jes ez good er Christian ez you. I went ter cherch. I prayed. We put our money in der money box. I visited der sick en prayed fer dem en so did Alburt. En wid all dat, God separated us. He tore us asunder his own self. Naw, I ain shame! Naw!

AMY—(*Sitting down again and continuing more quietly*) Yer sho wuz a good Christian. Der choir don seem right widout yer voice joined in. It jes don seem right. Couse I don mak no 'prtence er sayin I lak ebbrthing God's seen fit ter do ter me, but I ain complainin. I ain complainin. Dere's er lots mo dat's worse off den I iz en I thank der Lord fer dat. Dere's folks dat's starvin en sick er bed sence dey's born en full ob disease en achin wid pain dey en en day out, but I ain complainin. I got things ter be thankful fer too. I got my home en my two chillen well en sound. I got dead, too, jes lak you has, my mother is dead, mah pap is er cripple en dere—

CORRINNE—Yes, but yer got somebody! God ain got hit in fer yer lak he is fer me!

AMY—You jes goin crazy, Correen. God ain got nuffin in fer nobody. Lord, yer sho gits strange ideas in yer head. Yer ought ter stop stayin in en livin alone yer git queer notions in yer head in ye'll be stone crazy 'fore yer kno hit. You ought ter come out en git wid men folks en git marr'd agin. Odder women is los dere husbands en marr'd agin—

CORRINNE—Dat's dem! Dat ain me!

AMY—I sho wish yer would come back in der choir. Don seem right wid yer out. Revern misses yer too. He's always talkin 'bout how he used ter look at der back of yer neck en yer black hair glistenin in der lamplights. Yer sho got pretty hair en folks sho liked ter see it. Mah grandmother had long black thick hair lak yern.

CORRINNE—'Tain no use in all dat. I ain comin back ter der choir.

AMY—How come? Correen, yer ain cut dat pretty hair off is yer?

CORRINNE—I washed hit I tole yer!

AMY—Don' yer be gittin no queer spite notions in yer head en cut all dat hair of yern off. Yer sho would be crazy!

CORRINNE—(*Standing stock still*) What yer mean spite notions?

AMY—Jes seem like yer got er spite erbout somepun or somebody.

CORRINNE—Who I gon hav er spite erbout?

AMY—Well, I thout ez maybe folks tole yer Revern' was likin dat Macatown woman. I kno better. Revern' ain wanted er soul but you ebber since he put his foot in dat cherch en seen yer singing in dat choir.

CORRINNE—I aint studdin him!

AMY—He's er real nice man. Ain nebber been a better preacher in dese parts. Sho is too bad. I feels sorry fer him myself.

CORRINNE—(*Unsympathetically*) So does I.

AMY—Dey ain er soul could sing "Down by der Ribber side" lak yer kin, Correen.

CORRINNE—I don lak dat song no mo.

AMY—Yer don lak hit no more! Yer sho must be crazy. Yer been sayin yer crazy bout dat song fer years an ebber body knows hit.

CORRINNE—I don lak hit no mo. (*She puts another pie into the oven and slams the door vigorously.*)

AMY—Is yer ebber heard dat queer music does debbil worshippers sing? Yer ain been listenin ter hit has yer? Dey say if yer listen ter hit, dat a spell er'll come obber yer.

CORRINNE—Yer der one dat's crazy. How I gon heah hit?

AMY—Well, I ain knowin. There's been times late at night when hit seemed as do I heard hit myself, but I'd wake up en know I's jes dreamin. (*There is an approaching sound of humming. It is the deep voice of Reverend Simpson and he's singing "Down by the Ribber Side".*)

CORRINNE—(*Tensely*) Who's dat?

AMY—(*They both go to the window*) Hit sound jes lak Revern' Simpson. En dat's jes who hit is. Lor, gal, dat man sho is crazy 'bout you.

CORRINNE—(*More tensely*) I ain studdin 'im I tells yer!

AMY—Well, I don see no cause ter git all het up!

CORRINNE—I ain het up! (*She seats herself sideways on the edge of the table the skirts of her petticoats exposing a slim brown leg and ankle bound with a shining silver band.*) Yer ain finished yer pie. Don yer want er nudder piece.

AMY—Dis is er plenty, thank yer kindly. I mus be goin now.

CORRINNE—Yer ain got no cause te hurry. (*The Reverend enters.*)

AMY—Howdy, Revern! How you?

REV. SIMPSON—Jes fine, yes fine, Sistah Amy. Ain seen er better day. (*To Corrinne, in a voice of milk and honey*) Howdy, Sistah. How you been?

CORRINNE—Der same ez I wuz der las time yer come.

AMY—Well, I guess I better be goin. I been tryin ter git Corrinne ter come back in the choir. She sho needs er good talkin ter if yer asks me. (*To Corrinne*) Yer better look et yer pie. Good day ter yer, folks.

REVEREND—Dis pie sho does smell good. Kin er hungry preacher have er piece, Sistah?

CORRINNE—I ain carin. (*She doesn't move. He cuts the pie and eats it from his hand.*)

REVEREND—It sho is good, yes, sir, hit sho is. Yer kin sing en cook too. Is yer made up yer mind ter return ter de ways of der Lord, Sistah?

CORRINNE—Naw, I aint, en I ain gonna.

REVEREND—Der Lord 'ain got no use fer backsliders. Yer knows dat.

CORRINNE—Is he got use fer yer if yer ain er backslider? If he is I ain seen it!

REVEREND—Yer ridin high fer punishment. Yer ridin awful high. What yer wearin dat green rag on yer head fer?

CORRINNE—'Cause hit's my head en my rag!

REVEREND—Yer right dere, en er lot more could be yourn if yer would jes believe in der Lord. Yer wuz real happy—Yer ain happy now is yer? Now, jes tell der truf! Is yer happy der way yer livin?

CORRINNE—I'd be if twasn't fer odder folks tryin ter meddle in mah business!

REVEREND—Hit's God's business chile! Hit's der will en der wish of der Lord.

CORRINNE—Maybe 'tis but he ain done mah wishes en mah prayers. How come I gon do his?

REVEREND—Yer hard on God, chile.

CORRINNE—God's hard on me!

REVEREND—It ain right to put yerself up wid der Mighty.

214

CORRINNE—If he all dat mighty he ain caren what I do en I ain carin what he does!

REVEREND—But I cares, sistah, cause I's sent by God en commanded ter carry out his word en I's sorrowful over you backsliding en der whole church is prayin fer yer en dat you will be brought back ter der fold.

CORRINNE—I ain nebber comin back. Yer heah! I ain nebber comin back!

REVEREND—I ain gon take dose words, I ain gon eben heah dem. I's called ter face such ez dis en I kin bear hit.

CORRINNE—Yer ain called ternuffin! Yer ain called! Yer heah? I's tired er yer hypocriting I's tired!

REVEREND—Lord, let her come back ter der fold.

CORRINNE—Does yer want me back fer der Lord or fer yerself? Yer hypocrite!

REVEREND—Forgive her, Oh Father, fer she ain knowing der blasfemy she sayin! Forgive her!

CORRINNE—Dare ain no God! Yer heah me—Dere ain no God!

(He stops to look at her and her wild distraught expression, and quietly and emphatically he gets out of the chair and falls upon his knees, continuing his silent praying. Corrinne stands staring and shaking with a nervous trembling she can scarcely control. Steps are heard and Virginia Kelton, a raw-boned, skinny, dark, tall woman enters. Around her head is a green scarf similar but darker in color than Corrinne's. She steps in and both turn to look at her. She looks at the kneeling Pastor without speaking or making any sign of recognition and walking over to Corrinne says—(I must talk to yer alone.) They go into the other room. The Pastor rises from his knees, stares after them, brushes off his pants, takes another piece of pie, and after one bite drops both it and the knife as one who has been burnt. He chews the mouthful of pie thoughtfully. Virginia Kelton passes out. They stare at each other.

CORRINNE—I got ter be going now. (She gets his hat and offers it to him, he stands staring at her. Strange, weird music can be heard in the distance.)

REVEREND—De debbil worshippers! Yer been listening ter dere music!

CORRINNE—Heah yer hat!

REVEREND—En you got green boun' eround yer head! Take dat scarf off!

215

CORRINNE—Heah yer hat!

(He reaches out a hand and snatches the scarf from her head. She whirls around, screams and drops as a badly spun top. Her whole head is a sore red spot. She covers her face and head with her hands on the floor. The Pastor stands a moment in awed and trembling silence; drops the silk scarf as from the plague; and stepping back with his own hat, shouts: Der curse of Hebben upon her! Der curse of Hebben upon her! Er shaved'ed! Der sacrifice of er Heathen!

(CURTAIN.)

ABOUT THE EDITORS

Henry Louis Gates, Jr., is the W. E. B. Du Bois Professor of the Humanities, Chair of the Afro-American Studies Department, and Director of the W. E. B. Du Bois Institute for Afro-American Research at Harvard University. One of the leading scholars of African-American literature and culture, he is the author of *Figures in Black: Words, Signs, and the Racial Self* (1987), *The Signifying Monkey: A Theory of Afro-American Literary Criticism* (1988), *Loose Canons: Notes on the Culture Wars* (1992), and the memoir *Colored People* (1994).

Jennifer Burton is in the Ph.D. program in English Language and Literature at Harvard University. She is a contributor to *The Oxford Companion to African-American Literature* and *Great Lives from History: American Women*. With her mother and sister she coauthored two one-act plays, *Rita's Haircut* and *Litany of the Clothes*. Her fiction and personal essays have appeared in *Sun Dog*, *There and Back* and *Buffalo*, the Sunday magazine of the *Buffalo News*.